Small Miracles *of the*
HOLOCAUST

Small Miracles of the
HOLOCAUST

Extraordinary Coincidences of
Faith, Hope, and Survival

Yitta Halberstam & Judith Leventhal

The Lyons Press
Guilford, Connecticut
An imprint of The Globe Pequot Press

The Lyons Press is an imprint of The Globe Pequot Press.

Designed by Georgiana Goodwin

Mandelbaum, Yitta Halberstam.
   Small miracles of the Holocaust : extraordinary coincidences of faith, hope, and survival / Yitta Halberstam and Judith Leventhal.
      p. cm.
   ISBN 978-1-59921-407-8
1. Miracles. 2. Coincidence—Religious aspects. 3. Coincidence—Psychic aspects. 4. Holocaust, Jewish (1939-1945) 5. Faith. I. Leventhal, Judith, 1958- II. Title.
   BL487.M364 2008
   940.53'18—dc22

2008020634

Printed in the United States of America
10 9 8 7 6 5 4 3 2 1

For those who survived
And for those who didn't
We will never forget you.

For Pesi Dinnerstein
Hand-holder, mentor, friend
A blessing to the world
And a blessing to us.

In Jewish history, there are no coincidences.

—Elie Wiesel

In spite of everything, I still believe that people are really good at heart.

—Anne Frank

CONTENTS

Acknowledgments x

Introduction xii

Love among the Ruins
    by Tamar Snyder 1

My Pledge to Nachman
    as told by Rabbi Yosef Schwartz* 7

Sisters 16

Life in a Jar 28

A Robber's Redemption. 34

The Ren Twins 44

Number 7416. 51

An Unseen Blessing
    by Pesi Dinnerstein 54

The Miracle of the Muddy Seat
    as told by Louis Koplin 60

The Other Doctor of Auschwitz 65

A Question of Identity 71

Zayde's Travels
    by Azriela Jaffe 76

Mama Is Always Right
    as told by Nissan Krakinowski 79

The Swimmer
    by Dov Haller 89

The Last Candle 92

Lost and Found

    by Steve Eisenberg 96

The Love Story of Dovid and Shifra

    based on the testimony given by

    Dovid Landau to Shmuel Globa

    (from the original Yiddish) 103

Friend of a Farmer

    by Shoshana Goldwasser Schwartz and Azriela Jaffe 112

My Betrayer, My Savior 115

A Boy Named Yitzchak, Waclaw, and Jack

    by Liza M. Wiemer 123

Fall Prayers 130

Good Morning, Herr Mueller 134

Righteous among the Nations 137

The Search for Reb Burechl 144

The Philosopher

    by Yisroel Besser 153

Business Partners 155

Strangers on a Train

    by Shoshana Goldwasser Schwartz and Azriela Jaffe 160

Melvina's Dream

    as told by Bailey Lustig and Breindy Muller 163

Comrades 168

A Promise to Father

    as told to Tamar Snyder by Frank Hershkowitz 173

Subway Reunion

    as told by Ruth Fisher 176

Dancing with G-d 178

The Frequent Flyer 182
Seder
    as told to Tania Hammer by her Father 186
Shocking Discovery
    as told by Raquel Schraub 190
Getting to Know Germaine
    by Gerda Bikales 194
The Last Jew of Auschwitz 198
What's in a Name?
    as told by Masha Leon 202
The Hidden Child 207
Trunkful of Letters 212
The Gold Pendant 218
The Train of Lights
    by Pesi Dinnerstein 230
Miracle at the Gallows
    by Cantor Leo Fettman and Linda Ackerman 234
The War Artist 240
The Converted 247
The Namesake 250
A Dream Escape 253
"*Der Kranke Yingele*" (The Sick Boy) 259
Funeral for Baruch
    by Rabbi Binny Friedman 263
An Oscar for Oskar
    by Eric Saul 266

All names that appear in this book with an asterisk (*) have been
changed to protect identities.

ACKNOWLEDGMENTS

Our deepest appreciation and thanks go to:

Those who helped spread the word. Great leads and wonderful stories came our way through the help of two extraordinary women, both coincidentally named Naomi: Naomi Mauer, passionate, tireless advocate for the Jewish people and editor of *The Jewish Press,* who, in an amazing display of generosity, placed ads for us in the largest-circulation Jewish weekly in the United States; and best-selling novelist Naomi Ragen, who magnanimously included our call for submissions in her daily e-magazine. And a great resource for Jews all over the world, Luach.com, did the same. Without the help of the above three, we never would have gotten to first base. And Dr. Gary Neuman, what can we say: You get the "Biggest Mensch of the Year" Award! Thank you for everything.

Those who helped us with suggestions, research, and writing. Azriela Jaffe; Tamar Snyder; Yisroel Besser; Eric Saul; Rabbi Yossi Weiser; Elie Feuerwerker; LianSae Bloom; Doreen Nayman; Stefanie Stahl of the Righteous Gentiles Foundation; Masha Leon, cultural arts columnist for *Forward;* Dinah Shira Foster; Annette Grauman; Sheila Lowy; and Steve Eisenberg. Special grateful kudos to Nancy Porat, Israel-based researcher for *The Wall Street Journal* and other fine publications, whom we have hired in the past but who refused to take *one cent* for her efforts this time, because, as she said, "This is holy work, and a *mitzvah*." Nancy, we are humbled and overwhelmed by your beautiful spirit.

Those who have made our project a reality. Jane Dystel and Miriam Goderich of the Dystel/Goderich Literary Agency: You are warm, wonderful, caring, attentive, smart, and savvy agents; thank you for everything! Gary Krebs: We would follow you anywhere! You are an outstanding, brilliant, gifted, and punctilious editor with whom it is a privilege and pleasure to work! And Meredith Davis, project editor extraordinaire: Thanks for a great job, which you executed with both patience and grace. Kudos also to Melissa Hayes, for phenomenal copyediting.

Those who patiently overlook our erratic schedules and constant absences because of book tours and writing. Carol Sufian, exceptional executive director of EMUNAH, and Melanie Oelbaum, primary force—thank you for your tolerance, understanding, and graciousness, always.

Those who support us, champion us, put up with us on a daily basis, and make us who we are. Yitta thanks her extraordinary husband, Mordechai Mandelbaum, and wonderful children, Yossi, Henna, and Eli; extended family members Sima Mandelbaum, Miriam Halberstam, Chaya and Yeruchem Winkler, Moshe and Evelyn Halberstam, Chaim and Bayla Mandelbaum, and honorary sisters, the incomparable Raizy Steg and Bella Friedman.

Judith thanks her beloved husband, Jules Leventhal, and darling daughters, Arielle, Shira, and Tehilla. And family: Rose Frankel, Esti and her Aron Tzvi, Isser and Malku Handler; Hedy and Meyer Feiler; Yanky and Huvy; Aviva and her Tzvi, Yisroel and Rachelli, Duvy who has contributed so much to this book and Mimi; Anschel, Hershy; Shuly and David, Yoni, Michal, Avigayil, Arlene and Moish Fox and Emery.

And finally, the person to whom this book is dedicated, and who lived, breathed, and dreamed this book with us, who helped us in every conceivable and *in*conceivable way, our wonderful friend, mentor, and chief hand-holder . . . an angel and blessing to the whole world . . . our soul sister, Pesi Dinnerstein. This book is as much yours as it is ours.

INTRODUCTION

As members of the "second generation" of Holocaust survivors, we both grew up under the shadow of the Holocaust. Although we were born and raised in the United States, our respective childhoods couldn't have been more different from our American peers: We never knew what it was like to have grandparents. Most of our aunts, uncles, and cousins were people we got to know only through pictures and stories. And family milestones—birthdays, weddings, bar mitzvahs—were celebrated with a perpetual tear in the eye for those whose absence was so overwhelmingly present. Growing up as a survivor's child meant that you were only one step away from the abyss of hell. It meant that you had to struggle to find answers for questions that were too overwhelming to ask. It meant that you had to fill a void, a yawning vacuum left bare. And, finally, it meant that you were the scab on the open wound; that for those who had given up on the past, *you* were their only hope for the future.

Despite our youth, we carried a huge responsibility. With age we grappled with trying to understand that which cannot ever really be understood. "Coming to terms" with the Holocaust is an oxymoron, an impossible feat. How does one even begin to attempt to comprehend the incomprehensible?

And yet, amidst the great darkness, there were still pinpoints of light. The horrors, the atrocities, the heinous and brutal things that man perpetrated upon man...the accounts of these have been told and retold many times. But the sparks of human greatness that flared up during this nightmarish time...these have not been told enough. And the myriad ways these unknown incidences resulted in—or were the outcome of—"coincidences", or "God incidences" as we prefer to call them . . . these must be told . . . if for no other reason than to redeem the sullied image of Man during a time in which he seemed so absent. Hence this book, our gift to you—our dear readers—and to ourselves as well.

* * *

The mandate of the Small Miracles Series is to accentuate the positive in human nature, to emphasize the hidden goodness of G-d and his omnipresence. Too often we dismiss transcendent occurrences as quirky products of luck, fate, chance, or great timing. But who created the great timing? And why?

"Small Miracles" could just as well have been entitled "Small Mysteries." The stories contained inside these pages beg the following questions: Why do providential events occur to one person, but not to another? When one person is blessed with a life-changing or life-saving miracle as opposed to one who isn't, does it mean that the second person was less deserving? Or could both people have been blessed with an equal amount of miracles, but only one of them possessed the open heart to see them clearly and call them by their rightful name? Are we simply blind to the miracles that surround us every day, or do we blind ourselves deliberately in order to shrug off the formidable responsibility and the awesome message that these miracles convey? Alas, we do not know the answers; we only know how to pose the questions. But even the questions themselves are inherently valuable, as they hold the keys that help us open the doors where greater clarity awaits. And, without the question being posed, the answer could never be found.

This work is being published to coincide with the seventieth anniversary of *Kristallnacht*, The Night of Broken Glass. History views this horrific event as the inaugural date of the nightmare that engulfed the world. Seventy years later, there is a substantial canon of literature on the subject; yet new stories still continue to emerge from the rubble every day.

We began this project in a poignant effort to collect the untold stories of the last remaining survivors and to immortalize the testimony of those now in their twilight years. But we offer a special twist: Though framed in the context of the Holocaust, we specifically chose to include only those stories that ultimately proved to be positive and uplifting, and only those stories that centered around— amazingly—a single coincidence, or a series of them.

There are stories contained herein that defy the imagination and challenge credulity. How do we explain the miracles of siblings finding each other *fifty* years after the Holocaust; the stories of deceased relatives appearing in dreams with precise instructions on how to survive; reports of split-second, seemingly random decisions that made the difference between life and death? To label them as mere flukes dismisses their power, diminishes their spiritual significance, and takes away their wonder.

How do we explain the story of a man fleeing the Nazis, escaping deep into a dense forest that he had never traversed before, knocking on a random cabin door, and coming face-to-face with a gentile whose life *he* had saved years before? Is it possible, even right, to trivialize these kind of events, by relegating them to the realm of "coincidence"? To us these are all great mysteries, and even greater miracles, and though we cannot say why, or wherefore, or how, we can definitely say *who*.

Some seventy-odd years ago, Yitta's father, Rabbi Laizer Halberstam, then a five-year-old child in a Polish village, violated some tacit rule by playing with a non-Jewish friend. The two of them swapped stamps, coins, toys, and, one fateful day, decided to swap prayers.

Their respective parents would have been horrified had they discovered details about this particular trade, but blessedly, they never knew. Yitta's father taught his friend a Jewish prayer, and in turn, his playmate taught him a Christian one.

Ten years later, Yitta's father was fleeing the Nazis, traveling across Europe disguised as a Christian. One day, a German soldier boarded the train on which Laizer was a passenger and demanded to see everyone's documents. Her father was in possession of forged papers which had always passed muster, but for some reason aroused this particular soldier's suspicions. "Oh, really?" he taunted him. "You say you are a good Christian? Well then, why don't you recite a Christian prayer for me now, one that all good Christians should know by heart?" Fortuitously, the prayer he'd been asked to recite was the exact same one that Laizer's playmate had taught him ten years before, and Yitta's father—who had an excellent memory—recited it perfectly, and survived. Coincidence—or miracle?

Judith once asked her father, Herschel Frankel, why he had never written a book about his wartime experiences. Judith's father was well known for his spirited personality and his ability to regale audiences with an array of fabulous stories, bringing people to both laughter and tears. It seemed like he would have wanted to record his stories for posterity, seeing that he had miraculously survived Auschwitz and Birkenau death camps at the tender age of fifteen.

"*Totty*," Judith once asked him, using the Yiddish version of "Daddy," "surely you have much to say?"

Although it's been twenty years since her father passed away, Judith still vividly remembers his answer.

"*Yidisel*"—as he affectionately called her—"I *did* sit down to write my story once, and this is how I began. 'My name is Tzvi Yehuda.

This was the name given to me at birth. I was named after my grandfather, who in turn was named after *his* grandfather, and so it went back for generations, dating to the Frankel Tumim family, who were direct descendants of Rashi [the famous commentator on the Bible], who is a direct descendant of King David. I knew my lineage and I was proud of my name.'

"'But on June 1, 1944, I entered the Auschwitz death camp where the Nazis tried to strip me of everything, even my name, as they tattooed my arm with the number A-9975.'" Judith's father was silent for a moment, and then he said, "You know, *Yidisel*, when I read the words I had written on the first page of my book . . . I just couldn't continue."

This conversation is tattooed on Judith's heart, in her mind and soul, with the same indelible imprint that marked the number on her father's arm.

Today, she sends him a prayer: *Totty*, may the words in this book be a completion of yours.

LOVE AMONG THE RUINS

Tamar Snyder

For survivors of the Nazi concentration camps, the end of World War II and Liberation were not times of unheralded joy. In fact, the war's end created its own set of challenges. Those who had risen above the odds suddenly found themselves alone, bereft of every last family member. The thought of rebuilding their lives was a daunting one, as they were weak and frail not only in body, but also in spirit.

Howard Kleinberg was no exception.

It was the spring of 1945 and Howard was lying among the corpses in the fields of the Bergen-Belsen camp in Germany. The eighteen-year-old no longer had the strength to battle the typhus that choked his being. Death would be preferable to this miserable state, he thought to himself. Barely able to crawl, he lay down on the ground, begging his Maker to free him from his misery.

Out of nowhere, three women appeared. The youngest of the three was a girl, just sixteen years old. She stared at Howard with determined eyes. He was a mere skeleton, but his eyes flickered with life.

"I'll take him," she told the others. "I'll save him."

"It's too late. He's more dead than alive," the older women replied.

"But his eyes are open," said the teenage girl, persisting. "He's not dead yet."

Somehow, the women managed to pull Howard into their barracks. He was so weakened; all he could do was sleep. For days, he flitted in and out of consciousness. He could hardly speak. Yet the girl never gave up. She would spoon-feed him whatever morsels of food she could find. The food went in and went out. And the girl would get down on her hands and knees to clean up after him.

At some point, Howard awoke with a start. "I need a doctor," he announced, cognizant of just how ill he was. But there were no doctors.

"Don't worry . . . I'll save you," said the sweet, young girl, trying to reassure him. He fell back to sleep.

After three weeks of this twilight state, Howard felt a modicum of strength return. He opened his eyes. No one was in the barracks. *Where were the women, especially the girl who had saved him? Had they been forced to leave? Had they left on their own?* He couldn't believe that after all they had done, they would simply abandon him and disappear. But the barracks were deserted and he knew that if he were to survive, he would need a doctor's care. And so he took a risk. He rolled down from his bunk and, unable to walk, crawled through the fields, inching his way toward the middle of the road. There, he lay down. Either this cruel life would finally end, or maybe, just maybe, someone would find him.

Within minutes, a British military vehicle spotted him. They picked him up and rushed him to a hospital, where he spent six months in isolated care.

When he was healed, Howard returned to Bergen-Belsen to search for the young girl who had saved his life. But of course she was long gone, the camp now desolate, liberated months earlier. Howard was crushed. He needed to find the girl, to thank her, perhaps to repay her in some small way that counted, but now he doubted that he ever would. It was a time of turmoil; if you lost sight of someone, chances were you'd never see him or her again. All he had left of this girl was her name: Nechama Baum.

* * *

An only daughter, Nechama Baum—or Nachu, as she was called—had blond tresses and a determined spirit. She grew up acting as a second "mommy" to her five brothers. Before going to Bergen-Belsen, Nachu had been at Auschwitz, where she repeatedly risked her life by smuggling cigarettes. She'd sell them on the black market for a few sips of soup to spoon-feed to an ill friend. She shared any morsel of bread she could lay her hands on with her aunt, Toby, who slept alongside her in the same wooden barracks.

Once, while passing a can of soup to her friend over the barbed wire, Nachu's hands grazed the fence, and she fell to the ground, electrocuted. Girls rushed to her side, reviving her. The incident did not deter Nachu. She continued risking her life, trying to save herself and others.

As the Russians drew closer to Auschwitz, the Nazis led the remaining Jews out of the camp on a death march. Nachu snuck a pack of cigarettes to the kapo, the prisoner in charge of the inmates, in exchange for a guarantee that she wouldn't be separated from her aunt. They walked for three days straight in the January sun, without food or rest. At one point, her aunt collapsed, refusing to continue on.

"They'll kill us," Nachu pleaded with her aunt.

"Then I'll die," Toby said, resigned to her fate.

Nachu wouldn't let that happen. Weak as she was, she picked up her aunt and kept walking. That night, the Germans finally let them rest in a barn for a few hours. The next day, they were en route to

Bergen-Belsen. There was no crematorium there, but the camp was a nightmare nonetheless.

On April 15, 1945, Bergen-Belsen was liberated. It was a joyous occasion for Nachu, but that joy was short-lived. The realization that she would never see her parents again tore at her heart. There were dead corpses everywhere she looked. Nevertheless, Nachu tried to stay upbeat. With the help of friends, she took over a barrack that the Germans had left in their hasty flight. It had two bunk beds on each side and a small stove in the middle of the room. It was a palace compared to the cramped quarters they had lived in before.

It was around that time that Nachu spotted Howard Kleinberg lying in the field surrounding Bergen-Belsen, practically dead. She had been hunting for her beloved brother, searching for him among the mounds of corpses, when she saw one of them move. Drawing closer, she recognized the skeletal body as belonging to a boy from her hometown, an acquaintance of her brother's. She insisted on saving him, despite the misgivings of her aunt and another woman who accompanied them. *Maybe if I save him, someone else will save my brother,* she hoped.

Nachu gave up her bed for Howard and moved to the top bunk with her aunt and two other girls. She nursed him for three weeks. Then one day, when she returned from her daily scavenging for food, he was gone. She was disappointed, angry even. *What had happened to him?* she wondered. *To leave like that, without even saying good-bye?*

Day-to-day survival kept her from wondering for too long. After sending letters to an uncle in Israel that went unanswered, she received word from her cousin Yetta in Toronto: "Dear child . . . a room is waiting for you." Nachu was overjoyed. She took a children's transport to the United States in June of 1947. She spent several weeks in Buffalo, New York, where she lived with other relatives, waiting for a visa to Toronto. One month later, she arrived in Toronto at the home of Yetta and Izzy Horenfeld, a childless couple who adopted her as their own.

News of Nechama Baum's arrival spread quickly throughout the close-knit Jewish community of Toronto. Although today Toronto is a major metropolis with a large, flourishing Jewish population, in the immediate postwar years, Jews lived in a single square block, and everybody knew each other's business. And the business of arriving young survivors was especially palatable gossip.

Almost immediately, the spunky young woman gained a following. She quickly became very popular—especially among the young men. Unbeknownst to Nachu, her arrival was especially thrilling news for one young survivor: Howard Kleinberg, the boy she had saved, the one she had all but forgotten about. He just happened to have arrived in Toronto a few months earlier to live with relatives. And he had never forgotten *her*.

After searching the world over for his "angel," Howard couldn't believe his good luck in finally finding her. Now, if only he could summon up the courage to approach her.

A few days after Nachu (or Nancy, as she was now known) arrived in town, an unexpected visitor nervously rang her doorbell. It was Howard Kleinberg, all clammy hands and fidgety limbs. He had dragged his sister along with him, as a confidence booster.

As Nachu stood there in the doorway, Howard gaped at her, rendered speechless. She was as beautiful as he remembered her, perhaps even more so. Over the months, he had thought of her constantly, remorseful that he hadn't had the chance to thank her for rescuing him from the ashes. Yet here she was, right in front of him—some cosmic coincidence sending her to Toronto of all places, when there were so many other places in the world where survivors had gone.

He handed her a corsage and croaked:

"Hello . . . my name is Howard Kleinberg. Remember me?"

Postscript: Howard and Nachu (Nancy) Kleinberg recently celebrated their fifty-seven wedding anniversary. They are blessed with three sons, one daughter, and eleven grandchildren.

"It was *bashert*," Nancy Kleinberg says, invoking the Hebrew word for "destined."

The sages tell us that a *zivug* (soul mate) is determined in heaven forty days before a person is born. For the Kleinbergs, not even the horrors of the Holocaust could prevent the match. The Kleinbergs are proof positive that in the midst of darkness, love and compassion can shine through, sending healing rays to brighten even the most harrowing of circumstances.

MY PLEDGE TO NACHMAN

*As told by Rabbi Yosef Schwartz**
(Names have been changed at the request of the family.)

The name *Auschwitz* conjures up horror, revulsion, an immediate shrinking of the spirit. It is associated in most people's minds with the infamous concentration camp, but for me it will always be the name of the beloved town nearby where I was born and raised. Before the war, seven thousand Jews—almost all of them fervently religious—lived in Auschwitz, among them a large contingent of Bobover Chassidim.

On September 5, 1939, the Nazis marched in. The very first thing they did was burn the largest and most prominent synagogue in town and demolish the buildings around which Jewish life hummed. In the blink of an eye, Auschwitz was emptied of its Jews so that the Nazis could start constructing the camp; my parents and four siblings were slaughtered; and I was sent from one labor camp to another, until I ended up in Choow. I was thirteen years old.

As grisly as the conditions were, labor camps were better than the horrific concentration camps. There was more food, and there were no crematoria with the stench of burned flesh spiraling from tall chimneys, and instead of six people crammed into a single bunk, you only had to share your plank bed with one. This is how I first came to meet Nachman.

Nachman was twice my age, married, with two children—a six-year-old girl and a three-year-old boy. His wife was in the women's section of the same camp, and they were allowed visits from their children, who were staying with a Christian family on the outside. Perhaps it was because he was older, or because his family was intact while mine had been decimated, but Nachman was extraordinarily kind and attentive to me, a surrogate big brother. He took me under his wing and practically doted on me. When the lights were dimmed, we spoke long into the night. We would share intimacies, swap stories, discuss the Torah, give each other morale-boosting talks. We bonded deeply and became best friends. Nachman made me feel less alone.

I was taken aback one day when Nachman suddenly said to me, "I can't take living like this anymore—and I can't bear being separated from my family. I want you to know that I've arranged for a gentile friend of mine to help me escape from here, together with my wife and children, who will remain here and hide after their regular visit. We're going to make the break on Sunday night."

Labor camps were not as heavily guarded as the concentration camps were, and the fences were not electrified. Also aiding and abetting escape attempts was the fact that Choow was located at the edge of a dense forest, where one could easily find cover. Several prisoners had, in fact, successfully escaped from our camp, so the idea was not far-fetched. Although I would miss Nachman terribly, I understood his feelings and wished him well.

Nachman dug a hole under the fence. He and his family were crawling under it when someone observed them from afar. The alarms sounded. Nachman and his family sped toward the forest, but hordes of SS men with flashlights and vicious guard dogs were already in hot pursuit, yelling, "Stop! Stop!"

Nachman had prearranged a special signal with his Christian friend, and he whistled for him frantically. The German shepherds were already nipping at Nachman's heels when the gentile stepped out of the dark. Nachman knew that he would not be able to outrun the SS. He grabbed the nearest child—who happened to be the six-year-old girl—and threw her into his friend's arms. "Run, run!" he screamed.

The girl's name was Chayala.

* * *

Nachman, his wife, and their three-year-old son were captured, and the SS men determined that they should be killed at once. They were dragged to the outskirts of the camp where Nachman was handed a shovel and ordered to dig a large pit. The Nazis took sadistic pleasure in forcing their victims to dig their own graves before executing them.

At the precise moment the guards were raising their guns, the camp commandant appeared. "Are you crazy?" he yelled. "What are you doing? This is my best worker. He's the only one in the whole camp who knows how to operate the bulldozer. I *must* have him; you cannot kill him!"

"All right," the guards said, relenting. "But you don't need his wife or kid, do you?" they sneered.

Nachman was freed, but he was forced to watch the execution of his wife and son. They were buried in the hole he had scooped out with his own two hands. He was dragged back to our barracks, climbed up to the bunk we shared, and cried his heart out. Nachman's spirit was broken, but he did not become a *Muselmann* (walking dead). He continued to work hard, and he remained remarkably attentive and devoted to me, which was extraordinary in light of his terrible losses.

During the months that followed that harrowing night, Nachman spoke often about his murdered wife and son, but he also obsessed constantly about the whereabouts and safety of his daughter, Chayala. *Please G-d, at least let her be safe,* he prayed over and over again.

I will never forget the date of Nachman's death: *daled Tammuz* (the fourth day of the Jewish calendar month of Tammuz). On a Friday at four o'clock in the morning, members of the SS barged into our barracks, marched straight up to our bunk, pulled Nachman down, and dragged him out.

A few months had passed since Nachman's unsuccessful escape attempt. Apparently, an order had been handed down directly from Gestapo headquarters rescinding the original decision of the camp commandant to let Nachman live. I don't know whether it was out of a sense of irony or symmetry, but the Germans dragged him back to the grave where his wife's and son's bodies were buried, and ordered him to open it.

The entire camp had been roused and commanded to assemble in front of the grave and watch the execution. Right before he was killed, Nachman raised his face to the crowd, pinned me with his eyes, and screamed out, *"Yosef, gedenk ich hob a kind!"* (Yosef, remember that I have a child!) He was then shot dead. He fell into the pit, joining his family.

I fully understood that Nachman's last words had charged me with the mission of locating his daughter and taking care of her. I pledged myself to finding her. I vowed that if I survived, I would comb the ends of the earth until I met with success.

We were liberated in January of 1945, and I joined a group of young boys; we all returned to our hometown of Auschwitz together. It was only after Liberation that I was able to get in touch with Nachman's sole surviving sibling, a brother named Leibel, who had been incarcerated in a different section of Choow. He promised that while I looked for remnants of my own family in Auschwitz, he would immediately begin an exhaustive search for Chayala. He left for his hometown of Soisce, but said that if he did not find her there, he was prepared to hunt all over Poland—indeed, all over Europe—until he found his brother's child.

I returned to Auschwitz and started knocking on doors. My parents' home was empty, my uncle's home was empty, my grandfather's home was empty, all my cousins' homes were empty. Before the war, I had 150 close relatives living in the town of Auschwitz. None of them came back. I spent months looking for them, but couldn't find a single relative who had survived. Since there was no longer any reason for me to remain in Auschwitz, I decided to go looking for Leibel. In the Polish town of Sanz, someone told me that Leibel had been sighted with a little girl, and, as far as people knew, they had been taken on a Youth Aliyah mission to Israel.

I was thrilled to hear that Leibel had been reunited with his niece, but Nachman's last words had been directed at *me*, not him. His last request reverberated in my ears. I would not be able to feel that I had fulfilled my responsibility to Nachman's daughter until I found her myself. Perhaps I would adopt her as my own, if Leibel was not up to the task. I wrote letter after letter to as many Jewish agencies as I could find in Israel, asking for information about Leibel and Chayala. I placed countless ads in newspapers published throughout the Jewish state. In spite of all my efforts, I couldn't find a trace of either one.

Meanwhile, I began to rebuild my life. In Tarnow, I met my wife. We got married in Cracow, and, through the intervention of the Bobover Rebbe, received documents that allowed us to emigrate to the United States and settle on the Upper West Side of Manhattan. From there, I continued my relentless search for my friend's daughter.

In 1958, when the Bobover Rebbe visited Israel for the first time, I was among his entourage, seizing the opportunity to search for Leibel and Chayala firsthand. I scoured the country, but couldn't find them. I accompanied the Bobover Rebbe on his return visits in 1962, 1964, 1968, and 1970, each time intensifying my search efforts. I refused to give up. Nachman's last words still rang in my ears: *Yosef, gedenk ich hob a kind!*

During these intermittent visits to Israel to search for Chayala, I raised a family of my own—five children, four of whom coincidentally married Israeli spouses and settled in Jerusalem. My trips to Israel increased in frequency. I returned for engagement parties, weddings, *brisim*, and *bar mitzvahs*.

Whenever and wherever I went, I shared with people the story of my tenacious search for Chayala. Finally, in 1986, someone suggested that I visit the Diaspora Museum in Tel Aviv, which, they believed, stored the lists of the children who had come to Israeli via Youth Aliyah. There I finally found Leibel's name and address, and my joy was unbridled. I immediately took a taxi to his home, and we fell into each other's arms, weeping and shrieking in excitement. After I finally broke away, I asked him: "What happened to Chayala? Where is she?"

"*Oy*, Chayala," he sighed heavily. "She came with me to Israel and grew up to be a wonderful person. She got married, and then . . . she died of cancer at the age of twenty-three."

I was devastated. I couldn't believe it. I was not able to keep my unspoken pledge to Nachman, after all. And now his family line was completely gone. I felt a tremendous void, the deepest sense of loss.

"There *was* a daughter," Leibel said. "She was about three years old when Chayala died."

A daughter! I felt instantly reborn. I felt that G-d had given me another chance to redeem myself to him.

"Where is she?" I asked, wiping away my tears.

"*Oy!*" Leibel sighed, "another tragedy. Chayala's husband, the father of the girl, remarried very quickly, and his new wife cruelly insisted that she didn't want to raise another woman's child, demanding that she be placed in an orphanage."

"So where is she?" I jumped up.

He looked away from me; he could not meet my eyes.

"I don't know."

"You *don't know?*" I repeated.

"Chayala's husband and I didn't get along. We weren't on good terms, and he refused to tell me where she had been placed."

I redirected my efforts. I stopped looking for Chayala, and started looking for her daughter, instead. Every time I traveled to Israel, I stepped up my investigations, continuing to visit different agencies and organizations, but I always came to a dead end.

Many years passed, but I still refused to give up. By now, my youngest daughter Rivka accompanied me on these expeditions, as she spoke better Hebrew than I, and having lived in Israel for some time, knew how to navigate the system. During this time, Leibel died, but I continued to visit his widow and press her for information about Nachman's granddaughter.

"*Mazel tov, Mazel tov!*" she shrieked during one of these visits. "I finally have wonderful news for you! I've found Nachman's granddaughter!" She handed Rivka the slip of paper on which she had written the granddaughter's full name and address. When Rivka read it, she grew pale and fainted.

When she was revived, she rubbed her eyes and said, "Nachman's granddaughter Hindy is my *best friend!*"

Rivka had met Hindy five years before, when they were both blushing brides. Rivka had married the son of an illustrious *Rebbe*, and Hindy had married a *Chasid* (disciple) of the same *Rebbe*. Their husbands learned Torah in the same Yeshiva, and Rivka and Hindy had met in the shul where both prayed.

"We do *everything* together!" Rivka exclaimed. "We go shopping, take walks together, attend *shiurim* (lectures), study *seforim* (holy books) together, participate in the same *chesed* (charitable works) organizations—everything!"

I immediately called a taxi and we went straight back to Yerushalayim to see Hindy. The laughter and tears sprang forth as we told her the story of the deep bond that connected us all. Hindy became a fifth daughter to me. Our families became intertwined and we shared many family events together.

The story almost ends here—but not completely.

Several years ago, I participated in a Chasidic tour of Poland. Included in the itinerary was the holy gravesite of a saintly *Rebbe*. I prayed at his burial site and chanted *Tehillim* (Psalms) and then walked around a bit, waiting until the others were finished. It was then that I noticed a curious sight: A few feet away from the Holy Rebbe's *kever* was a small gate encircling three graves and one giant headstone. This was very strange, because old Jewish cemeteries in Poland *never* used headstones, and this was the only one in the entire place. My interest was greatly piqued, so I advanced toward the headstone to examine its inscription. As I read the engraved Hebrew words, I had to steady myself because I felt I would faint.

I was standing before the graves of my good friend Nachman, his wife, and his son.

Unbeknownst to me, Leibel had apparently gotten a court order to have the bodies exhumed from their graves in the labor camp and reburied in the old Chasidic cemetery. I began to shake and weep uncontrollably, and through my tears, to chant *Tehillim*. From afar, the distinguished Serreter Rebbe observed my highly emotional state and approached me to ask what was wrong. When I told him the story about Nachman and his family, he asked if he could have the *zchus* (honor) to say the *Kaddish* for them.

As the men gathered around the graves, the *Rebbe* began to chant the *Kaddish*. As we fervently answered "Amen," I could not help but think that on this day, finally, a circle had been completed—a circle of friendship and undying love.

SISTERS

They had never crossed paths before, despite the fact that many common denominators united them. Both had been born and bred in the same city of Kosice, Slovakia; they were teenagers close in age; they lived only a few blocks apart from each other; and they were Jews. It was the latter that defined them during the nightmarish war years, and brought them together for the first time in April 1944. Ironically, the Passover holiday had just ended the day before they were herded out of their homes into the grim, makeshift ghetto of Kassa-Kosice. Passover celebrated the Jews' redemption from Egyptian slavery, but for the Jews of Kassa-Kosice, oppression had only just begun.

The ghettos of the Holocaust conjure up stereotypical images of dilapidated houses huddled together, dirty streets swollen with sewage, and the detritus of hordes of people cramped into the confinement of a few square city blocks. The Kassa-Kosice ghetto was different; it was a single brick building, a former factory expropriated by the Nazis. In other ghettos, several families shared one apartment. In Kassa-Kosice, thousands shared one huge factory floor. The rows of straw mattresses that lined the cavernous hall represented the extent of each individual's personal space. Privacy, modesty, and dignity were nonexistent.

No one was allowed to randomly choose his or her "spot" on the floor. One of the strategies employed by the Nazis to demoralize the

Jews was the dividing and tearing apart of family members so they could not cling together for succor and comfort. To accomplish this, the Nazis assigned the straw mattresses, and it was along one such row that fifteen-year-old Miriam Beinhorn-Rappoport and sixteen-year-old Eva Lux found themselves on neighboring mats. Shared terror creates instant camaraderie, and the girls became friends. They spent much of each day with their respective parents and siblings (both were the eldest of their families, and each had two younger sisters), but when curfew was called and they returned to their assigned spots on the floor, they would often talk together well into the night. They could not know that from this time forward, their lives—and their destinies—would run on parallel tracks.

Several days before the Jewish holiday of *Shavuous* (they still counted out their days according to the Hebrew calendar), the transports to Auschwitz began. Miriam and Eva found themselves and their families in the group transported to Auschwitz-Birkenau. When they were shoved off the cattle cars, men and women were ordered to form separate groups. Then they were instructed to file past one of the most infamous men in Holocaust history for the dreaded "selection." They stared in horror as Dr. Mengele casually swung his baton back and forth and sealed people's fates with a simple flick of his wrist.

"Left!" Mengele dispassionately decreed, sentencing Miriam's mother Pearl and two younger sisters Rachel and Rivka, ages eight and twelve, to death.

"Right!" he pointed alternately at both the men's and women's groups, sending Miriam and her father Jacob to life.

"Left!" He swung his baton again, directing Eva's mother Devorah and twelve-year-old sister Susie to join the long procession of children, middle-aged women, the elderly, and the sick, for whom there would be no exit.

"Right!" Mengele's long, elegant, manicured hands waved Eva and her fifteen-year-old sister Vera to the group from which a pool of laborers would be drawn.

"Mama!" Eva screamed as she craned her neck for one last anguished look at the desolate group in which her mother and sister stood.

"Stay together!" her mother yelled. The last words Eva would ever hear from her.

In a matter of minutes, whole families were destroyed.

* * *

New inmates were taken to *Lager* C (Camp C), where they were quarantined for six weeks. From there they proceeded to *Lager B*, where they were conscripted into different labor forces. By some minor miracle, Eva and her sister Vera remained together as they navigated the move from camp to camp, from one work detail to the other. Coincidentally, Miriam always found herself in the same group as the two sisters.

Eva and Vera stayed together as much as was possible without arousing the suspicions of the Nazi guards. They shared the lice-infested bread and thin tasteless gruel that passed as soup; they took turns bolstering each other's spirits, and comforting one another. To survive in a concentration camp, a support system was imperative. Without it you deteriorated into what inmates called a *Muselmann*—a member of the walking dead, with lifeless eyes, who, as their life force dissipated and the will to survive disappeared, vanished into the furnaces.

Miriam had one family member left—her first cousin, Chavi—and they, too, held on to each other for dear life. But during roll call one day, as they stood in line waiting for their numbers to be called, Chavi stood with her arms folded. The Nazis, who expected the inmates to stand straight with their arms hanging limply at their sides, didn't like it. They deemed that Chavi was brazen and insubordinate. They pulled her out of line and she was never seen again.

Miriam was engulfed by despair at having lost her last living relative in Auschwitz-Birkenau. She stumbled dazedly to *Lager B*, where six hundred women were crammed into the barracks. Ten to twelve women shared the same "bed"—a few planks of wood cobbled together. When one turned over, all had to turn over. There was no privacy, no personal space; you were never alone. But for those who had no friend or relative beside them, the congested barracks were a lonely place indeed.

Miriam knew her chances of survival were that much smaller if she tried to wing it solo. Back in the Kassa-Kosice ghetto—a lifetime ago—she had felt tremendous admiration for Eva, a strong-willed, indomitable, tiny powerhouse of a girl who inspired confidence, even blind faith. She pushed her way through the swarming masses in the barracks, and approached Eva timidly. "Will you be my *lager* sister?" she asked.

"Well, we are both blonde, blue-eyed, same height and build," Eva said after a quick appraisal. "And you *are* two years younger than me. So I suppose we *could* pass for sisters. Yes, I'll be your *lager* sister." Eva knew it wasn't merely a symbolic position. She was pledging to take care of Miriam, to place her under her wing. Once Eva had "adopted" Miriam, she would be as protective of her as she was of Vera, her biological sibling. She had taken an oath of duty that day to risk her own life for her new sister.

Eva was strong, firm, disciplined. By contrast, Miriam was softer, more fragile. She grew increasingly depressed and apathetic each day, refusing to eat the meager daily rations—a crust of bread and some watery soup. Eva prodded her, forcing her to swallow down the food. "If you don't eat, I won't take care of you anymore," she threatened.

Miriam ate.

Their "luck" held out. All three were assigned to the same work detail together—the quarry—where they were forced to lug huge stones from one side of the excavation pit to the other. The quarry was a two-mile walk from Auschwitz-Birkenau, and they labored there from morning to night, returning by foot in the winter cold. With each day their exhaustion mounted as their energy and spirits ebbed away.

One morning, Eva looked at her two younger "sisters," sapped of strength and purpose, and impulsively made a decision. "Today," she told them authoritatively, "we are *not* going to the quarry. We are going to be completely broken if we continue any longer. We have to rest and try to restore our health." Neither Vera nor Miriam questioned Eva's judgment. She was their mainstay, their foundation, their support. Wherever she led, they followed.

The girls had been equally weak the day before, and the day before that, and Eva could just as easily have come to her snap decision earlier. What had prompted her to suddenly decide they should hide in the barracks on *that* particular day? Was it intuition . . . luck . . . G-d?

The three had been hiding in the barracks for a few hours when they heard the *Lagermaster* Zuzsi announce on the loudspeaker: "Everyone who is still in the camp should come out. We need two hundred girls with good eyes to work in a munitions factory in Reichenbach. This is a good thing—don't be scared."

Was it a trick? Would they be rounded up and shot for refusing to go to work that day?

"Let's go," Eva decided. "We don't have much to lose."

As Germany's war effort began to flag in the waning months of 1944, the Nazis sought more laborers to man the all-important munitions factories. Concentration camp inmates who still possessed a modicum of strength were pulled into the workforce. A transfer to these factories meant a reprieve from the ovens, a temporary ticket to life.

On that particular day, officials from the munitions factory had descended upon Auschwitz-Birkenau, demanding an immediate consignment of workers. Everyone knew what recruitment to this group meant, and they were frantic to join. But not everyone who volunteered was chosen. The women who came forward were subjected to yet another selection, and two separate groups were herded into a huge shower room guarded by SS men and their killer dogs. A large bench bisected the room, and each group was assembled on a different side.

Eva's heart sank as she beheld Vera and Miriam huddled together across the room. In all their months together, the three had never been split apart. The women watched each other warily. Which was the "lucky" group, the one slated for survival? They could not know what their selection meant until the showerheads on one side of the room first drizzled, then poured out a plentiful supply of hot, steamy water on their scrawny naked bodies. The women yelped with surprise, then delight—both for the luxury of the clean, hot water cascading down their grimy, lice-infested bodies, and also, for what it signified. Those assigned to factory work were always cleaned up before they left the camp.

On the other side of the room, the second group stood silently, engulfed by a sense of impending doom. The droplets of water streaming down Eva's face merged with the stream of her tears. For her there was no relief, no sense of triumph that she had escaped the jaws of death. Vera and Miriam were among the condemned. She could not stand idly by and watch her two sisters sentenced to certain death. But what could she possibly do?

Just then a loud noise reverberated outside the shower room and the two SS men guarding the women rushed to the door to see if anything was amiss. *This is it*, Eva thought to herself. *It's do or die. You have to seize the opportunity—now!* Eva ran to the bench that separated the two groups of women, toppled it over, grabbed a water hose that lay on the floor, and screamed, "Come on, everyone, get wet!" Pandemonium broke loose as bodies shoved, pushed, and rushed in her direction. She sprayed everyone with water, until all the women in the room were drenched. The two groups were now completely indistinguishable.

There had never before been a single instance of passive resistance in Auschwitz-Birkenau, and the Nazi guards had grown smug and lax. They had perceived the women inmates as being especially weak and powerless. Secure in that knowledge, they had turned their backs on them for a few fleeting seconds, which was more than enough time for the damage to be done.

Hearing the bedlam, the Nazi guards returned to their posts. Infuriated by what they found, they lined up the dripping women and demanded, "Who did it?" The concentration camp had become a dog-eat-dog, survival-of-the-fittest world where friends and relatives often denounced and betrayed each other. But in the shower room that day, no one said a word.

Under ordinary circumstances, the Nazi guards probably would have shot them all, but they knew that the girls were desperately needed for the munitions factory, and the orders for their consignment came from men higher up the totem pole. The guards did yet another selection, but this time Vera and Miriam were exactly where Eva had hoped they would be—right next to her, in the group designated for factory work, the group marked for life. They were disinfected and given clean clothes, and on December 28, 1944, they were sent to Reichenbach. Unbeknownst to them, they would be among the last work detail to leave Auschwitz.

From Reichenbach, they were sent on a death march to four more camps: Ravensbruck, Fallerleben, Porta, and Salzvedel. They walked in the dead of winter—hunger, cold, and humiliation their constant companions. But they also had each other, and, miraculously, they were never separated again. The girls remained with one another throughout the rest of the nightmare, stalwart and devoted to the end.

* * *

On April 14, 1945, they were liberated by the American Army and taken to a displaced persons camp. Their first immediate concern and priority—like everyone else's—was trying to find the remnants of their families. Miriam was told that someone had seen her father in Buchenwald, so hope still remained. She tearfully bade farewell to Eva and Vera.

"I will never forget you," she wept. She turned to Eva and said, "How can I ever thank you? I owe you everything. You saved my life."

"Well, we're sisters, aren't we?" Eva said. "How could I not?"

"Will our paths ever cross again?" Miriam cried.

"G-d's ways are mysterious," Eva said, smiling and wiping away a tear. "You never know."

Miriam made her way to Kosice, certain that her father would go back there, too, in search of her. She waited patiently until she finally learned the truth: Although her father had indeed survived the war, he had succumbed to typhus just one week after Liberation. She wept at the bitter irony of it all, and heartbroken, joined a group traveling to Transylvania, where a lone surviving cousin embraced her with open arms.

Meanwhile, Eva and Vera took a train to Budapest, where an uncle—reportedly the last remaining member of their family—had been sighted. Despite the fact that they possessed neither an address nor any real concrete information about his location, they hoped by some miracle they would find him. After all, they had been relatively blessed until now with their "luck" holding out.

But when the two disembarked at the Budapest train station, their "good fortune" faltered. Swallowed up by the hordes of people milling about, they became separated. Her heart hammering with fear, Eva began to frantically search for her younger sister, running up and down the station platform, indiscriminately screaming, "Vera! Vera!" Heads swiveled and fingers pointed in the direction of the crazed woman, but Vera's beloved visage did not appear.

Oh, no, Eva thought. *After all this time . . . after beating the odds over and over again . . . to have this happen, to lose each other now?*

Finally, someone tapped Eva on the shoulder, and she spun around joyfully with her arms outstretched, ready to scoop her lost sister into her arms. But it was a stranger who stood there, not Vera, a young woman who had heard her screams.

"Are you by any chance one of the Lux sisters?" she asked.

"Who are you? How could you possibly know that?" Eva demanded.

"I'm your uncle's sister-in-law, and he's been sending me to the train station every day to look for you, hoping that you knew he was in Budapest and were looking for him. He didn't have any photographs of the two of you, and I had no idea how I was going to be able to track you down, but he did tell me that your names were Eva and Vera. When I heard you scream for Vera, I hoped you might be one of the sisters I was looking for."

Eventually, Vera was found, and the two sisters were given sanctuary in their uncle's home, where they lived for a short time. Vera found refuge in Bratislava, Slovakia, in an Agudat Israel facility for girls orphaned by the war. From there she emigrated to the United States where she married Shimon Strauss and raised a beautiful Jewish family.

But Eva remained in Kosice; she had to find her father first. She haunted the halls of the Jewish agencies that had been set up in Europe to aid survivors, who formed a constant, daily presence that quivered with concurrent hope and dread. Here, bulletin boards inventoried the known living and the known dead. Homemade flyers scrawled with desperate messages plastered the walls, pleading, *Do you know? Have you seen? Looking for . . .* But Eva never found her father's name listed anywhere. She pored through the newspapers, carefully perusing each ad, every single news article, in the vain hope that they might yield clues to his whereabouts, or provide some suggestion that he was still alive. She searched the displaced persons camps, where the ragged tatters of Europe's Jews were given safe haven, but her father was not to be found. Finally, Eva determined to do what Miriam had done in the first place: return to her old hometown of Kosice and wait for her father there.

Eva wondered if Miriam would still be in Kosice when she arrived, but Miriam was long gone. In Bai-Mare, Transylvania, Miriam had found employment as a bookkeeper in a business run by the well-known Brach family, becoming a permanent fixture and beloved member of their household. Eventually, she married Sam Brach, one of their sons, and moved with him to Italy as refugees.

Eva and Miriam's paths kept on brushing against each other's, but never quite intersected. They thought about one another constantly, and wondered where each had gone.

Eva remained in Kosice, steadfast as ever, faithfully waiting for her father to return home. She waited for five fruitless years before she confronted her worst fears: He wasn't coming back. He had disappeared into the vortex and void of the Holocaust, a nameless number. There was no gravestone she could visit, no *yahrzeit* she could mark. It wasn't until 1950 that her last hopes flickered, then died. Eva finally recognized that she would have to try to rebuild her life without him, alone.

Eva moved back to Romania, where she was joyously reunited with the man to whom she had been engaged before the war—Eli Braun, a Holocaust survivor from Slovakia. After they married, they decied to leave Europe, from where most of the other Jews had long since dispersed. But where should they go? Survivors had scattered to new lives all over the world—to Israel, the United States, Canada, England, France, Australia, and South America—the majority preferring to leave the countries of Eastern Europe so drenched in Jewish blood.

"What do you think we should do?" Eva asked her husband. Her in-laws, Rifka and Baruch Braun, had moved to the United States, the *goldene medina* . . . the golden country. They insisted that the young couple join them in Williamsburg, Brooklyn, where they and many other transplanted survivors lived. They would make all the necessary arrangements. By the time Eva and Eli arrived in Williamsburg, their new apartment was painted, cleaned, furnished, and ready.

A few days after Eva had moved to Williamsburg, she stood on the doorsteps of her new home, breathing in the fragrant air of freedom, surveying the foreign street scene with curiosity and interest. It was then that she noticed a familiar and most beloved figure hurrying down the street.

"Miriam!" she screamed.

The two ran into each other's arms, kissed, wept, and gazed at one another in rapt wonder.

"But where do you live?" Eva asked, when they finally broke their embrace.

"Oh," said Miriam. "Right across the street."

Postscript: Sixty-three years after Liberation, Miriam Brach and Eva Braun—both living in Flushing, Queens—remain steadfast friends. They both have been blessed with children, grandchildren, and great-grandchildren, and they participate in each other's *simchas* (happy family occasions)—births, *bar* and *bat mitzvahs*, weddings. Every occasion is another personal victory, another spiritual triumph, a celebration, a declaration: "We are still here. And we have won."

What makes these exquisite moments even sweeter is their shared friendship—one that has spanned the dark years and the lighter ones. Miriam, gentle and sweet, looks up with admiration and gratitude at the still-fiery Eva, and says, "She is my hero. She saved my life." Eva smiles and expounds on the meaning of heroism. "Today, we equate heroism with apocalyptic acts of physical courage. We think of heroism in terms of Superman—leaping tall buildings with a single bound, holding up trains with a simple motion of the hand. But heroism can be moral resistance, too. And it can be something as small and simple as the mere raising up of an inconsequential water hose."

LIFE IN A JAR

The Warsaw Ghetto, the most infamous Jewish containment area during World War II, was created by the Nazis in order to expedite the mass murder of the Jewish people. The Nazis relentlessly amassed hundreds of thousands of Polish Jews and entrapped them in a mere sixteen-block radius, where even the most basic human rights were denied. Unbeknownst to the suffering souls holding on to hope for a better future, the ghetto was just a layover for those Jews who survived its brutality. Their destination would ultimately be the Nazi concentration camps, where they would be killed in the gas chambers. But even before their deportation to the Final Solution, Jews were dying by the tens of thousands in the ghetto. Starvation, disease, and random violence worked in tandem to kill them ahead of schedule.

One light shined amidst the darkness: Irena Sendler. Irena, a Catholic social worker, worked as the senior administrator of a social welfare department, which was a government agency. This job allowed her entry into the ghetto. Inside the sealed walls for the first time, Irena was overcome by compassion for the Jews—and fury at their tormentors. She could not just stand by helplessly and watch them die.

In 1942, Irena was one of the first recruits to join Zegota, an underground resistance movement formed to help Jews in Occupied Poland wage a clandestine war against the Nazis. She was recruited to head the children's division and she was now in charge of twenty-five people who helped in various capacities. To effect a change in the ghetto on any grand scale seemed impossible. But in terms of the children who dwelled inside its walls, saving them was an entirely different matter, and *not* a hopeless one. Irena began to dedicate herself to the sole mission of rescuing the Nazis' most defenseless victims, even if it meant risking her own life.

This is how she did it: Irena would approach a mother holding a baby in her arms and make her pitch, begging the mother to trust her to find a home for the infant. "Can you guarantee that my baby will live?" the mother would implore. "I can only guarantee that all Jewish babies will die if they stay," Irena would reply. For Irena, persuading parents to part with their children was in itself a horrendous task. She witnessed heartbreaking scenes. Sometimes the father would agree but the mother wouldn't; sometimes the reverse was true. One grandmother who was approached by Irena clasped the child tenderly to her breast and, weeping bitterly, said: "I won't give away my grandchild at any price."

In these instances, Irena had no choice but to leave empty-handed. Many times she would return the next day to find that this particular family—baby included—had just been transported to the death camps. But there were many families that *did* choose Irena's alternative and allow their babies to be placed in the hands of a total stranger. Irena endured the intense cries of both the parents and the babies as they separated, and then faced her next overwhelming challenge: smuggling them out of the ghetto.

The tactics used to usher the children out of the ghetto were perilous. Some children were sedated and taken out in body bags, while others were buried inside loads of goods. Many babies were carried out in potato sacks, coffins, suitcases, and, once, even a toolbox. A few were hidden under ambulance stretchers. The ambulance driver, a Zegota member himself, kept his dog beside him in the front seat and trained him to bark to camouflage any cries or noises coming from the babies hidden in the back. Irena prepared false documents, giving each child a false identity and then placing him or her in a private home or orphanage outside the ghetto, in Warsaw.

Irena's efforts did not end there. Her hope was that after the war, she would be able to reveal to the children their true Jewish identities and reunite them with family members who had survived. For this purpose, Irena methodically and systematically cataloged the names, family origins, and new identities of each child in coded form. Then she placed these tiny pieces of paper into jars, hiding the jars in the trunk of an apple tree in her neighbor's backyard.

On October 20, 1943, Irena was arrested by the Nazis, who had become aware of her prominent role in the underground movement. One of the Zegota members had been caught and tortured until she gave up Irena's name and home address. Irena was taken to the Gestapo, where the SS tried to coerce her into divulging the names of the other Zegota members, as well as the names of the families that had agreed to harbor the children she'd removed from the ghetto. Irena refused to give them any information. During the interrogation, the Nazis broke her legs, but they could not break her spirit.

Frustrated by Irena's stalwart position, the Nazis took her to Pawiak Prison in Warsaw, sentencing her to death. As she waited in her prison cell for the sentence to be carried out, Irena thought about the children whose only trace to their families would disappear with her death. How would they ever be reunited with their lawful biological relatives? She was the only one who knew where the children were hidden, and the only one who could decipher her coded files.

But the woman who had saved so many lives was destined to be saved as well. Irena was widely respected and admired by the members of Zegota, and they spared no effort in finding a way to have her death sentence rescinded. One high-ranking Gestapo officer proved susceptible to a large bribe, and he colluded with Zegota to secure her release. He falsified official documents stating that she had been killed by a firing squad, when, in fact, she had been snatched up by the underground and smuggled out of the seemingly impenetrable Gestapo jail.

Two months later, the Gestapo discovered that the papers that documented Irena's death were false, and they reopened her case. Irena obtained new identity papers and moved away from her home, taking her dying mother with her. The Gestapo was unrelenting in its hunt for Irena. Members of the SS even appeared at her mother's funeral, asking for the dead woman's daughter. Although she was now crippled as a result of the torture she had endured, with the help of fellow Zegota members, she persevered in her efforts to save Jewish children and adults from the ghetto, and continued to place coded records in a jar under the apple tree.

When the war was finally over, Irena dug up the jars and used the notes to track down the 2,500 children; she then tried to reunite them with their relatives. But by the war's end, a total of three million Polish Jews had perished, and less than 1 percent of the Jews who had dwelled inside the ghetto had survived the war. Sadly, most of "Irena's children" were now bereft of both parents *and* grandparents. Many were placed in Jewish orphanages, sent to Israeli youth villages, or dispatched to other relatives all over the world.

Although the war had ended, Irena Sendler's odyssey did not.

Other than being honored in Yad Vashem in 1965, Irena Sendler's story was essentially lost to history. In 1999, Irena was approaching the age of ninety and living alone in a modest room in Poland. She mourned the death of her son who had passed away at the untimely age of fifty-four.

Meanwhile, in an obscure little town in Kansas, four ninth graders named Megan Stewart, Elizabeth Cambers, Jessica Shelton, and Sabrina Coons were looking for a project to present on National History Day. The students' assignment included—among other things—finding a person who typified their classroom motto: "He who changes one person, changes the entire world." Their social science teacher, Mr. Conard, showed the students a brief reference to Irena Sendler in a five-year-old magazine article. The article stated that Irena had saved 2,500 Jewish children. "This number can't be right," was their immediate reaction. "It must be a typo. It probably meant to say 250, *not* 2,500, since we've never even heard of her." The girls pounced on the opportunity to bring this story to life. After a little research, they discovered that Irena did in fact save 2,500 children, not 250. Assuming that she must have passed away, they tried—via the Internet and international phone calls—to find the name of the cemetery where she was buried. They were stunned to discover that she was alive, although frail.

The girls produced a play about Irena and called it *Life in a Jar*. It was an immediate hit. The students dreamed of visiting Warsaw and personally meeting Irena, but lack of funds stood in their way. In January 2001, they performed the play again, this time in a city about a hundred miles from their school. A Jewish educator and businessman saw the performance and heard about their dream. Within twenty-four hours he had raised enough money to cover the cost of a trip to Poland for the students, their parents, and the teacher who had started it all.

In Poland, the girls were graciously received by Irena. She hugged them and showered them with blessings and good wishes. The Polish press embraced the story and it became international news. "Your performance and work is continuing the effort I started over fifty years ago; you are my dearly beloved girls," Irena said, overcome with gratitude for the hand that had brought these young women to her. They would return three more times to visit and care for her.

Postscript: Irena's deeds continue to live on: Since it made its debut, *Life in a Jar* has been presented to 50,000 people worldwide; both in Kansas and in Poland, there is now an official "Irena Sendler" week; an "Irena Sendler Award" has been established for teachers both in Poland and the United States who present Holocaust education in an outstanding manner; and a Web site, www.irenasendler.org, has been created to supplement Holocaust and tolerance education.

In 2007, Irena Sendler was one of the top contenders for the Nobel Peace Prize, nominated jointly by the governments of both Poland and Israel. She didn't win, but at the ceremony Poland's president Lech Kaczynski described her as a "great hero who deserves respect from our entire nation." Israeli ambassador David Peleg said after the ceremony, "I think that her courage is very special. I think she's a great lady . . . a model for the whole international community." Elzbieta Ficowska, one of the ghetto infants Irena carried out in a carpenter's box, read a letter written by her rescuer: "Every child saved with my help is the justification of my existence on this Earth, and not a title to glory . . . Let me stress most emphatically that we who were rescuing children are not heroes. Indeed, that term irritates me greatly. The opposite is true—I continue to have qualms of conscience that I did so little."

On May 12, 2008, Irena Sendler died at the age of ninety-eight in her home country of Poland.

A ROBBER'S REDEMPTION

The seven thousand Jewish residents of the Lvov Ghetto were growing increasingly tense, and some had even gone insane. Their already
circumscribed lives had shrunk even smaller in 1943, with the arrival
of SS Obersturmführer Gryzmek, infamously dubbed "the ghetto
liquidator." When new and harsher restrictions were set in place,
the Jews were sure that their days were numbered. But the turning
point—more than any other event—that pushed many of them over
the edge was an *Aktion* against the children of the ghetto, taking them
completely by surprise.

One morning, a contrived "work detail" comprised of all the adult
residents had been marched outside the concrete walls that fenced
them in. In their parents' absence, the Nazis had hunted and snatched
up the ghetto's young, hurling them onto the trucks that waited to
carry them into the jaws of the Gestapo killing machine. The roundup
had been efficient but slow, so the trucks were still standing there
with their swarming loads when the mothers returned.

Howling in anguish, frenzied women broke loose from the line
in which they marched, and, dodging bullets, flung themselves at the
trucks, screaming their childrens' names: *Sorah! Moshe! Miriam! Hershel!*
The ghetto reverberated with the mothers' screams, their children's
cries, and the Nazis' rough voices barking orders as they attempted
to regain control. The women clambered onto the trucks, frantic to

find their sons and daughters, and were either pulled off or shot dead. "Go! Go!" SS Obersturmführer Gryzmek, ghetto commander and mastermind of the *Aktion*, yelled to the drivers. The trucks rumbled away, crushing the bodies of the women who propelled themselves into their path. A stunned, paralyzed silence fell upon the numbed residents, and in that moment, many lost their reason to live, their will to fight. They shuffled back to their quarters and quietly, without fanfare, swallowed the vials of cyanide that had been prepared a long time ago.

* * *

Ignacy Chiger and his wife, Paulina, were among the few who were spared the heartbreak. Ignacy, blessed with both prescience and engineering skill, had built secret bunkers throughout his apartment months before in preparation for just such an occurrence. His two children—ages seven and four—had been carefully instructed to hide in the most impregnable one whenever their parents were away or missing. After the *Aktion* against the children, the Chigers called a meeting with their friends and relatives. "It's time to implement our plan," they said.

Several weeks before the *Aktion*, the Chigers and ten other people had begun chipping away—first with spoons and forks, and later with chisels smuggled into the ghetto—at the cellar floor beneath the room that belonged to a man named Weiss. Chiger and two other engineers he had recruited had correctly calculated that Weiss's room lay directly above their escape hatch—the sewers of Lvov.

It was common knowledge in the ghetto that a few desperate souls had already tried this route, but no one had been known to survive. Nazi soldiers, stationed at both the manholes in the streets and at the banks of the Peltrew River into which the sewers flowed, watched vigilantly for their quarry to emerge—for a breath of fresh air, a ray of sunlight, a morsel of food. When they invariably surfaced, as they always did, they were shot down in cold blood. The Chigers and their friends knew the odds, but still believed that the sewers of Lvov represented their one real recourse.

A few nights before, they had finished building a tunnel to the sewers, and several had slipped down the shaft to size up their surroundings. With a flashlight the men were able to find a three-foot ledge that abutted the raging waters of the Peltrew, and was in fact a pathway than ran along the underground river. They tentatively stumbled forward with the hope of unearthing a dried-out channel, pipe, or storm basin where they could hide. One of them retched, while another muttered: "Hades couldn't possibly be worse."

Inching their way along the ledge, a few men momentarily lost their footing and cursed. Another man plunged into the turbid waters below and screamed, almost swept away save for the strong arm of a comrade who pulled him out. It was the cursing and screams that drew the attention of three Polish maintenance engineers, sewer workers who were doing inspections further down the ledge. More surefooted and practiced than Chiger and his friends, the sewer workers accosted the men before they could flee. Although their faces were in shadow and unreadable, their voices held clear menace.

"Jews!" one of them exclaimed triumphantly.

"We have to turn you in," a second sneered. "There's a big reward. You're finished."

But a third came across as more amiable. "I must say, I'm much impressed by your ingenuity," he chuckled. His name was Leopold Socha. Of the three, his past had been the most checkered. He was also the most sympathetic to the Lvov Jews' plight and prevailed upon the others to follow suit.

"I think we can help you find a safe, dry place," Socha said, "but you have to pay us first. You have to understand: If we betray you, we are heroes; if we are caught, we—and our entire families—will be hung. Of course, as human beings, we want to help you . . . but the money would be a big incentive."

Chiger immediately pulled out a wad of bills. "I'll pay you on account," he said.

"We'll search for a suitable hiding place for you," Socha said. "Meet us here tomorrow, same time." As he turned to leave, he grasped Chiger's hand, saying with conviction, "Don't worry—everything will turn out well."

When the sewer workers disappeared down the ledge, Weiss turned to Chiger with dismay. "You gave them money in advance? Are you crazy? What if they betray us?"

"What else can we do?" Chiger asked. "Whether I give them the money or not, they can still betray us. We are in their hands. But don't be anxious, my friend. I'm a great judge of character. I don't know about the other men, but I do believe that we can trust Socha. And he is clearly their leader."

This conversation had taken place only a few weeks before the *Aktion*. Socha and his men had found a dried-up pipe filled with silt and infested with rats which they had deemed "suitable." Together with Chiger and his friends, they had removed the debris and brought down boards from the ghetto with which they had constructed makeshift benches and beds. Dry foodstuffs—cereal, barley, oats, flour, sugar—and sundry supplies (including a small kerosene stove) were stockpiled in a dry corner of their new home. With their preparations made and provisions in place, Socha and his friends now waited for a prearranged signal from the Lvov Jews. The *Aktion* had accelerated their original timetable, and they decided they could wait no longer. The moment had arrived to put their escape plan into motion.

When the plan had first been conceived by Chiger and his cohorts, their group had consisted of thirteen people. But by the time they assembled in Weiss's room to make their retreat, their ranks had grown to seventy. Somehow word had leaked out to other desperate Jews in the ghetto, and they had found their way to Weiss's escape hatch. Chiger knew Socha had not anticipated that their numbers would swell to such an amount, but how could he refuse a fellow Jew? One by one, they slipped down the manhole, grabbing at the slippery wall until their feet touched the solid ground of the ledge. When Socha met the group of Jews at a prearranged place on the ledge, he didn't say a word about their expanded numbers.

Socha led them to the secret shelter where their carefully laid plans were thrown into total disarray. The chamber that they had cleaned, equipped, and furnished, and where they had stashed hundreds of pounds of provisions, was *already occupied*. Hordes of other Jews had apparently slipped through manholes in the street and were already crammed into their space. Socha and Chiger looked at each other wordlessly. Socha squared his shoulders and said, "Come— we'll have to find a new place."

Another storm basin was soon found, but it made the first shelter look like the Hilton. Armies of bizarre-looking insects writhed on the walls, while the eyes of a pack of rats glinted forbiddingly in the dark. Damp slime oozed on the ground, and there was nowhere to sit but on a few limestone rocks. All of their equipment, supplies, and makeshift furniture was in the first shelter, which was now lost to them. Most important, the ample food provisions that they had stored in the other shelter were also gone. Chiger turned to Socha and said the words that everyone else in his group was thinking: "What are we going to do about food?"

The bargain that the Chigers had originally struck with Socha was that he would guide them to their sanctuary; food and supplies had never been part of the equation. But clearly they couldn't live without them, and now, they had substantially more mouths to feed. How could Socha possibly provide for *seventy* people?

"Don't worry," Socha said after they were settled. "I'll be back with food tomorrow."

The next day, Socha returned carrying two huge workman's bags. Normally used to hold tools, they were now stuffed with bread and potatoes. He handed the food out to Chiger's group, and then went looking for the other Jews hiding in the sewer, and fed them as well.

"The Germans know you're hiding here," Socha told everyone, including Chiger's group. "Keep away from the manholes. They're planning to throw grenades into the manholes to kill you or smoke you out. They've also decided to patrol the sewers, but they've asked *me* to lead them. Don't worry—I'll guide them away from you. I'll take care of you. They won't find you . . . don't worry."

A few days later, Socha—deeming the hiding place of Chiger's group too close to the manholes and consequently vulnerable to attack—moved them yet again to a still "more suitable" place: a large tunnel that broadened into an alcove, reeking with raw sewage and slithering with rats. "I know it's uncomfortable here," he apologized, "but it's safer." No one uttered a word of complaint.

Socha continued to go above and beyond the call of duty for Chiger's group. Sadly, there was no longer any reason to look after the other Jews who had hidden in the sewers, as they had all passed away. Some had starved to death; others had committed suicide, and those who had been driven out of their hiding place had been gunned down by the Nazis who waited patiently at the manholes. Still, the task of keeping Chiger's group alive and healthy under such abhorrent conditions was monumental. To get to Chiger's group, Socha and his men had to crawl through the narrow pipes with bags under their arms, their carbide lamps dangling from their teeth. They would arrive each morning, weighted down with food supplies. Although conditions were abysmal in the sewers, it was far better than the alternative. Tragically, however, an increasing number of Chiger's members succumbed to the same conditions that had ravaged their fellow Jews who were hiding in the sewers: starvation, hopelessness, insanity. Soon their group of seventy had diminished, returning to their original thirteen.

Socha and his coworkers brought Chiger's group more than just food and supplies; they became a veritable lifeline to the outside world. The men brought them news, gossip, and rumors, distracting them from their isolation and loneliness. Sometimes the news was overwhelmingly bleak; sometimes it was more encouraging. It was Socha who informed them that the ghetto above their heads had ceased to exist: It had been liquidated, its residents murdered, their quarters burned and gutted. It was also Socha who told them of the dramatic but slow Russian successes in the Ukraine, in his measured attempt to keep up the group's spirits.

Socha often visited the shelter without his comrades, spending up to two hours at a time talking with the Jews, encouraging them, bearing small gifts to brighten their days. He brought little trinkets to distract the children, and for the adults, used newspapers and books to keep them informed. And for Paulina Chiger, he brought candles and a carbide lamp (for fuel) every Friday for Shabbos observance. Socha's arrival was the highlight of their day. The Jews regarded him as their guardian angel. With his glowing eyes and luminous smile, Socha was a beacon of light in their dreary lives. Without him, they could never have survived.

And survive they did—for an astonishing full year, by which time, their money had run out. Socha continued without his payment.

* * *

During that long year of suffering in the sewers, the Chiger group exchanged many intimate secrets with Socha—and he did the same. In fact, his personal account proved to be the most surprising story of them all.

"I come from a very poor, low-class home," he told them, "and my parents threw me out into the streets—where I lived—when I was all of ten. The only way I could survive was by stealing. I fell in with a criminal element, and in their company, any conscience I had left was erased. I became a common thief, and was caught and arrested many times, but since I was so young, I was always released. My parents never took me back, and I always returned to the streets.

"As I got older and more experienced, my horizons expanded. I got into the big leagues. I no longer engaged in petty theft, but became a serious criminal. My name and picture appeared in the newspapers in connection with a particularly well-known bank robbery in Lvov. Perhaps you remember it?"

Chiger's group—all respectable, law-abiding, middle-class citizens before the war—nodded in stunned recollection, trying to hide their dawning horror about Socha's disreputable past.

"I was in prison three separate times, but released quickly," Socha continued. "I became adept at my trade. I kept on getting involved in crimes that were bigger and bolder than the ones before. I liked the risk; to me they were adventures. . . . Ah, I see by your faces that you are shocked. *This is the man who has been helping us all along?* you are thinking in disbelief. My friends, it is *precisely* because this is my past that I have helped you, and am helping you to this day.

"You see," Socha turned to them sadly, his usual easygoing, good-natured manner subdued by his own confession, "what I am doing for you represents my penance, my plea for the forgiveness of G-d. Despite everything, I always believed in G-d. And I feel terrible for everything I did. I am hoping that just like I have snatched you away from certain death, the angels are snatching sins away from my soul, and I will be redeemed. Today—after all this time we've spent together, all the ordeals we've undergone—I have great affection, even love, for all of you; I care tremendously about what happens to you. But when I first took on this mission, it was to make up for all the terrible deeds I had done in the past."

Socha looked at them with shame as he continued to recount his past crimes. "Perhaps you have heard of this famous case? A major robbery at a popular jewelry store in the district down by the main railway station? It has always remained unsolved—until today. Now I confess to you: I was the thief . . ."

Socha was so hell-bent on his own self-flagellation, so immersed in his own narrative, that he almost missed the flurry of emotions that flitted across Paulina Chiger's face. But when he heard her sharp intake of breath, her unmistakable gasp of disbelief, he looked up and locked eyes with her.

"What is it, Paulina?" he asked. "What's wrong?"

"This jewelry store, near the railway station . . . the jewelry store that was robbed—it belonged to my family."

Postscript: On July 28, 1944, after the city was liberated by the Russian army, Socha triumphantly led Chiger's group out of the sewers into the streets of Lvov. The Jews were emaciated, begrimed, foul-smelling, weak, and temporarily blind. As they stood blinking sightlessly in Bernardine Square, the Polish citizens of Lvov came running from all directions to surround and stare at these underworld apparitions. Socha stood proudly at their side and announced over and over again: "This is my work. All my work. These are my Jews."

On May 12, 1946, Leopold Socha and his daughter, Stefcia, were bicycling through Lvov when a Russian truck came barreling down the narrow street. Stefcia was several yards ahead of her father. Socha raced to her side, pushed her off her bicycle out of the truck's way, and took the hit himself. He was killed instantly. Although "his Jews" had already dispersed to all corners of the globe, they returned to Lvov for his funeral and marched behind Socha's wife and child in the funeral procession. Devastated by his death, the "sewer Jews" gathered in Socha's home after the funeral to pay their respects to his family.

It was then that they heard a voice ring out from the back of the room: "This is G-d's retribution. This is what comes from helping the Jews."

THE REN TWINS

In French, the root word *Ren* is a word laden with hope, for it means "reborn." No one knew if it was with a sense of irony or a spirit of defiance that Ita and Herbert Guttmann chose this word to name their newborn twins, for when they made their entrance into this world, it was dark with foreboding. It was December 1937, and Europe was quivering on the threshold of imploding. An imminent sense of death and destruction loomed over the Jews of Czechoslovakia, and everything they had once held dear was slowly slipping away. Hope seemed to be one of the few intangibles they would be able to hold on to.

Like many other Jews, Ita Guttmann did not believe that naming children was an arbitrary, casual matter. Names contained symbols, influenced destinies. Wanting feverishly to protect her twins from the coming storm, she carefully named their tiny son Rene and his twin sister Irene. "With the word 'reborn' at the root of both their names," Ita prayed, "may they be blessed to live despite the doom of the coming years."

For four years, Czechoslovakia withstood the coming onslaught, even as other countries fell to the Nazis. Because of the situation, the parents could not get work and the little support they had came from relatives. Despite this, the Guttmann home was an oasis, where life revolved around the twins and the ominous noises from the outside world were shut out. Ita and Herbert doted on their two growing children, taking tremendous pride in their small accomplishments, marveling at their growth, snapping photos every time they yawned, napped, laughed, ate, clowned around, played. In short, the Guttmanns were typical parents, and the twins were typical children. Though they lived in atypical times, Rene and Irene were oblivious to the sounds of war that grew louder with each passing day.

It was 1941 when Herbert was snatched by German soldiers who stormed the house one night. In front of his panic-stricken wife and children, two SS officers pinned Herbert's arms to his sides and pulled him roughly out the door. The children's and Ita's screams pierced the night, but not the Nazis' hearts. Herbert was hauled away to the Auschwitz concentration camp where he was later killed. Meanwhile, Ita and the twins were taken to the Theresienstadt concentration camp.

To ensure that the world wouldn't get in the way of their intentions to exterminate the Jews, the Germans had built this particular camp with a false facade that served as a gathering place for reporters and members of the Red Cross who had come to investigate. It was sheer propaganda, a "Big Lie." At Theresienstadt, families were shown spending "quality" time together, and working under normal circumstances. Behind the facade, however, a far different reality existed: The working conditions were intolerable and people were routinely being tortured, starved, and killed. Since Ita and the twins were housed in the area that was utilized for propaganda purposes, she was able to to have a little more time with her children.

But not too much time.

On December 15, 1943, Ita and her twins received orders to report for "resettlement to the East." This actually meant they were being sent to Auschwitz, the infamous death camp. Although a sign emblazoned on the front gate of Auschwitz announced ARBEIT MACHT

FREI (Work will make you free), nothing could have been further from the truth. No matter how hard you worked in Auschwitz, you were fated for extermination. The sign was yet another Nazi device designed to trick and deceive, and to quell the possibility of revolt.

The Guttmanns arrived in Auschwitz a few days before the twins' sixth birthday. They stayed together in the family *lager* until March of 1944, when their world fell apart. Ita's hands, hands that had been clutching on to her beloved son and daughter for dear life, were brutally ripped away. She didn't go silently, issuing forth a piercing, earth-shaking scream that would reverberate in her children's ears forevermore.

Although Irene and Rene were spared from the gas chambers, they were destined for a fate some might have considered even worse. They were placed in the "Mengele group." Dr. Mengele was notorious for his heinous experimentation with twins. Mengele used twins as laboratory guinea pigs in his obsessive search to perfect and produce a master Aryan race. Among many cruel and heartless procedures, he sterilized some twins, gave some organ transplants, ordered blood transfusions, and injected ink into some of their eyes to see if they would become blue.

Dr. Mengele worked with precision. He would experiment on one twin and use the other as the "control." Rene was the control subject, so he was continuously being brought in for observation. While he was weighed, measured, pricked, and prodded with cold, sharp objects, Irene was the subject of the invasive surgeries. At only six and a half years of age, with no loved ones around, Irene craved affection. When people are desperate for love, they will seek it—even from the devil. This little orphan was no exception. Incongruously, Irene sought to find favor in Dr. Mengele's eyes.

When she was called in for experiments, she followed orders exactly and behaved like a good little girl. Even when he put her naked on the cold steel table and her body writhed with chills. Even when he jabbed her arm with a long thin needle that was filled with poisonous fluids and it pierced deep into her frail body. And even when he repeated his experiments again and again, Irene bit her lip and cried on the inside. It all took place in a cold room surrounded with steel wires and machinery—cruelty committed by bitterly cold-blooded people with cold hands.

Since the camp was segregated according to gender, Irene and Rene had not seen each other since the fateful day when they had been ripped away from their mother. At the tender age of six, they watched in horror as the mounds of emaciated dead bodies strewn about the camp grew, like dead leaves falling from trees. They watched as the cattle cars kept rolling in, delivering hundreds of thousands of innocent people to their final destination. They watched the smoke from the furnace rise up into the heavens, a place where they hoped their parents now rested. A place they wanted to join because life seemed unbearable . . . until the day brother and sister saw each other across a barbed-wire fence. All the boys were on one side and all the girls were on another, yet somehow, they caught a fleeting glimpse, brief but life-sustaining. They didn't say anything to one another; they couldn't. They didn't even smile. There wasn't enough time, it all happened so fast.

But it was long enough to give each one of them enough hope to go on. Each now had a reason to live—someone to live for.

* * *

Of the 3,000 twins that had entered Auschwitz at the beginning of the war and passed through Mengele's hands in human experiments, only 200 survived. On liberation day, January 27, 1945, Irene and Rene were among them. Neither of them knew that the other had survived, since chaos reigned and they were still separated into different sections of the camp with no point of intersection. They had not seen one another since that short-lived moment across the barbed wire.

Soldiers from the Allied forces, officials from a multitude of Jewish agencies, and members of the Red Cross descended upon the camps to help with social welfare needs, resettlement, and—in the rare cases of orphaned children who had survived—foster care adoption. Irene was sent to an orphanage, where she encountered Rabbi William Novick, an official with Rescue Children. This organization's mandate was to find orphaned Jewish children and bring them to America, where they were more likely to be placed in homes with Jewish values.

Rabbi Novick decided that Irene was the perfect poster child for their cause. Her enchanting, soulful look endeared her to everyone. An unmistakable *joie de vivre* lurked behind her sad yet twinkling eyes, and the multiple contradictions that resided within her—hope despite horror, love of life built on death itself—made her a fascinating symbol of rebirth. Irene's jaunty manner even caught the attention of *Life* magazine, and a writer with the publication decided to track Irene's progress as she embarked upon her new life in America. A photographer for the magazine trailed her everywhere.

Life magazine was there when Irene looked up in awe at the famous Empire State Building. Photos were snapped of her in various department stores where she gazed in rapture at the endless racks of frilly dresses. Reporters traipsed after her as she examined, starstruck, the neon signs that winked from the tall buildings in Times Square, buildings that seemed to reach up to eternity. Dutiful as always, Irene twirled and pirouetted obligingly before the cameras, helping the photographers create a flurry of charming portraits.

She seemed to have adjusted easily to her new life in the States. Up until this point, she was called Renata. Now, she even had her name changed to a more American "Irene."

But what about her soul? What about the gaping hole in her heart that was left when she heard her mother's last scream? When would that be filled? Would it ever?

At a fund-raising dinner for the Rescue Children organization, it was announced that the Slotkin family of America had opened their hearts to Irene and had decided to adopt her. Irene moved in with the Slotkins and finally had a place she could call home. The Slotkins hoped it would be a place where she could heal completely.

Despite her cheerful personality, Irene remained silent about the personal trauma she had endured in Europe. She wasn't sure that anyone would want to hear her story, or, if they did, whether they'd believe it. So she kept it all inside. But just as a wilting plant can miraculously spring back to life with some water, so too did Irene. The Slotkins showered her with unconditional love and her aching soul began to mend. Even though she became increasingly comfortable in her new home, however, the hole in her heart could not be filled; she missed her brother so much. It was this intense longing to see her brother that finally allowed her to break her silence.

"I have a brother," she said one day.

"What?!" her newfound family exclaimed in astonishment. "What are you saying? Could this possibly be true?"

"I have a twin brother," Irene repeated.

The Slotkins believed her. They spared no expense in launching an international search for Irene's twin, spending over twenty thousand dollars to fund the operation. They hired private investigators to comb the world for her twin, instructing them to "leave no stone unturned." But where could they even begin to look? Amidst the rubble of post-Holocaust Europe, it seemed unlikely Rene would ever be found without any solid clues or leads. The investigation seemed to be an exercise in futility.

On November 17, 1947, a man walked past a newsstand in Israel and picked up a magazine to read at home. Seated in his favorite armchair, he leisurely leafed through *Life* while sipping a cup of tea. When he turned to the page that bore Irene's smiling face, something inside him clicked. It reminded him of another face vividly imprinted on his mind—one he had known well in postwar Europe and one he had wanted to adopt before he was forced to flee to Palestine from Communist Czechoslovakia. Without missing a beat, Dr. Kalina telephoned his sister, a woman who never had access to American publications in Czechoslovakia.

"Please put Rene on the phone!" Dr. Kalina told his sister, the woman who had been taking care of Irene's brother. With one hand cradling the phone and the other holding the magazine, Dr. Kalina stammered his news.

"Rene," he said, "I have found your twin sister!"

Postscript: Rene and Irene were both taken care of by the Slotniks. They grew up together and never grew apart. They have spoken every day since they were reunited, and haven't missed a day in over fifty years. Rene, trying to put the past behind him, tends to be silent about his experiences. Irene, on the other hand, considers it a great honor to have the opportunity to share her story with others and is now a nationally renowned speaker. Both live in the New York area, where both families combined have six children and twelve grandchildren.

Jerry Simon* first met Yehuda Finerman* at a kibbutz in Israel. Jerry had fled there after a brief stint in the U.S. Army, where he had encountered subtle and not-so-subtle forms of anti-Semitism. *"Just a few short years after World War II,"* Jerry had thought in anguish, *"and nobody seems to have learned any lessons. What kind of world do we live in?"*

One hot summer day, when the two were toiling side by side under the blazing sun and Yehuda's shirtsleeves were rolled up high, Jerry couldn't help but notice the numbers tattooed on his friend's forearm—7416. He gasped.

"What's the matter, Jerry?" Yehuda asked.

"I . . . I'm sorry, Yehuda," Jerry stammered. "I'm not trying to be nosy or anything, but I couldn't help but notice the numbers on your forearm."

"Surely you've seen them on other survivors before," Yehuda responded curtly.

"Of course I have. It's . . . it's just . . . Well, what struck me as odd is that your concentration camp numbers—seven, four, one, six—just happen to be the last four digits of my American social security number!"

"That's what you're so excited about?" Yehuda scoffed. "It's just a meaningless coincidence."

"Look, Yehuda," Jerry pleaded, "I know it's hard for you . . . but I care about you, deeply. Could you tell me how you got those numbers?"

Yehuda looked at Jerry thoughtfully. "Maybe it *is* a mistake for survivors to hide their experiences from the rest of the world. Maybe we *were* meant to serve as witnesses. . . . All right, Jerry. I'll tell you exactly what happened."

For the next hour, Yehuda told his story. "And then, we stood on line at selection—my brothers, my sisters, my parents, and I—and we were branded with these concentration camp numbers, in numerical order. I was next to last, followed by my brother. Afterward, we were split up, and I never saw any of them again. I was the only one in my family who survived the war."

Jerry was silent when Yehuda's recital of the terrors he had suffered came to an abrupt end. What could he possibly say in the face of such suffering? Now he understood why survivors were loath to recount their stories. Their nightmare was truly unutterable, unspeakable. But still, the story had to be told . . . didn't it?

Many years later, Jerry had left the kibbutz and was working in the Jerusalem–Tel Aviv area as a tour guide for wealthy Americans who wanted to be personally chaperoned around Israel in a comfortable limousine. Most of his clients were kind and amiable, and Jerry generally enjoyed his job. But one day, he picked up a new client at the airport whose behavior was downright insufferable. The man was domineering, rude, and harsh. He was a control freak, and continually shouted orders at Jerry from the back of the car. Jerry clenched his teeth and made an almost superhuman effort to remain polite. Finally, just when he felt he couldn't take it anymore, the man inexplicably shouted: "Pull over to the side of the road!"

"What?" Jerry asked, confused.

"I said, pull over! Look," said the man to Jerry, who had turned around to face his tormentor, "you don't like me very much, do you?"

Jerry was silent.

"I know sometimes my behavior is obnoxious, offensive. Sometimes even *I* can't quite believe what I've become. I'm sorry; I apologize. It's just that . . . I'm so alone in the world. I've endured so much. There are nights I think I just won't make it through . . ." And then the man broke down and cried. "You think I'm an arrogant, wealthy American businessman," he said. "What I really am," he sobbed, "is a Holocaust survivor." He rolled up his shirt to show Jerry the numbers.

7 . . . 4 . . . 1 . . . 7.

The last four digits of Jerry's social security number were 7416. He recalled the conversation he had had long ago with another Holocaust survivor, as the man cried: "I lost my whole family in the concentration camp; everyone was killed except for me. I have no one in the world!"

Jerry stared at the American in shock and whispered, "My dear friend, you are wrong. Number seven-four-one-six is very much alive . . . and I happen to know exactly where he can be found."

AN UNSEEN BLESSING

(As told by Rabbi Yaacov Haber,
grandson of Eliyahu Canyaz and Pesi Dinnerstein)
Written by Pesi Dinnerstein

"*Bonjour*, Monsieur Canyaz. Running a little late today, aren't you?"

"*Bonjour, mon ami.* Yes, running a little late, as usual."

Eliyahu Canyaz was a familiar figure on the streets of Marseilles. He traveled from home to home, a bit behind schedule most days, delivering fresh eggs to his Jewish and non-Jewish neighbors. An exceptionally tall and stately man, clean-shaven with his beret tipped slightly to one side, he looked as if he could have fit comfortably in either world. But any Jew living in France in 1942 knew exactly which world he belonged to; Hitler and his steadily advancing army made certain of that.

Eliyahu needed no reminding. An Orthodox Jew whose life was totally immersed in his religion, he never forgot for a moment who he was or why he was here. Even in these difficult times, his commitment remained unshaken.

Originally from Turkey, Eliyahu and his family found a warm and welcoming community of Sephardic Jews in Marseilles. Here, he also found the most beautiful synagogue he had ever seen in his life. And seeing was not something that Eliyahu Canyaz took lightly. Even with his bottle-thick glasses, he could barely recognize a figure two feet in front of him. Nevertheless, within his limited circle of vision, he managed to engage in most of the meaningful activities of his daily life. With a considerable amount of squinting and repositioning, he was usually able to see his family and friends, the customers to whom he sold his eggs, and the holy books from which he studied and prayed every day.

Beyond that point, however, the rest of his world seemed to be enveloped in a shadowy haze, a sad fact of life Eliyahu endured with relative equanimity. Except, that is, when it came to his synagogue. Not being able to experience the full richness of its beauty was profoundly disturbing to him. He knew that the synagogue was magnificent, embodying the simple elegance and fine craftsmanship of another age, an edifice worthy of the spiritual treasures it held. And he appreciated the special beauty of each element—the delicately arched windows, the hand-carved wood, the translucent tiles of polished marble, even the graceful chandelier spiraling down from the cathedral ceiling, far beyond the reach of his sight.

More than anything, however, he longed to see the majesty of his synagogue in one grand, expansive sweep—a never-experienced panoramic view. Instead, he had to settle for a series of individual close-ups, each frame disconnected from the next, as he drew near enough to bring the scenes, one by one, into his narrow sphere of vision. Only in his mind's eye did all the fragments converge into a single breathtaking image.

Although Eliyahu would never be able to see the synagogue as others did, he dedicated his life to caring for it and preserving its sanctity. Eventually, he became the official *shamash*, the person who enables the synagogue to function spiritually by attending to all of its physical needs. In the Sephardic community of Marseilles, this was a position second in importance and holiness only to that of the rabbi, and Eliyahu took the responsibility very much to heart.

The congregation of Orthodox Jews met three times a day in the synagogue for prayer, and Eliyahu—although not generally known for his punctuality—made certain that whenever everyone arrived, the large wooden door was unlocked, the teakettle was boiling, the chairs were neatly arranged, and the service was ready to begin. Even as Hitler's troops marched steadily through France, Eliyahu saw to it that the synagogue offered comfort and refuge to the Jews of Marseilles.

But by 1942, there was little left for Jews anywhere to call their own. And, so, it should have come as no surprise that one day, as the men of Marseilles approached their synagogue, they were greeted by a large sign announcing that the building had been officially confiscated by the Nazis and would henceforth be used as a clubhouse for their soldiers. Expected or not, the news came as a crushing blow.

However, a curious thing happened. Several weeks passed, and the Nazis never returned. Whenever members of the community walked by, they saw that the building was obviously not in use. But, still, to risk their lives and go in . . . no one was ready to do that just yet. Until, one day, Eliyahu could bear it no longer.

Determined to reclaim his synagogue at any cost, he showed up early one morning, as if nothing out of the ordinary had occurred, and started to prepare for services. Little by little, inspired by his courage, the members gradually came back. The Nazis, it seemed, had forgotten all about this building and had gone on to bigger conquests. Before long, the men were once again assembling for prayer three times a day, and Eliyahu was busy attending to their needs. Many months passed without disruption. Life seemed to have returned to normal.

But, as history has since shown us, for the Jews of Europe, life would never return to anything even remotely resembling normal. The day that would forever be remembered by the Jews of Marseilles began, as any other, with the men walking together to the synagogue and chatting pleasantly along the way.

"Spring is in the air this morning, Avraham, don't you think?"

"*Oui*, Binyomin. Any day now, I'll be planting my garden. I can already taste the tomatoes. An early spring this year, for sure, wouldn't you say, Yaacov?"

"*Non, non, mes amis*, not just yet. Winter, I'm afraid, will return once more."

As the men walked into the synagogue, they stopped—as Orthodox Jews traditionally do—to raise their right arm toward the ark that holds the sacred Torah scrolls, and then, to touch their fingers to their lips, signifying their love of G-d's holy words. Each man then donned his *tallit* (prayer shawl) and *tefillin* (phylacteries), opened his *siddur* (prayer book), and began to recite the morning blessings, the sweet harmony of their voices echoing gently throughout the room.

Suddenly, without a second's warning, the heavy wooden door crashed open. Before anyone had time to react, a group of enraged Nazis in full uniform burst into the sanctuary, with rifles raised and ready to fire.

"Jewish swine!" they screamed. "How dare you defy our orders and trespass upon our property?!"

The Jews of Marseilles immediately found themselves surrounded, with no chance of escape. Shouting at the terrified men in French and German, the Nazis tore the prayer shawls from their shoulders and pushed them to the back of the synagogue.

At that moment, the large wooden door began to open once again, but this time the movement was extremely slow and deliberate. A tense silence filled the room as all eyes turned toward the entrance. No one knew whether the door was being pushed open by Nazi sympathizers, armed partisans, or more unsuspecting Jews. Whoever walked in would surely be met by a scene never to be forgotten—a historical synagogue of legendary beauty about to become a blood-stained dot on Hitler's map.

Finally, the door opened all the way, and in stepped the one person incapable of beholding such a sight: Eliyahu Canyaz. Totally oblivious to what was transpiring, he did what he usually did when he arrived a bit late—he stood quietly in the doorway, gently placed his boxes of eggs on the floor, and raised his right arm toward the Torah scrolls. In that moment, two antithetical realities collided, and an unexpected miracle occurred.

In Eliyahu's reality, he was entering his beloved synagogue, for which he risked his life three times a day. And, as he always did, he lifted his arm in the direction of the ark to bring his mind and body closer to the Torah, to link heaven and earth in the service of G-d.

But the Nazis existed in a separate reality. When they looked at Eliyahu stepping through the door, they saw a tall, beret-clad French-man, whose only purpose in coming to the synagogue was obviously to deliver eggs to the Jews. And in his arm-raising gesture of connec-tion to a higher world, the Nazis saw an unmistakable salute to their Führer.

"Heil Hitler!" they shouted to a startled Eliyahu, as they raised their arms and sharply clicked their heels in response. Before Eliyahu could fully grasp what was happening so far beyond the range of his vision, one of the Nazis called out to him in French, "Leave immedi-ately, *Monsieur*! You have no reason to be here."

Without a word, Eliyahu Canyaz turned and walked away. As he stumbled toward the street, he began to pray intensely for all of his friends trapped inside. Then, with tears streaming down his face, he thanked G-d for helping him to escape—and, in the process, for answering the one question that had haunted him for as long as he could remember.

Now, at last, he understood that, rather than being a curse, his poor eyesight was, in fact, a very special blessing. It was, after all, only because of his virtual blindness, coupled with the Nazis' own distorted vision, that he was still alive. And it was also, perhaps, only because of his selfless devotion to a synagogue he could never fully see, that G-d chose to make it the site of the miracle through which his life was spared.

THE MIRACLE OF THE MUDDY SEAT

As told by Louis Koplin

"Life's a little thing," the poet Robert Browning once said, and how true that statement still rings today. Sometimes it's the trivial and mundane event that leads to apocalyptic circumstances and life-changing miracles. We can never predict when extraordinary denouements will suddenly spring up at us and take us completely by surprise. Such was the case with Louis Kopolovics, a survivor feverishly searching for his missing siblings in the aftermath of World War II.

Louis Kopolovics didn't consider himself fortunate when he was drafted into the Hungarian army in 1943, but ultimately it was his involuntary conscription that saved his life. While the rest of his family stayed behind in their snug, supposedly safe home in the Carpathian Mountains, Louis was sent to Komarno, a military installation situated on the banks of the Danube River. Although the Hungarian army didn't discriminate when it came to the race and nationalities of its draftees, it *did* attempt to protect the lives of its gentile members by exposing the Jewish ranks to greater risks and dangers. It was the Jewish soldiers, not the Christians, who were ordered to pick the mines scattered in the fields, and it was the Jewish soldiers who were among those deliberately selected for the most physically taxing work—labor that required them to be exposed to the brutal East European winters. Of the original group of Jews with whom Louis was first interned, only 5 percent survived.

Louis got his first break one day when an army captain lined up the one thousand Jews who were left and barked: "All shoemakers . . . step forward."

Five hundred men answered the call and pretended to be shoemakers in order to avoid working outside in the cold. They knew that if they were chosen, they could sleep indoors on blankets and have three meals a day. The captain chose five men, and Louis was one of them. There was only one real shoemaker among the group, but Louis's father had, in fact, worked at this trade. As a little boy, he had sat at his father's feet, watching and assisting with little tasks. Whatever he remembered helped him deceive his superiors.

Later, Louis ended up in Budapest, where he was arrested by the Germans and shipped to the Austrian-Hungarian border to dig ditches they hoped would waylay enemy tanks. From there, he was forced to participate in a death march across the entire length of Austria, to Mauthausen concentration camp. Despite these ordeals, Louis's earlier months in the softer shoemaking job had strengthened him enough to withstand the successive rigors to which he was subjected. When Mauthausen was liberated by Patton's army on May 6, 1945, he was among the skeletal figures who first welcomed the American troops.

But the nightmare wasn't quite over. The next phase of his Holocaust trauma would unfold as Louis began his frantic, desperate search for the scattered remnants of his family, if indeed anyone had survived. All over Europe, this search was replicated by tens of thousands of people—mostly teenagers and young adults—hunting for scraps of their old life.

Like many survivors, Louis hopped on trains to search for relatives. They didn't need identification papers, and the tickets were free. He constantly went back and forth between Prague and Budapest, where the United Nations Relief and Rehabilitation Administration (UNRRA) and the Jewish Joint Distribution Committee (known as "the Joint") had set up safe havens for refugees. Not only could you find food and shelter at these places, but they were also great sources of information. There was always the possibility of running into someone who knew something about your loved ones, and the walls and bulletin boards were scrawled with messages:

Have you seen . . . ?

Does anyone know the whereabouts of . . . ?

Do you know anything about . . . ?

One day, while Louis stood in line at one of these soup kitchens, a man came up behind him and tapped him on the shoulder. "Your father's dead," he told him, without prelude.

"How do you know?" Louis asked, starting to shake. He knew this man from his village, so he believed the information to be true.

"I was with him in Buchenwald until the end. He died two weeks after Liberation."

The man had no news about the fate of his mother and five siblings.

Louis continued to search. He would not give up; he *could not*. False alarms, wild goose chases that led nowhere, possible sightings that were never confirmed . . . his post-Holocaust days were a wild roller-coaster ride, filled alternately with hope and despair, faith and doubt, as he tried in vain to find at least one member of his family who was still alive.

One day, Louis boarded a crowded train bound for Budapest. His shoulders sagged as he sought an empty seat. He was so bone-weary and drained after all his fruitless trips that he was finally considering giving up. Perhaps it was time to stop looking . . .

All the compartments were filled. Louis kept opening and closing doors until he finally found one with a vacant bench. Expelling a sigh of relief, Louis was about to lower himself onto the seat when he suddenly realized why it hadn't been occupied: It was covered with mud. Louis had no more energy to try to find another seat. *I'll just clean it up myself*, he thought. *But with what?* With all the postwar shortages, he possessed no tissue or napkin, nothing that could remotely serve as a *shmattah* (rag). *I just have to sit down; I can't stand another minute*, he thought. *There has to be something, somewhere . . .*

It was then that he spotted a discarded piece of paper on the floor. Louis bent down to pick up the stray paper and saw that it was a torn page from some kind of official document. He gave it a cursory glance, and then stood still in his tracks. A name leapt off the page, a name he knew well: Lenka Kopolovics, his sister. *His sister's name on a random page. What did it mean?* There were dozens of other names listed on this page, but his eyes were fixed only on her name. The letters seemed to dance before him, doing a little pirouette, taking a winsome bow. The document bore the official seal of the Swedish Red Cross and was a record of patients sheltered in their facilities—and his sister was among them.

Louis jumped off the train at the next station. He made a U-turn back to Prague, where telegraph services had been restored. He didn't know whom to contact, so he simply sent a telegram addressed to "The Swedish Red Cross." Somehow, Lenka received the message and telegraphed him back twenty-four hours later.

He was alone no more. And the wonder of it all: something as trivial and mundane as a muddy seat had brought him back his sister.

Postscript: When Louis and his sister were reunited, she told him that their family had been rounded up from their home in the Carpathian Mountains, where they were sent straightaway to Auschwitz. Louis's conscription into the Hungarian army turned out to be a blessing in disguise, as his trajectory was much milder than theirs.

Louis's mother and three of his siblings died in the gas chambers. Just minutes before she disembarked from the cattle cars and was marched to her death, Louis's mother said to her children: "I hope and pray that Duddy is safe," using her pet name for Louis.

A few months after he found his sister, Louis discovered that one other sibling—a brother named Bernie—had also survived, and had either returned to their hometown of Szolyva or their birthplace, Nelipeno, a few miles away. Although he was loath to go back, Louis traveled to Szolyva and began to look for Bernie. He didn't have far to go. As Louis walked on a small bridge from Szolyva, headed north, he collided with his brother, who was walking south from Nelipeno. They fell into each other's arms and wept. The three siblings eventually emigrated to the United States and annually winter together in South Florida.

THE OTHER DOCTOR OF AUSCHWITZ

He had been sent to the left, and she to the right. She had survived, so she understood immediately what *his* selection meant. She looked up at the ashes spurting out of the crematoria of Auschwitz and wondered which flecks belonged to *him*—her beloved husband of just seven months.

Esti Magid* had been a young bride, only nineteen, but the wedding had been far from joyous. Too many relatives had already vanished, sucked up by the maelstrom of the Holocaust, and the dark cloud of death and uncertainty that hung over the hurried wedding party had eclipsed the happy occasion. Still, she had loved him, loved him dearly, and had savored their time together, fearing it would be brief.

Esti thought that if she somehow miraculously managed to survive, she would hoard her remembrances of their time together in the treasure trove of her heart. But in Auschwitz, she discovered that she was carrying more than poignant memories: She was also carrying a child. When she told the women of her barracks about her pregnancy, they were aghast. While she believed that the birth of this child would transcend her beloved's death, her companions knew with certainty that if she went through with it, she would be courting her own.

"Don't you know," they scolded her harshly, "that the moment the Nazis discover a pregnant Jewish woman, they kill her instantly? There is no reprieve. If they find out you're carrying, you have absolutely no chance—you're dead."

Esti's eyes filled with tears. She wanted this child so badly. She had somehow deluded herself into thinking that she could deliver and raise a baby in the camp. Through this child, her husband would live on . . . the Jewish people would have lived. Children were guarantors of the future. But right now, here in Auschwitz, the Jewish people *had* no future.

The women's blunt words rained down on her like hammer blows. They were right, of course; no pregnant woman ever lived in Auschwitz once her condition was revealed. Dr. Mengele had special scorn reserved for Jewish "breeders" and subjected them to vicious, sadistic medical experiments before he finally had them killed in the most horrific of ways. He tortured their fetuses, and the rare live baby, too, pulling them out of their mothers' bellies (without anesthesia) and using them for target practice, then throwing them into the furnaces, together with their mothers, while they were still alive. *She is so naive*, the women in the barracks thought silently. *Doesn't she know what goes on? How can she be so blind?*

"What should I do?" Esti begged the women.

Their harsh countenances softened for a moment as they regarded the sweet, innocent girl, far too young to have been orphaned and widowed at the same time. They looked at her and remembered the babies that had been torn from their arms, not long ago. Most of them had been mothers themselves, before their capture.

"We'll go get Gizelle Perl," they said.

Dr. Gizelle Perl, beloved obstetrician from the town of Sighet (Transylvania), was known among the inmates as the "doctor of Auschwitz"—the same appellation used by her nemesis, Dr. Mengele. Dr. Perl plied her profession silently, surreptitiously, moving quickly through the concentration camp inmates to heal and cure, wherever and whenever she could. She was loving and kind, a beacon of hope and light in a place and time of utter darkness. She had been summoned hundreds of times to help pregnant women in despair.

"Esti," Dr. Perl whispered softly to the young girl, "your pregnancy is too advanced, and I cannot perform an abortion. You will have to hide your pregnancy, and when it is time, I will deliver the baby." She paused, gently caressing the young girl's face. "And then I will do what I have to do in order to save your life." Averting her eyes from her patient, Dr. Perl rose and vanished.

"I don't understand," Esti said anxiously to the other women who hovered nearby. "What is it that she's going to do after she delivers the baby?"

They threw piteous glances in her direction, and then looked at one another in mute despair. One woman's harsh voice finally broke the silence. "As soon as the baby is born, Dr. Perl will do the only thing she *can* do to save your life: She'll suffocate or strangle the baby to death."

Months later, Esti went into labor. Dr. Perl led her to the floor of the latrine—the only safe place in the camp where she could work undetected. Esti beseeched the doctor: "Please, can't you let my baby live? Just this once . . . just this one baby. Please? I'll hide the baby where no one will see it. I'm begging you—please!"

"*Esther'le*," Dr. Perl answered with tears in her eyes, "do you know how much this hurts me to do? I'm a woman . . . a mother . . . a Jew. I'm an obstetrician committed to bringing forth new life. But this is the only way I can save the lives of pregnant Jewish women in Auschwitz. Over and over again, it's always the same. Every single time the Nazis learn a woman has given birth to a baby, they torture them, and then they kill them both in the most brutal ways. There is never an exception, *never*. This is what happened repeatedly before I arrived at Auschwitz.

"Now at least I can save the mother. There is no recourse, Esti. I am so sorry. If I let the baby live, both of you will die. Alone, maybe you have a chance."

Esti struggled to raise her head when the baby was born.

"It's better that you don't look, *mameleh*," Dr. Perl said. "You'll only suffer more."

But Esti managed to catch a glimpse of the newborn, a boy with her husband's face. The woman assisting Dr. Perl clamped her hand over Esti's mouth to muffle her sobs.

"*Esther'le*," Dr. Perl said softly. "I know that right now I am taking away life, but I promise you, if I ever get out of this hellhole, I will dedicate myself to bringing it back. And you, Esti . . . I know how your heart breaks now, but I promise you—if you miraculously survive, you, too, will bring forth new life again one day."

And then, grimacing, Dr. Perl stretched out her two hands that had just delivered the child and did the unthinkable: She strangled it to death. It was the only option, given the brutal alternatives in a Nazi death camp.

* * *

Esti survived the war. She was in Auschwitz when it was liberated, and from there she was sent to a displaced persons camp in Sweden, where she remained for two years. She eventually emigrated to the United States, ending up in Borough Park, a fledgling Jewish neighborhood in Brooklyn, New York, in the 1950s. Like millions of other survivors, she tried to put the war behind her and begin anew. She married again, and soon she was pregnant.

Her husband urged her to find an obstetrician, but she had difficulty making the decision. She asked her friends, relatives, and neighbors for referrals, and conscientiously kept a large and growing list of recommended names while still continuing to procrastinate. One day, Esti was strolling down a street in Borough Park when she spotted a small white placard on an apartment building. She drew closer and read OFFICE OF DR. GIZELLE PERL, OBSTETRICIAN.

She stopped short. *Could it be? Was it really her?* Had Dr. Perl also survived and made her way to Borough Park? Perhaps it was just a coincidence—someone else bearing the exact same name. She had to know. Esti rang the bell impatiently and pushed the door hard. Inside, bending over the receptionist's desk with a file in her hands, was none other than Dr. Gizelle Perl—the doctor of Auschwitz. Esti's eyes widened and filled with tears as she gazed at this ghost from the past. She couldn't speak, she was so overwhelmed with emotion. Feeling the intensity of Esti's stare, Dr. Perl looked up from the file she was studying, and then she too froze. Their eyes locked in recognition. They rushed into each other's arms, embraced, and wept.

"Esti Magid! So you too survived!" Dr. Perl exclaimed. "I am overjoyed to see you!"

"And I am overjoyed to see *you*," Esti said. "I cannot believe you're here—right in Borough Park! How did you happen to come here, of all places—do you have family nearby?"

Dr. Perl shook her head no. "Only my extended family from Auschwitz," she said softly. "The remnants. *They* are here." She explained: "Many Holocaust survivors have settled in Borough Park. I came here to keep my promise—to bring back the life I had to take away in Auschwitz."

"You will keep your promise to me, as well?" Esti asked.

Once again, Esti Magid was taken under the wing of Dr. Gizelle Perl, obstetrician. But this time, the birth of her baby did not take place in a filthy latrine in Auschwitz, but in a clean, sterile, antiseptic delivery room at Maimonides Hospital in Borough Park. And as Dr.

Perl delivered Esti's baby, she screamed out an epithet that was at once a proclamation and a manifesto; an expression that would become her trademark, one that she would hurl out to the heavens every single time she delivered a Jewish baby from that point forward.

"A life for a life!" she shouted as Esti's baby slid into her hands—the hands that had taken away life, and now would spend decades restoring it.

"*Mazel tov*, Esti!" Dr. Perl whooped joyously. "It's a baby boy, a fine, healthy, strapping baby boy. I have kept my promise to you, Esti. We have both brought forth new Jewish life, together. *L'chaim!* (To life!)"

"Chaim . . . Chaim," Esti murmured, half hallucinating, half dreaming on the delivery bed. "I had an uncle named Chaim who perished in the Holocaust. Yes, that's what I'll call this child . . . Chaim." And then she looked up at Gizelle Perl with light shining in her eyes and said, in a firm and resolute voice, "His name will be a symbol, yes. He will be our mutual act of defiance. Yours . . . and mine."

Postscript: To this very day, Dr. Gizelle Perl remains a relatively unknown and unsung heroine of the Holocaust, although it is estimated that she saved close to 10,000 pregnant Jewish women in Auschwitz. In the United States, she practiced at Maimonides Hospital in Brooklyn, and Mt. Sinai Hospital in Manhattan, later moving to Jerusalem, where she served as director of obstretics and gynecology at Sha'arei Tzedek Hospital. Every time she delivered a Jewish baby, she would shout, "A life for a life!" as her own personal motto of triumph and revenge. Dr. Gizelle Perl died in Israel in 1984.

Esti Magid ultimately gave birth to and raised four children in Borough Park, Brooklyn. She died in 2005 at the age of eighty-four.

A QUESTION OF IDENTITY

Barbro Karlen should never have been born. Her mother Maria was stricken with multiple sclerosis, her body paralyzed for years. The doctors with whom Maria consulted predicted two things with absolute certainty: She would never be able to walk again, and she would die an early death. Defying both forecasts, Maria rehabilitated herself using a series of exercises that she devised, and she lived a full life. Physicians also said that it would be impossible for Maria to conceive and carry a healthy baby to term. When she announced that she was pregnant, they gasped and urged her to have an abortion. Maria dug in her heels and stood up against them all. It was into such a contentious atmosphere that daughter Barbro was born in 1954 in Gothenburg, Sweden. The incongruity—and the miracle—of Barbro's birth may have been a harbinger of other strange things to come.

Barbro was a bright, precocious, gifted child with excellent verbal skills. (By the time she turned sixteen, she had already published eleven books; her first book, written at the age of twelve, was *Man on Earth*, the best-selling poetry book of all time in Sweden.) In fact, it was her verbosity that first disturbed the composure of the household. When she was two years old, Barbro strangely began to refuse to answer to her name. "My name is *not* Barbro," she insisted to her parents. "My name is Anne. And when am I going home?"

Barbro's alarmed parents took her to various psychiatrists and psychologists who pronounced their little girl to be a highly functioning, intelligent, well-adjusted, and healthy child. "She's perfectly normal," everyone declared. "But what about this Anne thing?" her parents persisted. "It's probably some kind of imaginary play situation," the professionals said, trying to soothe the anxious parents. "Don't worry about it."

As the slew of practitioners ably predicted, Barbro's insistence that her name was Anne dissolved over time, and she never gave her parents cause for concern again. On the contrary, she made them proud. She excelled in her studies and showed a remarkable aptitude for writing at an early age. Her teachers called her a prodigy.

When Barbro was ten, she and her family went on holiday to Amsterdam, where Barbro found the surroundings achingly familiar. The city infused her with a sense of *déjà vu*—the indescribable impression that she knew this place, that she had been here before.

As first-time tourists in Amsterdam, Barbro's parents eagerly sought to visit all of its famous sites. "Let's go see the Anne Frank house," Barbro's father suggested one day. "I'll call the front desk and ask the hotel clerk to call a taxi." Maria agreed. From her perch on the bed, Barbro suddenly jumped up with alacrity and announced with airy self-assurance, "Oh, you don't have to call a taxi. The Anne Frank House is not far from the hotel at all, only a few blocks away. I know how to get there. Come, I'll show you."

Barbro's parents exchanged alarmed looks. This was their first trip to Amsterdam; they had no friends, relatives, or even acquaintances living here. As far as they knew, Barbro was not in possession of any maps, and how many ten-year-olds could read them properly, anyway? Her behavior was strange, disquieting. Still, their curiosity was sufficiently piqued that they allowed her to lead the way: out of the hotel, down a few winding streets, and around one corner, until Barbro stopped in front of a building that resembled a former factory or storehouse.

"Here it is," Barbro announced triumphantly. "My house." She bounded up the steps with quick, sure steps and tugged at the door that was tightly shut while her parents watched warily, foreheads furrowed in consternation. What did this bizarre conduct mean? As they scrutinized the nondescript building that had so excited their daughter, their eyes rested on a small, discreet plaque they hadn't noticed before: ANNE FRANK HOUSE, the sign announced. Barbro's parents exchanged stunned looks.

"Let's go in . . . I'll show you my room!" In an almost hypnotic state, Barbro tried to shove the heavy doors open, but they were securely locked. She rang the bell impatiently.

"What in heaven's name is going on?" Barbro's parents whispered in concern as an elderly man—the curator of the museum—opened the doors.

"I need to see my room!" Barbro cried, whipping past the man as she sped up the stairs.

"Oh, we have another Anne Frank here now, do we?" the curator chuckled. "I can't even count them anymore; I've lost track of all the different people claiming to be her reincarnation. And when did your daughter first read the diary? Are you Jewish?"

As the import of the curator's words pressed down upon them, Barbro's parents paled considerably. "Is that why she insisted she be called Anne? But how is this possible?" they asked one another.

"Sir," Barbro's father drew himself up indignantly, as he addressed the curator. "First of all, I'll have you know, we are *not* Jewish. We live in Sweden, and we have no Jewish friends or neighbors. Second, my daughter has never read Anne Frank's diary, nor has she read any literature pertaining to the Holocaust. You are entirely mistaken. My daughter does *not* think she is Anne Frank; she doesn't even know who Anne Frank is. There must be some logical explanation. It's probably just a crazy coincidence."

"Well, let's go find her," the curator sighed. "All those other Anne Franks turned out to be frauds, and I don't believe in reincarnation, anyway. So how did you find our place?" he asked over his shoulder as they trudged up the stairs. "Read about us in a tourist book?"

Barbro was snuggled up in a chair in Anne Frank's room, gazing at the bare walls with a mixture of confusion and intense concentration. "What happened to my posters?" she asked the curator. His eyes widened with something akin to fear, and he scratched his head in puzzlement. "Well, I'll be darned, young lady," he said. "Now how did you know about that?"

"What is she talking about?" Barbro's parents demanded.

"This *is* a little strange," the curator confessed. "How could she possibly know about the posters?"

"What posters? What are you talking about?"

"While she was hiding here, Anne Frank pinned up pictures of her favorite movie stars. They were just pages torn out of fan magazines, and after many decades, we had to take them down; they were all crumbling into dust. But how in the world did your daughter know?"

Postscript: Barbro Karlen's story was eventually leaked to the Swedish press, and she became an overnight sensation. She was one of Sweden's best-selling writers, and published many popular books. To this day, she continues to maintain that she is the reincarnation of Anne Frank, and she frequently appears as a guest speaker at many past-life regression conferences throughout the world. The mystery of how the little girl came to find the Anne Frank house has never been solved.

Although many people remain skeptical, Barbro Karlen's claims have been at least partially supported by one of Anne Frank's surviving cousins, Buddy Elias, who lives in Basel, Switzerland. In an interview in a popular Swiss magazine, Elias stated: "I am generally very skeptical about people who claim to have been this or that person in another life. With Barbro, it was different. Our meeting was very emotional. I felt something very special and positive while I was in her presence. I felt like I was being reunited with a kindred spirit. The impression she made on me was of someone I could trust. I don't rule out the possibility that she could have been my cousin, Anne Frank."

Barbro Karlen now lives in the United States under an assumed name. Her autobiography, *And the Wolves Howled: Fragments of Two Lifetimes*, has been published in Germany, Norway, Sweden, and the United States. In it she tells of her recurrent nightmares about men in uniform breaking into the house where she is hiding with her family and brutally dragging her into a waiting vehicle. She says that, to this day, she cannot shake the fear.

ZAYDE'S TRAVELS

Azriela Jaffe

Today, as Holocaust survivors age and watch their older peers struggle with the infirmities endemic to the twilight years, they know it's time. Even if they have been silent all these decades, as so many of them have been; even if they could not bear at an earlier age to relive the nightmare by retelling it; even if they wished to spare their children the anguish they experienced—they know that the sands of time are quickly seeping out of the hourglass. They know that they are the last witnesses, and they cannot postpone sharing their narratives any longer. And so, now, they speak.

Hersz Hanfling, a survivor nearing his nineties, is eager today to tell his amazing story of survival to anyone who will listen—but it wasn't always so. His son, Marc, grew up with a father who *never* spoke about the Holocaust. *Not one word.* And Hersz's grandchildren never heard about his experiences during World War II, either, until one pivotal day in 1990 when he started talking.

Aviva, Marc's daughter and Hersz's oldest grandchild, was then a student in the Rabbi Pesach Raymon Yeshiva of Edison, New Jersey. She was in the sixth grade and had been given a school assignment: to put together a poster presentation for a Jewish fair, with the theme "My Zayde's Travels through the Holocaust." She asked her grandfather to help her with her school project. He was ready to talk, at last.

The end result of several conversations with her grandfather was Aviva's proud production: an oak-tag poster that mapped out Hersz's journey through several concentration camps in Poland: Mielec, from April 1944 to July 1944; Wieliczka, from July 1944 to September 1944; Plaszow, from September 1944 to October 16, 1944; Schachwitz, from October 1944 to April 1945; Litomerice, April 1945; then an eight-day march to Theresienstadt, in Czechoslovakia, where on May 9, 1945, he was liberated by the Russian army.

On the day of the school fair, Aviva stood proudly next to her poster as all the students' parents and grandparents walked by and studied her work. One man, whom she did not know, stopped by and identified himself as the father of a girl in a different grade in the school. He studied her poster with interest, and then suddenly shouted for his father, the girl's grandfather, to come and take a look.

"Dad, check out this poster! Weren't you in many of these same camps?"

The grandfather, Marvin Balsam, sauntered over to Aviva's table and peered at the oak-tag exhibit. Tears came to his eyes as he read off the names: Mielec, Wieliczka, Plaszow, Schachwitz, Litomerice, Theresienstadt. This was his exact same journey, too, each and every camp! And then his eyes came across the name of the survivor who had journeyed there: *Hersz Hanfling*.

"Hersz Hanfling?!" he shouted. "Hersz Hanfling saved my life! He gave me a potato when I was starving. Because of Hersz Hanfling, I lived!"

Incredibly, Marvin Balsam hadn't seen or spoken to Hersz Hanfling since their liberation. But he remembered well the day when Hersz had risked his own life to steal a potato for Marvin from a roomful of them in Schachwitz concentration camp where they had both been interned. That single raw potato had made the difference between life and death for Marvin Balsam, and he'd never forgotten it. Coincidentally, from that moment on, he and Hersz had been deported to all the same camps at the same time, and they were constantly at each other's side until they were finally liberated.

Marvin couldn't wait a moment longer. Right then and there, he asked Aviva for her grandfather's phone number, and after the fair, he called his old friend whom he hadn't seen or spoken to in forty-plus years.

He began the conversation this way: "Hey, Hersz—I owe you a meal!"

MAMA IS ALWAYS RIGHT
as told by Nissan Krakinowski

When he first emigrated to the United States, Nissan Krakinowski watched a segment of *The Art Linkletter Show* on television with wonderment and disbelief. During the program, Mr. Linkletter asked a number of teenagers whom they would love to have as parents, and why. "Rockefeller," one ambitious boy answered instantly, "because then I'd be so rich." "Sophia Loren," a homely-looking girl said dreamily, "because then I'd be so beautiful." One after another, the group of teenagers delivered their answers with certainty and assurance, readily summoning up the names of various icons of the day.

"What stunned me then, and still continues to stun me to this day," recalls Nissan, "was that not a *single* one said their *own* parents. I couldn't get over it. If I had been there, that would have been my answer for sure. I never wanted another set of parents. To me, my mother and father were just perfect. I idolized them." It was this fierce love and adulation that would ultimately save Nissan's life during the Holocaust.

"We led a simple but idyllic life in prewar Kovno (Kaunas), Lithuania, a city of forty thousand Jews. My mother Pessie was a devoted homemaker; my father, Shimon, a respected custom tailor. But it was what my father did *after* work that brought droves of people to our home. He was a renowned storyteller, exceptionally gifted. Television hadn't been invented yet, and few people owned radios. For recreation and relaxation, neighbors, friends, and relatives streamed to our house every night, where my good-hearted mother would serve tea and pastries while my father would spin tales that held everyone in their thrall. I was blessed to grow up with extremely warm and loving parents who doted on their two sons—my older brother, Chaim, and me. These halcyon days ground to a sudden halt one night in 1941, when an urgent knock on the door ended life as we knew it."

Shimon Krakinowski's friend Aaron, whose son was a government official with "connections," stood on the doorstep, nervously wringing his hands. "Oy, Shimon, Shimon!" he cried out when Nissan's father opened the door. "I have very bad news. The Germans have declared war on Russia, and they are advancing rapidly. In three days they'll be in Kovno."

"What should we do?" Shimon asked, struggling to remain calm as his wife and children peered anxiously over his shoulder at their trembling neighbor.

"There's no time to think. My son called me and said we have to leave immediately. It's very serious. Take whatever you can and let's go together, now."

"Aaron," Shimon said mildly, "I myself was a soldier during World War One, and I don't believe this can happen so fast. Besides, I have a big family in Kovno . . . my mother, my in-laws, my brothers, my sisters, and all their families… How can I get up and leave them without saying good-bye? My whole life is here—my work, my house, my reputation—everything I know and love is here. I think you are overreacting, Aaron, but go gezuntheit (with my blessings)."

Aaron and his family fled their home that night, but the Krakinowskis stayed. Three days later, just as Aaron had predicted, the Germans were in Kovno. They burst through the Jewish homes with machine guns, screaming "Everyone out!" herding them into the streets where they were marched to De Gele Turme, an infamous jail.

"What hurt the most during that march," Nissan remembers, "was not what the Germans were doing to us, but what our Lithuanian friends, neighbors, and customers were doing to us. They stood on the sidewalks and cheered. They cursed at us, laughed at us, kicked us as we passed. Just a few days before, some of these same people had been in our house, drinking tea."

The Jews were confined to De Gele Turme for three days without food or drink. From there they were transferred to a valley guarded by young Lithuanian hooligans who stood sentry on the nearby hills. For sport, they randomly shot at the 25,000 Jews milling below, using the dreaded dum-dum bullets that expand on impact, creating greater trauma and blood loss. "Every day, the corpses of hundreds of people would fill the valley floors," Nissan remembers bitterly. "For no reason other than the Lithuanians were bored."

On the seventh day of the Jews' internment, in the middle of the night, German military vehicles rolled into the valley. The soldiers who emerged from the vehicles barked sharp orders: "All boys under the age of thirteen come to this side!" The women and girls had been removed to a different section a few days before.

"Go," Shimon Krakinowski enjoined Nissan, who stood resolutely at his father's side. "You just turned thirteen."

"No!" screamed Nissan. "I don't want to leave you."

"Nonetheless, you must," Shimon said gruffly as he pushed his son to the other side, turning his back so Nissan wouldn't see the tears streaming down his face. Shimon also tried to push fifteen-year-old Chaim in the same direction, which he deemed the safe place to be—but a soldier blocked his attempt. "This boy is older than thirteen! He stays with you." But Shimon was not to be deterred. He engaged another soldier in conversation, in an attempt to distract him, and, as they spoke, he motioned to Chaim to join his brother on the other side.

Under the cover of the dark, Chaim was able to successfully steal over to the section where Nissan stood. The three huddled together and vigilantly kept their eyes pinned on the already-stooped figure of Shimon Krakinowski, standing alone on the other side. They followed each movement he made, every step he took, fearing that if they lost sight of him for a moment, they would lose sight of him forever. Although many yards separated them, Shimon was acutely aware of his children's unwavering scrutiny—their eyes boring into him, their tension, their fear. He made reassuring motions, signaling that they would be together, soon.

Shimon Krakinowski had been wrong that fateful night when he had confidently told his friend Aaron that the Germans could never advance so quickly to Kovno. But this time, he was prescient. The men were led up to the hills, where the dreaded *rat-a-tat-tat* of a dozen machine guns reverberated for a very long time. Afterwards, the women and children—now widows and orphans—were freed. The soldiers herded the boys out of the valley and, after a twenty-minute walk, Nissan and Chaim found their mother wandering dazedly with a group of women searching for their families.

"Where should we go?" Pessie asked her sons. "We have *nowhere* to go." She didn't know anyone in the nearby region. "Kovno is only about eight kilometers away. Maybe the best thing to do is return home, hide there, and wait out the storm. We have lots of food stored away that can keep us for a while . . . Yes, let's go home."

"It was not so much a preposterous decision as it was a desperate one," Nissan Krakinowski reflects today. "We hadn't eaten in days. We were hungry and homeless. We had only been away from our home for about ten days; how could my mother begin to imagine the radical changes enveloping her old friends and neighbors, the simmering hatred that the Nazis had unleashed in the townspeople's hearts? She probably hoped that the Nazis had stormed through the town, emptied it of its Jews, and then left. She never dreamed that we couldn't return because of the local residents. My mother was such a good person, so naive and innocent, that she was unable to fathom the full extent of man's capacity for evil, man's inhumanity to man. Maybe she thought that the terrible things we had witnessed in Kovno when we were rounded up that last day was an aberration, that it couldn't possibly be repeated again. It was when we returned home that the world of goodness in which she had always dwelled was permanently turned upside down."

Back in Kovno, Pessie found their apartment house padlocked, so she rang the bell that summoned the superintendent.

"How come you are still alive?" he snarled at her as he opened the door. "Get lost!" This was the man to whom she often gave small gifts, generous tips, kosher delicacies—the same man she often invited to their home for festive meals.

"Please," she begged, "we just want to go to our apartment."

"It's not yours anymore," he answered.

"Please . . . just let me look through my apartment to see if I can find some food for my children. They're so hungry; they haven't eaten for days."

The superintendent looked at Pessie with contempt and slammed the door.

Their journey took many difficult twists and turns, including living as vagrants in the public gardens and a brief tenure in the Kovno ghetto where they worked on its airfield. Here they were allotted one crust of bread each day and one bowl of watery soup. Pessie

Krakinowski tore her own piece of bread into two parts, giving each of her sons an extra quarter.

"Mama, what are you doing?" Nissan begged, when she pushed the extra crust into his mouth. "You can't live on half a piece of bread a day. I don't want it."

"Nissan," his mother said tenderly, "I have lived my life already. Maybe this extra crust of bread will save yours."

The Krakinowskis were able to remain together as a family until "that terrible day in 1944 when all three of us were shipped to Stutthof concentration camp in Danzig, Germany. Immediately upon arrival, the men and women were separated into different lines. When my mother's column was ordered to march away, she broke out of line, and ran towards us. I, in turn, broke out of my line, and met her halfway."

They only had a moment to say good-bye. Pessie hugged Nissan tightly, planting soft, sad kisses on his cheeks, her eyes damp with tears. As she caressed his forehead, Pessie urgently whispered into his ear: "Listen, my son, listen well. Even though Chaim is older, you have always been the stronger one—physically and emotionally. Promise me that you'll take care of your brother. Wherever you go, make sure he goes with you. I feel in my heart that you are going to survive, and if *you* survive, *he'll* survive. Promise me you'll *never* leave him alone. Promise."

"Yes, Mama," Nissan choked.

"Promise?"

"I promise."

Nissan never saw his mother again.

Chaim and Nissan were shipped to one of the satellite camps of Dachau. Here the Nazis seemed especially brutal, and the prisoners were whipped, truncheoned, pummeled, and kicked for the tiniest of infractions. "Inmates dropped like flies," Nissan says, shuddering in recollection. "Corpses were strewn all over the camp's grounds." Chaim fared poorly under these savage conditions. His mother had been correct in assessing that he was the weaker son; he was less able to withstand the atrocities to which his body and soul were subjected. Thoroughly demoralized (which was precisely the point of many Nazi tactics), Chaim constantly cried out to Nissan: "We're finished. We're going to die, so what's the use?"

Nissan worked hard to bolster Chaim's spirits and infuse him with hope, but deep inside he knew that Chaim had become the ghostlike apparition that everyone feared becoming: the dreaded *Muselmann*— the living dead, one of the walking corpses who no longer possessed the will to fight, the energy to care. With his hollowed-out eyes and dragging feet, the *Muselmann* was doomed. His loss of spirit almost always led to loss of life. Nissan was his brother's watchful protector, knowing full well that Chaim was easy prey for those Nazis wishing to shove a few more Jewish bodies into the ovens before their own time ran out.

Legs swollen and black with gangrene, Chaim could barely walk or show up for work anymore. Nissan constantly covered for him. "Maybe it was because the Nazis knew the end was near that the guards became increasingly lax at roll call and Chaim's absences weren't noted," conjectures Nissan. "Whatever the reason, their carelessness was a G-dsend. No one asked where Chaim was, why he hadn't come to work." Nissan kept plying Chaim with gentle words of encouragement, desperately trying to help him hang on. "Chaim, we're going to make it, I promise you . . . it's almost over," Nissan would reassure him every day. "The war is going to end soon—everybody says so. The Allies are approaching. Do you hear the planes overhead? They are Allied planes. They're almost here. Don't give up."

On the morning of April 26, 1945, the Nazi commandant issued a proclamation ordering the Jewish inmates to evacuate the camp at noon that day. The prisoners were to be taken deeper into Germany, after which the camp would be dynamited to the ground to remove evidence of the atrocities. "*Everyone* must leave," the commandant said.

Nissan ran into the barracks where Chaim lay lifelessly on his bunk bed. "Chaim," he said, "we have to leave now. The camp is being liquidated."

"No, Nissan," Chaim moaned, "I can't walk—I can't move."

"Chaim, you have to be strong; you have to force yourself to walk. I'll help you. I'll carry you part of the way, as much as I can."

"No, Nissan, I can't go," Chaim said. "Please go without me. I'll be all right. Go yourself."

"But Chaim," Nissan pleaded, "they're going to dynamite the camp after everyone leaves. You'll surely die if you stay here." Nissan flung his arm around Chaim, raised him out of the bed, and walked a few steps with him, until Chaim slipped out of his grasp and flopped onto the floor, crying. "I beg of you, Nissan, leave me."

Demons suddenly emerged from a place Nissan hadn't known before. They taunted his steadfastness. *Your brother is close to death anyway*, the strange voices inside his head whispered to him. *Your mother will never know. You took care of him all this time; you did your duty, but now you should go. Why should you both die? Don't be a fool. Leave him. Go!*

The whispers inside Nissan's head were loud and urgent, but louder still were his beloved mother's last words: *Promise me you'll stay with your brother always; promise.* And his heartfelt answer: *I promise, Mama; I promise.*

Nissan bent to pick Chaim off the floor, and resolutely said, "No, Chaim, I am not leaving you alone; I am staying with you, no matter what."

They remained inside the barracks, listening to the soldiers laying dynamite outside, stringing wires. They heard the roar of the motors as the Nazis' vehicles sped away from the camp, the footfalls of their brethren as they marched out the gate. By noon, only a few individuals—the weak and the sick—remained in the barracks with them. They chanted prayers together as they prepared to die.

They waited for the explosions, but none came. Miraculously, a few days later, the Americans came instead. They heard the rumble of tanks and the shouts of American soldiers as they poured through the gate and liberated the few inmates still left in the camp. The camp was never dynamited, after all. No one ever discovered what had gone awry. No one really cared. They were *alive!*

A few days after Liberation, Nissan met a fellow inmate who had left with the others when the camp was evacuated by the Germans on April 26. At the time of his departure, the man had walked on his own, but now he supported himself on crutches.

"When did you get wounded?" Nissan asked him in confusion. "And how?"

"Oh, you didn't hear what happened to those of us who evacuated the camp?" the man responded. "We were walking along the road when Allied fighter planes bore down on us and attacked. They must have mistakenly believed we were a German convoy. We were sprayed with machine-gun fire. Most people in our group were killed. You were very lucky you stayed behind."

As the man limped away, Nissan thought: Lucky? No. *Obedient*—to the final wishes of his revered mother, whose love and wisdom had safeguarded her children, even when she was no longer present.

Postscript: Nissan Krakinowski and his brother Chaim both survived the war and emigrated to the United States, where they settled in

New York. While Nissan married and raised two daughters, Chaim remained a lifelong bachelor. The two, however, were inordinately attached to each other, working together in the same business, living in the same Brooklyn neighborhood, and speaking to each other on the telephone several times a day. They were extremely close and devoted to each other until Chaim's death five years ago. Nissan, now eighty years old, still speaks of his parents with tears in his eyes.

THE SWIMMER

Written by Dov Haller

The walls of the impressive stone house on the banks of Germany's Rhine River were saturated with the history of the Solomon family. They had seen four generations of Solomon men marry and raise children—had watched four generations of this German-Jewish elite family succeed at the family's bakery. They had seen the parties and rejoicing, the good and happy times. They had observed young Arthur Solomon, an athletic and vigorous young man, emerge as one of the greatest swimmers in the country.

Young Arthur had set his sights beyond the bakery: He would become an Olympic swimmer, a champion who would bring honor to his family and his country. In time, Arthur achieved national renown, winning swimming meets across the country. He competed with the celebrated champion, Johnny Weissmuller, who played the famous title role in the *Tarzan* films. The future looked bright.

It was a late summer's evening, a mere two months before the night that would forever change the landscape of the country: *Kristallnacht*, The Night of Broken Glass. The cursed night upon which dozens of defenseless Jews were beaten to death, 30,000 Jewish men were led off to the concentration camps, and over 1,500 synagogues were ransacked and set ablaze. Arthur was walking along the banks of the river, lost in thought, when he heard a weak cry. He looked out into the expanse of water and made out the shape of an overturned boat and its lone passenger, struggling against the powerful current. He didn't hesitate.

With confident, powerful strokes, Arthur swam out toward the helpless man, placing a strong arm around his weary body. "Don't worry," he assured him, "I will get you to shore, into a warm, comfortable bed." Minutes later, the man was sipping hot tea by the fire, unable to believe that he had been plucked from the jaws of death by this stranger.

* * *

Months passed and the situation worsened for Germany's Jews. Those who had considered themselves privileged soon learned that no privilege was sufficient to make up for the curse of Jewish blood. All of them, professors and doctors, industrialists and athletes, were equally tainted in the eyes of the Germans, and thus, equally unwanted.

Arthur Solomon, fourth-generation German, one of Germany's most promising young athletes, was taken to Dachau that winter. Dachau was the first concentration camp, the prototype for all the concentration camps that would follow, and close to 200,000 people would perish within its blood-stained fences.

But Arthur Solomon's wife refused to accept the inevitable. The family had papers to travel to the United States, and she was determined to get her husband out of the camp so that they could escape Germany. She was mocked for her innocence, derided for her naiveté. The camps were the dark hole from which none would return. How would she get him out?

Undaunted, she traveled to the office of the head of the Nazi division in Cologne, Germany, a feared man. He was, however, the same man that Arthur Solomon had rescued from drowning that night. The officer had not forgotten Arthur's selfless, heroic act. He arranged for Arthur to be taken out of the concentration camp and over the border into Holland. From there, he, his wife, and their young son Otto traveled to America.

As he took his last step on the blood-soaked German soil, Arthur paused, remembering the shouts for help on a summer's evening—cries that would herald his salvation.

THE LAST CANDLE

It was brutally cold outside, and only a few degrees warmer inside the little room where Brocha Rivka hovered over her sleeping children at night. Hundreds of adults and children had been crammed into the small room in the 21st Bezirk concentration camp in Vienna where they lived while the war raged on. At night, they all slept on straw mattresses on the floor, blessed by the oblivion that came with slumber. All except Brocha Rivka. Her husband was taken to Munkatabor, a slave labor camp, but she and her four children had miraculously survived and remained together, and it was because of them that she could not sleep. Even at night, she kept vigil over them, making sure they were safe. Despite the fact that her eyelids were leaden with fatigue, she kept herself awake by thinking of all the things she could do to make their lives better. On this particular night, she was thinking of shoes.

Chana, her eight-year-old daughter, had no shoes; they had been destroyed. Brocha Rivka couldn't bear to see her little girl walking barefoot, so she thought of ways she could fashion a pair of her own. As everyone else slept, Brocha Rivka scavenged the room for remnants of cloth, scraps of paper, and anything else she could possibly use to piece together makeshift shoes.

* * *

In April 1945, on a chilly spring morning, Brocha Rivka and her children, along with everyone else in the concentration camp, were herded out of their quarters and forced to go on one of the infamous death marches. Barely clad, starved, disease-ridden, and cold, they marched, not knowing their fate. Many fell to the side of the road, dead. Like so many others, Brocha Rivka became ill. She felt chills throughout her body and every muscle ached, but she continued to march on, knowing what would happen if she stopped. She also urged her sons and daughter to keep walking. She gave them hope when their spirits waned and solace when they cried. Finally, her fever was just too high, and she was too weak to continue.

"Mommy," her young son wept, "if you stop here, we'll surely die. Mommy! Keep going!"

"Baalt, mein kindt." (Soon, my child.)

She kept on repeating *Baalt, mein kindt*, but she couldn't get up. She had sunk into the earth and, despite all her efforts, couldn't muster the energy to get up. As Brocha Rivka sat there, unmoving, she saw another family that had also lost their footing. The father had become too ill to continue on the death march. As they began to speak to one another, little Chana started to wander away. As she listened to the murmurs of her older siblings urging her mother to get up, she kept walking although she knew better than to wander too far. Suddenly, from a far distance, Chana noticed a Nazi soldier running toward her in great haste. She screamed out and all eyes turned toward Chana's direction, terror seizing them as they watched the Nazi hurtling toward beautiful, blond-haired, blue-eyed Chana.

"Gevalt!" Brocha Rivka cried out. "This is the end of us!" She began to recite the *Shema Yisrael* prayer—"Hear, O Israel, the Lord is our G-d, the Lord is One," the blessing one says when one senses

that death may be imminent. The Nazi picked up speed as he raced directly toward little Chana. When he reached her, he stood there in front of her, unmoving. Everyone else froze in place. Chana boldly returned his stare, expecting to see the expression of fury she had often encountered with Nazis. She waited for the Nazi to pull his gun from his holster. She braced herself for the bullet that she knew would come. And yet . . . there was no rage in his face. He did not go for his gun. Instead, he began to weep. "Your hair—it's so blonde. You look exactly like my daughter; you could be her twin. I swear, you look just like my little girl—her spitting image. I miss her so much. I didn't want to be part of this killing machine . . . They drafted me . . . I had no choice."

Everyone watched the Nazi with bated breath, unsure of what he would do next. After only a few moments—that seemed like an eternity—the Nazi came to a decision. He approached Brocha Rivka and her children, who stood huddled together in fear.

"Take off your Star of David emblems and call yourselves Hungarian refugees. Don't follow those people on the march; they are being led to their deaths. Instead, go toward that mountain." He pointed to one of the highest mountains in the region, adding, "You will find refuge there."

Then he planted a kiss on Chana's forehead and said: "Good luck to all of you!"

Brocha Rivka hugged her daughter as everyone let out a unanimous sigh of relief. Stunned by their twist of fortune, they fled to the mountains and found refuge in a barn belonging to an elderly Christian lady. She allowed them to stay in the barn until the war was over.

On the last Friday night before the war ended, Brocha Rivka lit her Shabbos candles, as she did every week. These candles were among the few things she had taken with her when she had been herded out of her home. As she packed her bags to leave, she didn't even think of taking her jewelry. She left behind everything of monetary value except the candles and a few necessary articles of clothing for her children. As for spiritual value, that was a whole other matter. Brocha Rivka took along with her the one thing she knew she could not live without, the one thing she knew would bring her strength through the trying times she could already foresee: her Shabbos candles.

Against all odds, she and her children had survived. Now she could continue to light the Shabbos candles, as did her mother, grandmother, and great-grandmother before her—every ancestor back to Sarah, the matriarch.

On this last Friday night before the war ended, Brocha Rivka lit the very last candle that remained to usher in the Shabbos.

LOST AND FOUND

As told by Steve Eisenberg

Union, New Jersey, is a drab, gray, blue-collar town—not a place I would ordinarily visit. But a business meeting had been scheduled in this most unlikely place, so I left my usual stomping grounds in Manhattan and hopped on a bus from Port Authority. The meeting, which had been extremely challenging, was now over, and I was brooding about it. Deep in thought, I was standing at a windswept bus stop with two other commuters: a middle-aged woman and a stooped, elderly man.

"When's the next bus to Manhattan due?" the woman said as she approached the man. Perhaps the older gentleman was hard of hearing, or perhaps he was trying to collect his thoughts. At any rate, he didn't answer right away. Instead, he gazed at the woman with a blank stare.

She went ballistic. "You &*$%*% idiot! What's the matter with you? Don't you have any common courtesy? What are you, stupid?" She went on and on, hurling a volley of insults, curses, and epithets at the bewildered man. Noticing the yarmulke on my head, he motioned me to his side.

"Do you speak Yiddish?" he whispered in a thick, guttural accent.

I nodded yes.

"Ze's an achta meshuggeneh." (She's crazy.)

I smiled in commiseration.

The bus arrived, and I boarded quickly. I looked forward to my solitude and the opportunity to review the sequence of events that had led to the abysmal conclusion of my meeting. The bus was nearly empty, so I snuggled into a corner and closed my eyes.

"Ah, so good to find a *landsman* in Union, New Jersey!" a voice sighed into my ear.

The elderly gentleman had settled into the seat next to me, clearly seeking companionship.

"Not too many Jews in Union, you know. Where do you live?" the man asked.

Probably a lonely Holocaust survivor, I thought. *It's a* mitzvah *(good deed) to give him a little attention.* I would have to reassemble my thoughts some other time.

"I live on the Upper West Side," I said with a smile.

"Ah, the Upper West Side," he said, fumbling for a connection. "Do you know Rabbi Schacter? Do you attend his *shul?*"

"You mean the Jewish Center? I don't happen to attend that particular synagogue, but certainly I know of Rabbi Schacter. He's a renowned and highly respected Rabbi. Why do you ask?"

"I knew his father, Rabbi Herschel Schacter," the man said with obvious pride. "He was the one who liberated me from Buchenwald. I will never forget that day for as long as I live."

"Can you tell me about it?" I asked. I was interested, as Holocaust stories have a particular resonance with me.

"It was the eleventh of April, 1945. Buchenwald was eerily quiet. We were all in our barracks, waiting for roll call. We didn't see or hear any of the Nazi officers milling around, but we were still too afraid to venture outside to investigate. Then we heard the roar of military vehicles as the front ranks of the American troops stormed Buchenwald. Rabbi Herschel Schacter, the Jewish chaplain, was among the first to enter the gates. He immediately made his way to the administrative offices where the PA system was housed, and broadcast this message in Yiddish over the camp's loudspeakers. I will never forget what he said: "'Yidden (my fellow Jews, my brothers), it's over. Yidden, you are free. Yidden, we are the American troops here to liberate you. Yidden, you can come out now.'

"But few of us did. We were frightened. Most of us thought it was a trick. We couldn't really fathom that the nightmare had truly ended. I was one of the few who came forward, and I trailed behind Rabbi Schacter in wonderment as he began inspecting the camp with the American generals at his side. An American soldier who spoke Yiddish. Amazing!"

The American officers and Rabbi Schacter were clearly devastated by the carnage they saw. They walked around with dazed expressions of disbelief. With stricken eyes, they stared alternately at the mounds of corpses piled neatly in rows and the skeletons strewn haphazardly on the ground. They reeled from the stench that came from the furnaces, still hot, from the ashes still smoldering in the air. Groans of horror and gasps of shock issued continuously from their lips. Despite all of the reports they had heard in advance, they had never conceived of such depravity, such evil, as they witnessed now.

"At one point, Rabbi Schacter stood paralyzed in front of a mound of corpses, unable to go on. Suddenly, a slight movement caught his eye. He touched the arm of the general accompanying him. 'I think I saw one of the corpses move,' he said, trembling with excitement. 'I think one of them is still alive!'

"'Rabbi, it's impossible,' the general gently remonstrated him. 'Even if the person was still alive when he was thrown into the pit, the weight of all the other bodies on top of him would have suffocated him to death.'

"'No, no no,' Rabbi Schacter insisted. 'Don't you see some movement? I see it, I see it even now!'

"'Rabbi,' the general repeated patiently, 'I know how much it would mean to you to be able to save even one life, but it's your imagination, sir. All those people in the pit are dead.'

"But Rabbi Schacter was not easily persuaded. He drew closer to the mound of corpses and began circling it slowly. It was then that he stumbled upon a small child, wide-eyed with fear, who had been hiding behind the pile of bodies, and whose slight motion Rabbi Schacter's eagle eye had detected.

"'I found a child! I found a child!' he yelled to the officers. 'A child in Buchenwald, alive! It's a miracle!'

"Rabbi Schacter knelt down before the child and embraced him gently. 'What is your name, sweet child?' he asked in Yiddish.

"'Lulek,' the child answered, eyes averted.

"'And how old are you, Lulek?' Rabbi Schacter asked.

"'What's the difference?' the boy said sadly. 'What are numbers? Believe me, with what I have seen and what I have experienced, I am older than you. You can laugh and you can cry, but I can no longer do either.'

"Rabbi Schacter later discovered that the boy—perhaps one of the youngest known survivors of the concentration camps—was only eight years old. Against all odds, this one child had clung to life. One and a half million innocent children had been brutally murdered by the Nazis, who routinely killed all children below the age of fifteen as soon as they entered the camps. The discovery of this lone child was both a shock and a triumph. A combination of miraculous circumstances and his own steely resolve had kept young Lulek alive.

"Rabbi Schacter insisted that Lulek stay at his side; he didn't want to let him go. He asked Lulek to accompany him to the prisoners' barracks, where the inmates were still hiding, so that he could personally reassure them that it was true: They were liberated, they were free . . . It was finally over. The Rabbi held Lulek's hand tightly as they walked from one barrack to another, announcing the same message over and over again: *Yidden*, you are free. *Yidden*, it is over. *Yidden*, you are free.

"And do you know who this little child Lulek turned out to be?" the elderly gentleman asked me with a triumphant smile, as our bus rolled into Port Authority. "Israel Meir Lau, Chief Rabbi of Israel!"

* * *

Although I regularly pray at a different synagogue, a few weeks later, I happened to attend Shabbat services at the Jewish Center, which is presided over by Rabbi Jacob Schacter, Rabbi Herschel Schacter's son. At the end of the davening, Rabbi Schacter stood at the doorway greeting congregants as they filed past. *You know what?* I thought. *He's here, I'm here, let me tell him the story.* Although I hadn't doubted the elderly survivor's sincerity, part of me wondered if he hadn't somehow dreamed up the episode he had recounted to me. Quite simply, it had seemed too amazing to be true. Had it been real? As I told Rabbi Schacter about my encounter on the bus with the Buchenwald survivor, he began weeping, and he pumped my hand in gratitude.

"You know, my father told me this story thirty years ago," he said, "and of course, I believed him. But it means so much to me to have it corroborated by a witness, and to hear the events that occurred from this man's perspective. You don't know what this means to me. You have given me a gift."

That summer, I traveled to the Catskills for the weekend and stayed at our summer home in a resort called Vacation Village. Every Shabbos, Vacation Village hosts a different distinguished guest, and unbeknownst to me, the scholar in residence on that particular weekend just happened to be Rabbi Herschel Schacter, liberator of Buchenwald.

After his speech ended, I raised my hand and asked if I might recount a story that I had recently heard about his experiences in Buchenwald. He graciously gave his assent, and I proceeded with my tale. I felt privileged to be able to tell the four hundred people in the audience how Rabbi Schacter was responsible for the rescue and well-being of the current Chief Rabbi of Israel. The audience oohed and aahed, and Rabbi Schacter beamed. It was an honor to be able to give him the public acknowledgment he so richly deserved, and to corroborate a story few people know about today.

There was only a short interval between this and my penultimate experience with the story. Not many days had passed when I was summoned to a fund-raising dinner I was reluctant to attend. My tentativeness, however, immediately vanished when I entered the ballroom and saw on the dais none other than "Lulek"—Israel Meir Lau, the Chief Rabbi of Israel. Sitting next to him was Rabbi Herschel Schacter.

Rabbi Lau was called to the podium to deliver a speech, but before he launched into his opening remarks, he introduced Rabbi Schacter to the audience. "You see this man over here?" he said, pointing to the Buchenwald liberator. "He saved my life."

I thought this would be my last encounter with the story, but it seemed to have taken on a life of its own and kept me in its thrall. Five years later, in January 2008, I was on an El Al flight en route from Israel to New York. After the plane had reached cruising altitude and we were free to move about the cabin, I went hunting for Rebetzin Esther Jungreis, whom I knew was on board. After we exchanged greetings, she told me with excitement: "Do you know who's sitting right behind me? Chief Rabbi Lau."

"Rabbi Lau . . .," I stammered. "I know you probably want to catch a nap or just relax, but I have got to tell you a story. . . ."

THE LOVE STORY OF
DOVID AND SHIFRA

Based on the testimony given by Dovid Landau to Shmuel Globa
(from the original Yiddish)

In a small city in Galicia, Poland, during the 1930s, a Jewish dentist by the name of Dr. Dovid Landau established a thriving practice in Piaskes, a thoroughly Christian neighborhood. A warm and genial man, Dovid formed friendships quickly and easily with Jews and non-Jews alike, and patients came to his office not only to have their teeth fixed, but also to unload their hearts and ask him for advice. His wife, Shifra, was a beautiful blonde who shared her husband's charisma. When she finished her advanced degree in elementary school education, she opened a Jewish kindergarten in the heart of town, and, like her husband's practice, it, too, flourished.

These halcyon years for the young couple came to a swift end with Germany's invasion of Poland in 1939, and the subsequent merciless attacks on the Jewish communities. The German soldiers in Piaskes constantly feasted on stolen Polish delicacies and liquor. Soon their stomachs started to swell and their teeth began to rot. Even though patronizing a Jewish doctor was strictly forbidden, they heard that Dr. Dovid Landau was a good dentist and surreptitiously went to him for treatment. They befriended him, and as a result of these "connections," he was able to help the Jewish community by having a number of harsh decrees annulled. He used his friendships with his Nazi patients to ensure a somewhat easier life for his brethren.

But the day arrived when even Dovid could no longer influence events. Three Jews had been arrested for some minor infraction and were condemned to be hanged. No amount of pleading, bargaining, or bribing could effect any positive change. All the Jews in the town were ordered to witness the hanging, a tactic frequently used by the Nazis. The Nazi commander looked at the masses of frightened Jews gathered in the square, and, for some reason, his eye fell upon Dovid Landau.

"You!" he pointed. "Step up!"

Dovid didn't know why he had been singled out.

"Put the nooses around the necks of these Jews!" the commander barked sharply. Dovid stepped out from the rows of Jews and said, "I cannot do this."

Infuriated, the commander's wrath now spilled down upon Dovid himself.

"Shoot this dog!" he instructed two German soldiers. They grabbed his arm and pulled him forward. "We'll take him to the fields and do it there," they told the commander.

Fortuitously, both men happened to be Dovid's patients. When they arrived at the outskirts of town, one whispered to him: "Don't be afraid. We'll dig a shallow grave. Climb in, and stay there until it gets dark. Run deep into the forest; we know there are Jewish partisans hiding out there, and maybe you can join them. But remember, whatever you do, don't ever show your face in our town again."

Then they took out their guns, shot twice into the air, returned to the site of the hanging, and told the commander the job was done. Everyone gathered in the square had heard the shots, including Shifra. Her body had tensed, but her face remained expressionless; she did not collapse into tears or fall onto the ground in hysteria as everyone had expected. Rather, she stood there, calm and stoic. As far as she or anyone else knew, Dovid was verifiably dead.

* * *

Dovid wandered through the forest at night, when it was safer, and rested during the daytime, hiding between tall stalks of wheat. Hunger gnawed at him, and he felt faint and weak. After several days, he felt ready to surrender to death. When he spotted a small cabin in the distance, he made a decision: *Whatever is going to happen, let it happen, but I must try to get some food and water.* He knocked on the cabin door and was greeted by an elderly peasant man whose face registered shock.

"Oh, you must be so hungry," he said instantly, in sympathy and quick understanding. "Come inside; I'll give you some food."

Dovid told the peasant his story, and the man gave him food, drink, and fresh clothing. The man took Dovid to an empty barn, and told him that he could sleep in the hayloft. "In the morning, I'll point you in the direction of the Jewish partisans," he said.

When Dovid finally found the partisans, they were as excited as he, declaring his arrival to be "providential." Many of them knew him from town, and knew him to be a skilled dentist. Hiding out in the forest for so long, their teeth had become neglected, their gums badly swollen.

The next day, two of them ventured out of the woods to steal dental equipment and medicine, and Dovid thus began a second thriving practice—in the forest. In addition to his dentistry work, Dovid also fully participated in partisan activity against the Germans, and was involved in skirmishes where many of his comrades were mortally wounded. He was nearly captured or killed several times himself, but somehow he always managed to escape death at the last minute.

Throughout his five-year ordeal, Dovid thought constantly about his beloved wife, Shifra, wondering if she was alive, and, if so, where she was. During the moments of high drama that had preceded his staged shooting, Dovid had forgotten to ask the two German soldiers who saved him to contact his wife. He hoped that they would seek her out and tell her the truth about his so-called death so she wouldn't mourn needlessly. But the soldiers never told Shifra that they had helped Dovid escape. While the war raged on and Dovid fought with the partisans, Shifra grieved the loss of her husband.

Dovid searched for Shifra the moment he was liberated, but the beloved place of his youth was now empty of Jews. Not a single Jew from his town had survived the Nazi purge. As he walked the streets of his old city and returned to visit old haunts, he felt hollow. He had expected to be joyously greeted by the local citizenry, to be showered with *bravos* and *hurrahs* for having survived. But the dead eyes of the villagers did not warm at the sight of him, and their faces turned stony as he walked by. In fact, wherever he went, he felt rabid anti-Semitism directed at him—even from his former patients and friends.

There was nothing left for him here. Shifra was gone, his friends and relatives were gone; the life he'd known was over. There was no reason for him to stay. Dovid emigrated to Israel, and joined the *Haganah* (the fledgling Israeli Defense Forces), the first Holocaust survivor to volunteer. Having honed his combat and intelligence skills during his years as a partisan, Dovid was ably suited for his new role. At the same time, he watched other survivors marry one another and start anew. He knew he should try to rebuild his personal life, but he couldn't stop wondering about Shifra. In Europe, he had tried tenaciously to track her down, both through Jewish organizations and on his own, but all his search efforts had proven futile. His spirit was restless, and he knew no inner peace. Turmoil vibrated through every fiber of his being. He obsessed about Shifra and the question— always the same question—*Is there any chance she could be alive, after all?*

From afar, the astute and observant captain of Dovid's brigade watched one of his finest soldiers pace, clench his teeth, and often bury his face in his hands. He felt his pain. When the captain was asked to dispatch two competent intelligence men to Poland to retrieve three Jewish children who lived in a Christian orphanage in Cracow, he instantly knew the name of at least one whom he would appoint. The captain decided this mission would provide Dovid with the perfect opportunity to return to Poland and launch a new search for Shifra. He welcomed the providence that would give Dovid a second chance to find his wife.

Dovid and his friend Mordechai were given British passports and instructed to pose as a pair of English journalists writing a feature story on Christian orphanages during the postwar period. Soon, they were en route to Poland.

* * *

A few weeks after her husband Dovid had been executed in the forest, Shifra Landau returned to her apartment one afternoon to find a sealed envelope on her kitchen table. When she opened it, she found a false Polish passport, a genealogical history of her pure Polish ancestry, and one hundred German marks. No letter was attached, and she could not guess the identity of her mysterious benefactor. Stunned, Shifra sat down at the table to ponder her options. She made a beeline to the local rabbi to seek his advice. "I am, of course, overwhelmed and tremendously grateful for this opportunity," she told him, "but I feel guilty about abandoning my kindergarten. Who will take care of the children?" she asked.

"My dear child," the rabbi said, "it is very commendable of you to care so deeply about your people, but according to Jewish Law, we are commanded to do everything possible to save our *own* selves first.

And, maybe," he added, in an attempt to console her, "just maybe, from your vantage point as an Aryan, you will also be able to help other Jews as well. You *must* cross over to the other side."

Shifra followed the rabbi's counsel and traveled to Cracow, where she obtained employment as a teacher in a Christian orphanage brimming over with blond-haired, blue-eyed cherubs. Three children—one boy and two girls—immediately stood out from the rest. They were dark-haired and dark-eyed and, somehow, they just seemed different. *Could they possibly be Jewish?* Shifra wondered.

When she was asked to help bathe the children, Shifra was able to ascertain that the little boy was circumcised, as she had suspected. Now that her instincts about the boy had been validated, she was even more determined to find out the truth about the two little girls, as well. One night, Shifra broke into the office where the children's files were kept and discovered once again that her intuition had been correct. The two little girls were also Jewish, the files listing their real names as well as those of their parents.

After Dovid's death, Shifra had become listless and depressed, but now she was reinvigorated with new purpose—to mother these three Jewish orphans, to nurture them as she would her own children. A regenerative energy pulsed through her, helping her overcome the tremendous tension she had felt while living her double life. Shifra watched over the three children for the next several years, until Poland was liberated in 1945.

A few weeks after Liberation, Shifra visited a hastily organized Jewish aid society in Cracow to ask for assistance in smuggling the three children out of the orphanage. "Look," the foreign staff members told her, "we just got here, and we don't really know how to deal with this kind of situation. Go back to the orphanage, continue to pretend that you're Christian, and we'll send a delegation to the manager of the orphanage, asking that the children be returned to the Jewish community."

The Poles, however, refused to cooperate, vehemently denying that these three children were Jews. The Jewish organization tried to negotiate with the manager, offering a large sum of money to "redeem" the children, but this tactic also failed. Finally, in desperation, the Jewish aid society contacted the *Haganah* in Israel and asked for help.

In response, a telegram advised the Jewish organization that two *Haganah shluchim* (messengers) were being sent to Cracow, with orders to spirit the children away in the middle of the night. They would be masquerading as British journalists. Shifra was told about the plot, and asked to be on the lookout for two messengers from the *Haganah*. Their names were not mentioned.

Upon their arrival, the two British journalists were given a warm welcome by the orphanage's manager, who affably offered to give them a tour of the premises. When Dovid noticed the lone figure in the study hall, sitting with her head down, immersed in a book, a muscle twitched in his face, but he said nothing. It had been five long years, and she had grown much thinner, but Dovid instantly recognized his beloved wife, Shifra.

Shifra, engrossed in her book, had been oblivious to the men. But Mordechai, Dovid's comrade, immediately noticed that Dovid had started to shiver inexplicably, and his face had blanched white.

"Dovid, what is it?" he asked.

"Shifra, my wife . . . she's in the study hall."

* * *

After the tour was over and the manager had left them to their own devices, Dovid and Mordechai conferred. They agreed that if Dovid were to directly approach Shifra, she might sustain too great a shock. Beyond her personal welfare, they were also concerned about jeopardizing their operation. They decided that Mordechai would speak to Shifra first in order to gently give her advance notice and psychologically prepare her for the great miracle that was about to take place.

Shifra, like her husband, was made of iron stock. When Mordechai gave her the news that Dovid was alive and outside, she blushed deeply and tears sprang to her eyes. In a heroic effort to control her emotions and not give anything away, she nodded curtly, continuing to sing the song with the children that Mordechai had interrupted when he'd entered the classroom.

He whispered one more thing in her ear: "Two o'clock tonight."

Shifra had prepared the three children's clothing, and a little before 2:00 A.M., she opened the front door of the orphanage. Her heart sank when she saw the night watchman posted at the door.

"What are you doing up so late, Shifra?" he asked. "Don't you usually retire early?"

"I have the most *awful* headache," she said. "I thought that perhaps I could get rid of it by going outside. I need some fresh air."

"Enjoy your walk," the guard said, politely doffing his cap.

A few minutes later, Shifra returned to the watchman's side and told him that she had found a drunk Englishman sprawled outside on the sidewalk. Could he help her and the Englishman's friend drag the man inside? The guard obligingly stepped away from his post and helped Mordechai pull Dovid—the supposedly drunk Englishman— into the orphanage hall. Mordechai also pretended to be a little drunk and offered the guard a shot of whiskey from his bottle. The guard was happy to take a drink, and soon fell into a heavy sleep.

"There is enough medicine in that whiskey to keep him asleep for several hours," Mordechai said.

It didn't take long to sneak the children out of the orphanage and into a jeep that was waiting down the block, its motor running. A few hours later, they were in Czechoslovakia, from whence they would be whisked away to Israel.

Only then did Dovid and Shifra finally allow their emotions to take over. They hugged and kissed each other, with hot tears flowing down their cheeks.

Postscript: For decades, a sheaf of precious documents gathered dust in the corner of an attic belonging to Etta Ansel, daughter of a Polish survivor. Her father, Shmuel Globa, had founded a Jewish historical society in the aftermath of the Holocaust and had recorded the testimonies of many survivors. It was not until Etta decided to help us unearth these heretofore unknown stories for this volume that she discovered a set of pages entitled *Nissim*—both the Yiddish and Hebrew word for "miracles"—which told the story of Dovid and Shifra. A miracle indeed.

FRIEND OF A FARMER
Shoshana Goldwasser Schwartz and Azriela Jaffe

My mother, Miriam Kolodny Goldwasser, now eighty-five years old, comes from a small village in the Ukraine. Thanks to her uncle's excellent relationships with the local gentiles, most of the family was given warning before the final roundup of Jews from the Kamen Koshorske ghetto began in 1942. My grandmother decided that she and her seven-year-old daughter (my mother's younger sister) were too frail to live life on the run, and would take their chances with the Germans, staying put in their native town. They were later killed.

My mother chose a different path. At the age of nineteen, she left the village with her uncle, aunt, and the rest of the family to hide wherever they could find shelter. For three months, my mother and her three-year-old cousin found a haven in the hayloft of a neighboring gentile farmer. He was very kind to them and gave them whatever he could to eat. He was their link to the outside world and kept them informed.

One day, the farmer approached them nervously. "I have bad news," he said. "Some townspeople have told me that I'm under suspicion; there are rumors circulating that I'm hiding Jews. I fear for the safety and well-being of my wife and children. If it were just *me* at risk, I'd have you stay, but I cannot put my family in jeopardy." He apologized profusely. Clearly, he was torn.

"I understand," my mother said, sensitive to his quandary. "You can't endanger your family, and I don't want to see you come to any harm, either. We'll leave tomorrow morning."

My mother and her young cousin spent the next two years of the war hiding in the forest until Russia was liberated in 1944. After it was safe to leave the forest and travel freely, my mother returned alone to her village, Jervey, and the area where her aunt had lived, Kamen Koshorske. She decided to visit the Polish farmer who had hidden her and her young cousin, to thank him for his kindness and for saving their lives.

When she arrived at his home, she walked straight into a horrifying scene. Soldiers of the liberating Russian army had descended upon the house, and their rifles were raised against the farmer.

"Collaborator!" they spat at him. "Now it is *your* turn to be killed!"

My mother could not believe her timing. "No, no, it isn't true!" she cried as she rushed to his defense, putting herself in the line of fire. "Stop, stop!" she shrieked. "You have the wrong man!"

"And exactly who are you?" A Russian soldier asked her sternly, as the men slowly lowered their guns.

For once, her identity would serve both her and the farmer well.

"I am a Jew. This man hid my cousin and me in his hayloft for three months!" she said, vindicating the farmer. He fell to the ground crying. "He hid us for as long as he could without arousing suspicions, and he fed us, too. He took care of us in every way, and because of him, we are alive today! He was *never* a collaborator with the Nazis, but a *friend* to the Jews."

As my mother finished her story, the Russian captain also began to cry. "I, too, am Jewish!" he tearfully exclaimed. "I thought all the

Jews had been wiped out . . . I never expected to find a single Jew who had survived Hitler's hell."

The Russians halted the execution and left the house. My mother was thus able to repay the Polish farmer's kindness by saving his life, just as he had saved hers. "You came to my rescue more than once," she said. "You saved *my* life, so it is only just and fitting that I be able to repay your kindness by saving *your* life in turn." My mother stayed in touch with him for the rest of his life, and to this day, she continues to send money to his great-grandchildren.

MY BETRAYER, MY SAVIOR

The village of Vladimirets in the Ukraine was a warm and friendly place, where everyone knew your name and said hello. But there was one particular home that teemed with people and extra cheer.

"Hot danishes for everyone! Come, gather round. Some *kave* (coffee)? Maybe some milk?" Breindel Schwartzblatt's hands always seemed to be holding a tray filled with freshly baked cookies and hot drinks that she proffered to the gentile guests who frequented the dry goods store she ran with her husband, Reb Berel.

"Delicious, Breindel!" everyone would declare enthusiastically. "The chocolate *rugelach* are baked to perfection!"

Coming to Breindel and Reb Berel's store was like coming home. The dry goods store and tailoring services that Breindel offered were only the secondary reasons people frequented their shop. The primary reason was the warm welcome the two offered, enhanced by Breindel's goodies and Reb Berel's storytelling. Within the bosom of this cozy environment, no one was able to hear the distant sound of the German soldiers who would put an end to this way of life—forever.

In the summer of 1941, the Germans arrived with orders to round up all the Jewish residents and herd them to the ghetto in the town of Vladimirets. Almost as soon as they were settled, they were once again rounded up, this time for a march. The Jews had no way of suspecting that they were marching to their deaths. Unbeknownst to them, a huge pit had already been dug near the outskirts of town. The plan was to shoot them by the edge, and then, one by one, they would drop neatly into the pit.

As the townspeople marched to their fate, one voice rose above the crowd. *"Yidden! Radivit zich!"* (Jews! Save yourselves!) No one knows who he was or how he came to know about the pit, but, in any case, he repeated his warning. Suddenly, people started running toward the forest. Whole families, holding on to each other's hands, ran as fast as the youngest could go. Breindel, Reb Berel, their fifteen-year-old daughter, Chana, and their twelve-year-old son, Chaim, were among those who ran to the forest for cover. The Germans, armed with rifles, chased after the unarmed Jews and shot at them. Bodies fell dead, families were split apart.

Breindel and Reb Berel tightly gripped Chaim's hands, but he tripped and lost his footing, landing in a pigsty. Mired in the mud and unable to rise, Chaim heard gunshots and the screams of his parents as they were killed, but above all else, he heard the familiar voice of his sister, Chana, pleading for her life.

"Vyedor! Please don't kill me!" she cried.

In the pigsty, Chaim froze with disbelief. Vyedor, whose name had been called by his sister, was a gentile friend of the family—and a Ukranian policeman working for the Germans. He had just recently been in his parents' home, partaking in his mother's delicacies and enjoying the camaraderie of the household. Chaim couldn't believe that this was the same person now standing over his sister with a bayonet, poking her in the ribs. Vyedor had just taken his parents from him without mercy. Now he was about to kill the only family member Chaim had left.

"Vyedor," Chaim heard his sister plead, "how could you do this to me? You're my friend . . ."

"You're going to die anyway," Vyedor sneered, readying his gun. "I'll do you a favor—I'll kill you right now." Chaim watched the sickening tableau unfold through a little hole in the wooden fence behind which he now crouched, hiding.

"Vyedor!" she cried out again. "You don't have to—"

Chana was cut down in the midst of her tearful pleading, silenced by a single shot from Vyedor's gun. When the shooting finally stopped, the ground was littered with dead bodies. Chaim watched as the corpses were systematically loaded onto the back of a truck and hauled away. He was now irrevocably alone at the tender age of twelve.

Somehow, his survival instincts kicked in. Day after day, he scrounged for food and water in the depths of the forest, and he continued to soldier on. One day a young boy about the same age as Chaim called out to him: "Who are you?"

"Why, I'm a shepherd," replied Chaim.

"Oh yeah?" the young boy said in mockery. "If you're a shepherd, then where are your sheep?"

"Over there," Chaim said, pointing in the direction of the hillside. The boy slipped away and Chaim was relieved.

The next day, he saw the boy again: "So . . . how come I don't see your sheep?" With a sickening feeling in his stomach, Chaim realized that he had been found out. It seemed that the only way to get through this might be to tell the truth.

"I am a Jew," Chaim said, "and I am in hiding." With that, the young boy retreated once again.

The next day, the young boy emerged from the thicket into the clearing where Chaim stood. He studied Chaim up close, and then wordlessly presented him with food and drink. The food sustained him, but even more important, provided Chaim with the reassurance that someone in the world still cared about Jews. He was overwhelmed with gratitude.

The boy came regularly for several days, but one day someone else appeared in his stead. Chaim was surprised when he heard an unfamiliar voice call out to him, instructing Chaim to come out of his hiding place.

"My name is Draka," the man said. "I am the father of the boy who has been helping you." Chaim trusted the man, and accepted his invitation to accompany him home. Chaim was unaware of Draka's malevolent intentions.

"You are a Jew, my son tells me," Draka said in a threatening tone, suddenly clamping a strong hand on Chaim's shoulder.

"Yes, I am," Chaim replied, trying to break free of Draka's strong grip.

"I was promised a sack of salt if I brought in a Jew . . ."

After having successfully evaded the Nazis and their collaborators all these months, Chaim had let his guard down this one time, and it had led to his capture. He knew Draka planned to hand him over to the Nazis as soon as they reached his town. There was no way out; he'd been captured. What Chaim did not know, however, was that the Nazi guard anxiously awaiting his arrival was none other than Vyedor—the man who had mercilessly murdered Chana and his parents. When Chaim was shoved into the home of his betrayer, Vyedor's eyes gleamed with sadistic pleasure.

"Well, well, what have we here?" Vyedor said, his voice dripping with mockery. "How did you manage to hide all this time? You may have lived a bit longer than your family, but you're going to end up dying just like them. I'm taking you back to the town where everyone was killed. There, the Germans will take care of you, too."

"Vyedor," Chaim pleaded, "don't you remember how nice my mother was to you? You were always in our house. My mother gave you pastries. My father used to entertain you with his stories. You smoked in our living room. We gave you cigarettes! How could you do this?!"

Vyedor was unmoved. He slipped a rope around Chaim's neck, attached it to the wagon, and forced Chaim to walk alongside the horse-drawn carriage for ten kilometers. Upon arriving at Gestapo headquarters, Vyedor was greeted as a hero.

"You are to be congratulated! You did a great job! You will get your reward."

Chaim was thrown into a dark cell. As the doors closed behind him, he heard the faint sounds of classical music drifting through the air. Chaim prayed for his life to the strains of Brahms.

Killing one or two Jews at a time didn't seem efficient enough for the Germans. They preferred to round up a large number and then kill them all at once, burying them in the same pit that Chaim had already escaped. Another mass murder was scheduled to take place the next day. Chaim was contemplating his fate when the door suddenly opened and another prisoner was thrown into his cell. The man had been brutally wounded and lay on the floor, gasping for breath. Not a word was exchanged between the two.

Overcome with fatigue, Chaim fell into a deep sleep. *Don't sleep, my Chaimele,* his mother whispered in his dreams. *Get ready to escape. They're going to kill you.* Startled out of his sleep, Chaim opened his eyes, almost expecting to see his mother at his side. Instead, he saw only darkness, and soon fell back asleep. Again, his mother appeared, speaking with even greater intensity.

Don't sleep, Chaimele! she insisted. *Get ready to escape.* She continued, giving him specific instructions: *There's a stool in the cell. Find it. Climb up on it, and you will be able to escape through the window. Chaimele, I know you are so hungry. The man that is lying in the cell with you, he will surely be dead by tomorrow. He has a piece of bread on him, and some matches. Take the bread and eat it so you will have some strength, and take the matches, too. You will need them along your way.*

Chaim awoke, infused with a sense of courage he had not known before. Inspired by his mother's words, he got down on all fours to search for the stool. He followed the rest of his mother's instructions, searching for the piece of bread and matches hidden in the man's pockets. Both were right where his mother said they would be. He ate the bread, put the matches in his pocket, and then stepped on the stool to climb up to the window. The iron bars were close to one another, but he managed to push his head through. Suddenly, the stool fell from under his feet, making a loud noise that aroused the prisoner on the floor.

"The Jew is escaping!" the wounded man called out to the German guards. "The Jew is escaping!"

But no one heard him over the classical music that played on through the night. With his head through the bars and the rest of his body hanging in midair, Chaim knew that it was only a matter of minutes before he would be caught. He heaved his entire body against the iron bars with all his might. Somehow, they gave way under his weight.

"The Jew is out—he's getting away!"

The Germans could now clearly hear the prisoner's screams, and the guards came running. With flashlights in hand, they searched the room and discovered, to their utter amazement, that Chaim was indeed gone. They were incredulous that Chaim had succeeded in squeezing his way through such a tiny space. Chaim lay outside the cell, panting, hiding between the wall and several bushes that made for perfect camouflage.

"Catch him!" The call went out to the guards outside. The dogs began to bark. The German guards started up their motorcycles. Flashlights beamed all around, and the hunt was on.

When the moment was right, Chaim made a dash for the forest. The same forest that had been his refuge before now stood waiting to receive him once again. Chaim reached the cover of the trees and continued to run, the sound of the guards' voices and the dogs' barking following him. After what seemed like a very long time, the sounds grew fainter, until they completely faded away. But that didn't stop Chaim from running. Something compelled him to keep going until he saw the sun peeking up from behind the mountain range.

Chaim didn't know where he was, but he felt certain that he had put enough distance between himself and his Nazi pursuers. He felt safe, and for the first time that night, paused to catch his breath. But he had miscalculated. He had simply run in circles. As the sun rose to illuminate his surroundings, Chaim felt deeply shocked and betrayed by his own feet as he beheld the one person he never thought he would see again: Draka, the same man who had corralled him in the forest the day before and turned him over to Vyedor. He stood only a few yards away from Chaim and pierced him with his gaze.

Chaim's first impulse was to pick himself up and flee again. But before he could even get his feet under him, Draka fell to his knees, clutched his hands in front of his chest in prayer, and cried, "Thank G-d you escaped!"

Chaim could hardly believe what was happening. *Is Draka really kneeling before me?* In order to save himself, Chaim quickly dissembled. "No, no, you are wrong, I didn't escape. The police let me go once they saw that I was a little boy. They decided not to harm me."

"No!" Draka said firmly. "That is not the truth. I *know* you were in jail, and you escaped. I know exactly what happened because last night, your mother kept coming to me in my dreams. She kept yelling at me. She kept saying 'What did you do to my child?! For a bag of salt, you turned him in! For a mere bag of salt?' I couldn't sleep all night because your mother wouldn't relent. She haunted me all night."

Chaim's terror now melted into an overwhelming feeling of love for his mother—a love that could not be stopped by death. "From now on, I will make sure to keep you safe," continued Draka. "I will pay with my life if I have to, but I swear, you *will* be safe."

Draka took Chaim to his brother, who was the mayor of the town. Together, they devised a plan: In order to ensure that no one would turn Chaim in, *everyone* in the village had to be involved in this mission. Each day, a different family would take Chaim in to live with them. This way, everyone would be equally responsible for him, and no one would be foolish enough to turn him in, as it would expose everyone in town.

The plan was instituted promptly, executed perfectly, and it was the way that Chaim lives to tell his story.

A BOY NAMED YITZCHAK, WACLAW, AND JACK

Liza M. Wiemer

In the fall of 1941, terrifying rumors of liquidation, murder, and mass graves buzzed throughout the Strzegowo Ghetto in northern Poland.

"We must make arrangements to escape immediately," ten-year-old Yitzchak (Jack) Dygola's mother said.

A partially nailed-down wooden slat in the ghetto wall moved easily and concealed his family's escape route. Under the blanket of a moonless night, Yitzchak, his mother, his younger brother Shmuel, two aunts, and three male cousins slipped through the narrow gap at various intervals, each running in separate directions to test their fate.

"We will meet up again soon, after the war, in Dobrzyn," were Mrs. Dygola's parting words to her sons.

With newly bleached hair, Yitzchak had a survival plan, which he revealed to no one. "May I have a cross and a Bible, please?" he asked the gentile farmer's wife who periodically supplied cow's milk for Yitzchak's baby cousin back in the ghetto. She gave him the icon and Bible without any questions. Yitzchak silently declared, "I am now Waclaw Dulczewski!"

The real Waclaw had been the son of Christian neighbors who had moved from Yitzchak's hometown, the Polish village of Dobrzyn, right before the war. During sleepless nights and endless days, the new Waclaw memorized the prayers from his small Polish Bible.

Life on the run was terrifying and lonely. Sporadically, a farmer would offer a night of shelter, a discarded shirt, or a pair of tattered shoes. But Waclaw could never stay in one place for very long. Anyone caught with an unregistered individual under his roof would face the Nazi shooting squad.

A few times Waclaw worked alongside a Polish farmer to earn a bit of food. Conversations sometimes focused on "the Jewish problem."

"There's not one filthy Jew left in these parts, and soon there won't be a Jew alive," an accommodating farmer declared while Waclaw hoed the man's hayfield.

"It's a darn good thing," Waclaw agreed.

Later that evening, alone, Waclaw sat by a raging river with tears streaming down his face. His voice was drowned by the rapids as he practiced the Hebrew prayers he had learned in religious school. *Yisgadal viyiskadash shimay rabbah* . . . (The Mourner's Prayer) and *Shema Yisrael, Hashem Elokeinu, Hashem Echad*—"Hear, O Israel, the Lord is our G-d; the Lord is One."

Waclaw thought to himself as he prayed: *I must survive, I must remember . . . I am the only Jew left!*

Two brutal winters passed and it was now early spring, 1943. Waclaw looked more like a wounded animal than a human being. Starvation, bitter cold, loneliness, inadequate clothes, and constant fear had nearly broken Waclaw's spirit. "I'm not going to make it," he moaned out of utter despair. Sitting in a cornfield near a river, Waclaw stared at his infected black and blue hands. "My fingers are going to fall off . . . I'm going to die!"

In the late afternoon he somehow managed to get to his feet and walk along the river. Off in the distance Waclaw saw a Polish woman washing clothes against a rock. *You can trust her,* he heard a voice say out of nowhere. *She will help you. You can tell her who you are.*

Waclaw cautiously approached the woman, holding out his swollen, frostbitten hands. "Are you a Jew?" she asked, staring at his disfigurement.

"Yes," he nodded. More than two years had passed since he had revealed his true identity to anyone.

"Hide in the cornfield until it is pitch dark, and I will come back for you with my daughter. You can tell no one in my family that you are a Jew. Do you understand?" Again, Waclaw nodded.

The hours seemed endless as Waclaw hid in the cornfield, but the kind Polish woman, wife and mother of eight, came back for him. For nearly six weeks she nurtured him—body and soul—feeding him, soaking his hands and wrapping them after applying salve, which she procured from a local doctor by bartering with some of her hand-churned butter.

"It's time for you to go," the kind Polish woman told him one afternoon. "But I know of a widow living across the river who could use some help on her farm. Her two sons are doing forced labor for the Germans. You will need to get proper documents if you are going to stay with her."

In the town nearby, Waclaw bravely walked into the Nazi head-quarters. "I'd like to get identification papers," he said.

"Why don't you have papers already?" the stern German behind the desk asked.

Waclaw quickly made up a story. "My father died before the war and my mother went to look for work. She died, and now I am an orphan."

Staring into Waclaw's face, the Nazi thought he would trick the boy. "Recite the morning prayer," he demanded. Waclaw flawlessly recited the Christian prayer. With dubious glances the officer gathered the documents and filled in the name and residence of Waclaw

Dulczewski. He could now legally live with and work for the Polish widow.

But life did not improve for Waclaw. The embittered widow treated him like a slave, fed him little, and worked him until he was bone-tired. The hayloft above the stables provided little rest or comfort with the constant looming fear that Nazis might discover his secret.

One night Waclaw was awakened by a shout: "Come down from there!" A flashlight blinded his terrified, bleary eyes. Scrambling down the ladder, Waclaw saw men carrying guns. "Come outside now!" they said. To Waclaw's surprise, these men were not Nazis. They were freedom fighters, partisans! Standing in her nightgown, the widow watched stone-faced from her front door as the partisans raided the farm, taking horses, chickens, and other supplies. A partisan stood by, a gun pointing toward her.

"I know you!" Waclaw said to one of the men who stood near him. "You're Chaim Polsky.* You were in the Strzegowo Ghetto with me! I'm Yitzchak Dygola."

"You're not staying here anymore," said Chaim. You're coming with us."

Yitzchak, now nearly fourteen, became a junior member of the partisans. Too young to fight, the group leaders assigned Yitzchak to help out around camp. His constant hunger pains subsided. The partisans were well supplied with guns, ammunition, and dynamite, allowing small groups of men to destroy German railways and buildings. Their numerous successful attacks forced German tanks and trucks to retreat on the northern road to Germany.

Within eight months of joining the partisans, Yitzchak's group met a Russian corps made up of young women. They yelled to the partisans, "The war's over! It's truly over!"

Yitzchak immediately began to search for any surviving family members. He made his way back to Dobrzyn, but found no one. Only a handful of Jews from the nearly 2,500 who used to live there trickled home. One day, however, he reconnected with a World War I Polish officer whom Yitzchak's family had known before the war. "Go to Warsaw," the officer suggested. "That's where you might find your family."

Several months passed as Yitzchak tried desperately to discover any information about his kin. He put his name on lists of survivors, and eventually he heard the horrible fate of his brother, Shmuel. He had been hiding on a Polish farm when someone betrayed him and turned him over to the Nazis. He was murdered by firing squad.

Alone and heartbroken, Yitzchak left Warsaw for Lodz, a city with an abundance of Polish refugees. Sadly, he found no family members there. His father had died from a heart attack in 1937, and, after an exhaustive search, Yitzchak concluded that the Nazis had murdered his mother.

Eventually, Yitzchak joined a Zionist kibbutz for orphans in Lodz, Poland. The group planned to illegally immigrate to Palestine, as soon as arrangements could be made. He learned to speak modern Hebrew, sing Zionist songs, and develop the skills needed to help build Palestine. The kibbutz leaders put Yitzchak in charge of entertainment. In 1946 Poland came under Russian control and the kibbutz leaders moved the group to to Landsberg, Germany, a town near Munich, which was under American leadership. The group was also one step closer to reaching Palestine. In Landsberg, they took over an abandoned school, which was large enough to house the near 100 children. Ironically, across the street stood the prison where Adolf Hitler had written *Mein Kampf*.

One afternoon in 1947, Yitzchak waited in the Munich train station after picking up theater tickets for his kibbutz. Suddenly, he overheard two American soldiers speaking Yiddish.

"Excuse me," Yitzchak said in Yiddish. "Where are you from?"

"Brooklyn," they said in unison.

"Well, then, you must know my *tante* (aunt), Sara Newman. She lives in Brooklyn!" Yitzchak declared.

The men laughed. "You've got to be kidding! Do you know how big Brooklyn is?"

Yitzchak had no idea.

"Listen," one of the soldiers said, "we can write to our parents and ask them if they know a Sara Newman. Give us your address and we'll see what we can do for you."

A few months later a letter arrived for Yitzchak. It was from his Aunt Sara. "Come to Brooklyn," she urged. Subsequent letters followed. "Don't go to Palestine. You've survived so much. Do you want to get yourself killed there? You're the only living Dygola." Unfortunately, his aunt was poor and could not afford to become his sponsor. Her words did have a powerful effect on Yitzchak, however, so he contacted the American embassy to inquire about immigrating to the United States.

"The process to get a visa could take two years," Yitzchak was told by the secretary. But he would not give up. Soon, he knew the names of the secretaries at both the Canadian and American embassies.

"Great news," said the secretary from the Canadian embassy upon seeing Yitzchak for the second time that month. "The Jewish Congress of Canada is sponsoring five hundred orphans. I'm putting your name at the top of the list!"

After a grueling fourteen-day journey, Yitzchak arrived by boat in Halifax. Following good-byes and best wishes, the orphaned boys and girls left for new homes spread throughout Canada. Yitzchak was taken in by the Fogelbaum family of Montreal, along with another boy named Yitzchak. That's when his name was changed to Jack.

Time passed and Jack continued to believe that he was the only survivor in his family. He learned the furrier trade and to speak and write English. During the summer of his nineteenth year, some of his new family's friends invited him to leave the heat of Montreal for their summer cottage in the cool Laurentian Mountains. Soon after they'd arrived, Jack received an urgent call from an acquaintance he had met on the boat to Canada.

"Yitzchak, you're not going to believe it! Today I saw an ad in the *Jewish Forward* saying 'Eva Chava Dygola from Milwaukee, Wisconsin, is looking for any survivors from her family.' You're the only Dygola I know; are you related to her?"

"It's got to be my mother! She's alive!" Jack shouted with joy.

Eight months later, philanthropist Harry Bragarnick sponsored Jack's emigration to the United States. On September 24, 1950, Jack and Eva Dygola reunited in Milwaukee, Wisconsin, with copious tears and hugs.

Five out of the eight relatives who had run from the ghetto survived. Sadly, however, Jack lost nearly seventy other family members in the Holocaust.

FALL PRAYERS

David Seitelbach's bright blue eyes and light blond hair became his passport to survival during the war. At the tender age of thirteen, he was forced to leave his hometown of Galicia in the south of Poland, near the Russian-Ukraine border. His town had been turned into a ghetto by the Germans. His father, mother, sister, and uncles were bound for the concentration camps where, unbeknownst to David, they would all be exterminated.

David, however, roamed free. His "Aryan" coloring allowed him to blend into the Polish landscape. The young boy wandered aimlessly throughout the war, working as a farmer's helper whenever and wherever he could, all the while feverishly trying to hide his Jewishness. Any slight hint of exposure meant certain death.

During one "Thanksgiving" dinner at a Polish farm where he had secured temporary employment, David was invited to join the family and partake in the meal. While everyone else enjoyed the ham set in the center of the table, garnished with herbs, David ate only vegetables, remembering his family's clear admonishment against eating ham—the quintessential un-kosher food. Not wanting to rouse any suspicions, he simply said that he wasn't too hungry when he was asked if he'd like some more food.

It was the fall of 1942 and David worked unceasingly, tending the land with horse-drawn plows. As he fed the cows, minded the chickens, and brought in the harvest from the fields, he took special note of the season: The green leaves on the trees were turning into a rich kaleidoscope of color; the air was growing colder; the sun set earlier and rose later. It was the time of year that David had learned to associate with the Jewish High Holidays. He vividly recalled going to the synagogue with his father, mother, and sister where they beseeched G-d to bless them with a good year ahead.

David thought yearningly of the solemn High Holiday prayers. Despite the brutality of the war and his own tender years, David clung to his faith, and longed to give expression to it in some small way. But while grown men probably knew the prayers by heart, he was too young to have had the opportunity to memorize them.

"I wish I had a Jewish calendar," he reflected one day. *"Who knows? Maybe today is Rosh Hashanah, the New Year . . . or maybe it's Yom Kippur, the Day of Atonement. It should be somewhere around now. How sad it is that I don't know and don't have anyone to ask. If only I knew the exact words of the prayers so I could say them anyway, and just hope it was the right day . . ."* David was thrust out of his reverie when the farmer, his boss, asked him to go to the market to fetch some goods. David traveled by horse and buggy, and once he'd arrived, he hitched the horse to an adjacent tree and went inside to buy the goods requested by the farmer.

"Please give me half a pound of salt, one pound of sugar . . . and . . .," David's voice began to falter as he watched the grocer package his items. Although he knew that the war had created a huge paper shortage in Poland, he could not have imagined what was being used as its substitute. David watched, horrified, as the grocer casually reached for a volume of Jewish Holy Scriptures that lay on a nearby shelf and ripped out a few pages to create some paper cones into which he poured the salt and sugar. While many supplies were scarce, Jewish holy books were plentiful since the synagogues, Jewish schoolhouses, and Jewish homes had all been laid to waste and looted by the Nazis and the Poles. Clever uses were devised for all Jewish property. What better way to wrap grocery goods than with the holy pages of the Jewish scripture?

David felt as if he had been punched in the stomach. The violation of the sacred book was almost too much to bear. Not wanting to show his dismay for fear of revealing his identity as a hidden Jew, David kept his voice steady and his face stoic even as his innards churned. "And please," he continued, "some yeast." David paid the sum and, with hands shaking, placed the packages under his arm and exited the store.

Once outside and back in the buggy, away from the store and anyone's view, David opened the packages to see exactly which holy text was being used in this sacrilegious way. He took the cone of yeast in his hand and gingerly untied the string. With loving care he beheld the sacred Jewish pages in his hands, then began to read the words that lay therein. He trembled with excitement as he realized that the storekeeper had randomly wrapped his packages with pages torn from the High Holidays prayer book.

Let us tell how utterly holy this day is and how awe-inspiring . . . The great shofar is sounded . . . a gentle whisper is heard . . . On Rosh Hashanah their destiny is inscribed and on Yom Kippur it is sealed.

These words were considered to be among the most powerful prayers of the High Holidays. David read each word as if for the first time. As he prayed, he recalled the holidays of a better time, when all the congregants in the synagogue had stood erect while chanting these holy words.

Who shall live and who shall die . . . Who shall come to a timely end, and who to an untimely end . . . who shall perish by fire and who by water . . . who by hunger and who by thirst . . .

For David, these words were real. At his tender age, he had already witnessed "untimely" deaths, had already experienced the ravages of hunger and thirst. So many of the people he knew and loved had "perished by fire" (the furnaces) and "water" (the showers that spurted gas instead).

David knew it was the fall season. He knew the holidays were around this time; he had wanted to observe them in some meaningful way. He was too young to know the prayers by heart but yet he wanted to access the prayers that would lift him up from his dismal surroundings and propel him to a higher plane. Now these same prayers had miraculously appeared in his hands, and David knew without a shadow of a doubt that his question about whether it was, in fact, the High Holidays had been answered. He knew that this was his personal miracle.

David raised the torn, violated, sacred pages of the Rosh Hashanah *machzor* before him, and with his pure, sweet voice, he prayed on.

Postscript: David is now seventy-eight years old and lives in Toronto. Though his life's path has taken him on a circuitous journey and he's had his share of trials and tribulations, he still reflects back on that day in Poland a long time ago when those powerful words appeared and brought solace and deep comfort to his aching soul. They still do today.

GOOD MORNING, HERR MUELLER

It is a Jewish dictum to always try to be the first to greet everyone you meet. When you greet someone heartily, with a warm smile and friendly salutation, all is well in that person's world—if only for a fleeting moment. The individual feels a sense of validation, that his existence in the cosmos has been acknowledged and recorded, that he is *known*. There are tales told of revered Jewish sages who scrambled to greet each other first in almost comical ways. One should never underestimate the power of "hello."

Rabbi Israel Shapira, a renowned spiritual leader in Poland in the 1930s, took this directive quite seriously. Wherever he went, he regaled his fellows with wholehearted greetings, always making sure to be the first to say "hello." This practice extended to *everyone* he met—Jew and non-Jew alike. Almost everyone returned his cordial greeting, with the notable exception of one man.

Long walks were the rabbi's only recreation, a time for him to reflect and refresh himself. His doctor had also recommended regular exercise as beneficial to his health. Rabbi Shapira would wander through the familiar village streets, and then continue on his daily constitutional to the less-traveled outskirts, where the stores and houses gave way to verdant meadows and rolling hills. It was here that he often encountered a Polish peasant named Herr Mueller, a rabid anti-Semite. The townspeople avoided him, but Rabbi Shapira was undeterred. Whenever he would chance upon Herr Mueller tilling the soil or planting new crops, he would stop for a second and sing out: "Good morning, Herr Mueller!" Stony-faced and grim, Herr Mueller never answered. He would turn his back on the rabbi, pretending that he hadn't heard the greeting. Surprisingly, Rabbi Shapira remained undaunted by Herr Mueller's hostile behavior. He continued to greet him effusively, every single time he passed him on the road.

Years passed, and the rabbi's customs never wavered. Eventually, the rabbi's unflinching resolution to bequeath human dignity upon every soul he encountered began to wear Herr Mueller down. Cracks began to appear in his armor. First, he began to nod his head in acknowledgment of the rabbi's greeting; later, he doffed his hat. Finally, Herr Mueller began to grudgingly answer back, "Good morning, *Herr Rabbiner.*" Rabbi Shapira was the only Jew Mueller ever addressed or interacted with—even in the smallest of ways. For everyone else, he harbored a deep and abiding hatred that was soon to find an outlet.

The Nazis' rise to power sparked and inflamed the simmering hatred of other Polish peasants much like Herr Mueller. When they invaded Poland in 1939, the Nazis capitalized on this hatred, counted upon it, manipulating it toward their own evil ends. In Eastern Europe, the Jews of Poland were the first group to be rounded up and deported, and soon, entire villages were emptied out. Rabbi Shapira was among those ensnared by the Nazi web, and the day arrived when he too was shipped to a concentration camp from which few Jews emerged alive.

As soon as Rabbi Shapira disembarked from the cattle cars, he was directed to wait in a long line for "selection." From a distance, he saw an officer's baton swing alternately to the right and left, and Jews being separated into two different groups. Whispers made their way down the line: one group was destined for death, the other for life. It sickened Rabbi Shapira to realize that his fate would be sealed within a matter of seconds by the officer with the baton. *Who was this man*, he wondered, *who could so easily and dispassionately send a human being to his death for no other reason than the fact he was Jewish?*

He watched as the people at the beginning of the line approached the man for inspection. Some of them averted their gaze, avoiding eye contact with the Nazi, but Rabbi Shapira determined that *he* would not go to his death in utter submission. No; he would look boldly into the Nazi's eyes, pin him with his stare, and try to make him see the human being standing before him.

The line moved forward. It seemed to take only a second to condemn a man to the chimneys, the group waiting on the left.

The rabbi's turn came. He stared into the officer's eyes—eyes he knew well.

"Good morning, Herr Mueller," said the Rabbi.

A muscle twitched on the Nazi's face, the only hint that he had heard the rabbi speak. He paused for a heartbeat before responding, "Good morning, *Herr Rabbiner!*" And then: *"Recht* (right)!" Herr Mueller swung his baton toward the group of able-bodied men and young women designated for hard labor, even though Rabbi Shapira was neither young nor able-bodied anymore.

RIGHTEOUS AMONG THE NATIONS

Things were not perfect in eleven-year-old Solly Ganor's little world. Yes, it was the joyous Hanukkah holiday, and the smells of frying oil and burnt wicks filled the house. Sure, he had received the traditional Hanukkah *gelt*, the money from friends and relatives that filled his pockets and made him feel ten feet tall. But still, he felt a vague sense of unease, of impending doom. The appalling tales of a war in faraway Poland, the accounts of Jews beaten and imprisoned, had made their way into young Solly's idyllic little paradise. Every so often a broken Jewish refugee from that country would come into the synagogue in their Lithuanian hamlet, living testimony of the horrors of war.

So when the neighborhood women came collecting for a Jewish refugee fund, though it was Solly's mother they were looking for, he felt like he should be a part of it. On a sudden impulse, he reached deep into his pocket and handed over his entire fortune. The ladies were overwhelmed by the gesture and promised to use the sum, which was a generous one by all accounts, to help buy visas for people trying to leave Lithuania.

Solly had mixed feelings: On the one hand, he felt noble and proud of what he had done, comfortable with the knowledge that his money was going to help people. Yet, at the very same time, he was just a child, and he missed the feeling of money in his pockets. He had given away every last coin, and now he himself had no money for his interests and activities.

There was a brand-new Laurel and Hardy film showing in the local Metropolitan movie house, and Solly watched the other kids run off to see it with a trace of envy; he had no money left. His last hope to see the movie was his dear aunt Anushka. She knew how much he loved the humorous characters, and she was the type of adult who would understand his dilemma.

He hurried off toward her store, an upscale food market that stocked expensive food items from around the world. The shop was usually filled with foreign dignitaries who came to purchase their native foods. Solly opened the large glass door and entered, enjoying the sudden warmth of the store after the chill of the outdoors. Aunt Anushka immediately noticed him and welcomed him warmly.

"It's my favorite nephew," she said. "I bet you he is here for his Hanukkah money," she added good-naturedly. As she greeted him, she pointed at a distinguished-looking gentleman standing next to the counter. He was dressed immaculately and carried himself with an air of importance. Solly stared at him.

"Solly, say hello to the consul of Japan, Mr. Sugihara."

Solly extended his hand and looked up into the face of the diplomat. He remembered what his grandfather had always said: The eyes are the mirror to the soul. Solly decided that this man's eyes spoke of a soul filled with humor and generosity, with hope and sacrifice. Solly felt like he had found a friend in this elegant man with the unusual eyes.

"So, you need some money, little fellow?" the consul asked. He reached into his pocket and withdrew a *lit*, handing it to Solly with a smile.

Solly spoke solemnly. "I cannot take your money; you are a stranger."

"Then consider me your uncle for the holiday," replied the man with the smiling eyes. Solly hesitated for a moment, and then accepted the shiny coin.

"If you are to be my uncle," Solly said, "then you must come join in the family Hanukkah party on Saturday night; everyone will be there."

Anushka heard the last part of the conversation and looked embarrassed at his childlike naiveté. "I am sure His Excellency is very busy," she said. Then she looked at the dignitary and smiled shyly. "Of course, you are cordially invited to join us."

His eyes lit up. "Oh, then I will certainly come. I have never before been to a Hanukkah party."

On Saturday night, the large mahogany table was laden with heaping dishes of food. Family members sat in groups, chatting and laughing, enjoying each other's company. The Hanukkah lights burned brightly in the corner, adding to the sublime atmosphere in the room. There was a knock at the door, and there stood Mr. Chiune Sugihara, and his wife, Yukiko. They made an elegant picture: She wore a stylish black dress, and he was dressed in a formal striped suit. They were warmly welcomed by the extended Ganor family. Most of the people spoke Russian and German, languages with which the Sugiharas were familiar, so conversation flowed freely.

Anushka had brought home some Japanese food from the deli, and it occupied a place of honor on the table among the more traditional dishes. Uncle Jacob took out his harmonica and everyone joined in the joyous Hanukkah songs, with lyrics proclaiming the victory of good over evil, odes to the triumph of the human spirit, and songs of gratitude to G-d. The consul was visibly moved by the scene of the large family singing together heartily, and he expressed his admiration to Solly's mother. "It is evident this family loves each other very much," the consul commented.

Later on, as the evening was drawing to a close, Abe Rosenblatt came into the room. Abe was a refugee from Poland who had come to stay with the family for a while, and he looked out of place in a borrowed suit that was several sizes too large for his bony frame. He asked to be introduced to the consul. Solly's father rang the servant's bell and it was silent. "This is Mr. Abe Rosenblatt," Solly's father announced, "and he would like to say a few words."

All eyes were on the dilapidated figure, who was clearly uncomfortable. At first Rosenblatt spoke softly, as if he himself couldn't believe his words. He described how the Germans had bombed his native Warsaw, acting with inhuman brutality. He recounted how his wife and eldest daughter were killed in the attack, and how he was trapped under the rubble of the fallen house for three days. His voice gathered strength as he continued, describing the persecution and beatings. He recalled how he and his surviving daughter, Lea, had moved in with a cousin, and how the Germans entered and took possession of the home, shooting the cousin in full view of everyone else.

As Rosenblatt spoke, Sugihara listened intently, his horror evident. Rosenblatt spoke with emotion, shedding the tears of a million people who had been silenced. After he completed his narrative, he turned to Mr. Sugihara, and implored him to issue him a visa. The consul promised to look into it.

The very next day, Mr. Sugihara cabled his country and told them of the atrocities being perpetrated by the Germans. He requested permission to grant visas to help the Polish refugees. The foreign ministry cabled back, denying his request. Sugihara repeated the application again, and then a third time, but each time the answer was the same. Sugihara was well aware of the consequences of disobeying his government. He knew that it would bring him shame and punishment. He understood the grave risks for his family and himself. But he did it anyway. Each day, he handed out hundreds of visas, granting them to those with proper identification and those without. Many applicants came with just the tears on their faces, but for him, that was enough.

He felt driven to help, saying that he had orders from a higher authority. "I still have no permission from my government to issue visas, but under these circumstances the humanitarian needs of people take precedence over my received instructions," he said. Among the recipients of those visas was the entire student body of the Mirrer Yeshiva, some three hundred students. When all was done, Sugihara had issued over 3,000 visas.

* * *

The Nazis eventually marched on Lithuania as well, destroying homes and lives, and more significantly, hope. Solly Ganor, the boy who had given his money to help refugees, was deported to the concentration camps, where he, like so many others, was slowly deprived of his basic rights. He grew emaciated and cynical, barely surviving, sometimes wishing that he wouldn't.

At the very end of the war, when the footsteps of the American liberators could already be heard, the Nazis led the inmates from Dachau on the dreaded death march, forcing them to continue walking even as they could no longer stand.

The American forces arrived, and Solly Ganor collapsed. He lay there, too weak, too weary, too skeptical to believe in a new day. A strong American soldier hurried over, placing an arm around the skeletal figure of Solly Ganor. Solly looked into his eyes. For the second time in his life, he saw Oriental eyes.

And then, he knew that all would be well. For he remembered the heights that the human spirit can scale, the power of hope and goodness, the selflessness of man. And with the confident arms of the Japanese-American soldier beneath him, he began to believe again . . .

Postscript: After the war, Sugihara was no longer allowed to serve his country as a diplomat. He had toiled on his country's behalf for decades, but at the age of forty-seven, he was left without a career. His prestigious position was no longer available to him because of his decision to save lives.

This elegant, princely man was forced to take menial jobs to support his family. He lived out the rest of his life in obscurity, broken and bitter at his country's refusal to rise up to the challenges thrust at them. He had to leave his own family to work in Russia, just to make a living. When he finally returned to Japan and his family, he was old and weak. Toward the end of his life, the community of Holocaust survivors wanted to honor him, but he resisted the accolades. He played down his historic role, saying that "though I may have disobeyed my government, there was no choice; otherwise I would have been disobeying G-d."

In 1985 Sugihara was recognized as a "Righteous among the Nations" by Yad Vashem, the Holocaust memorial in Israel. He died later that year. A few years later he posthumously received the Nagasaki Peace Award, and the Japanese government issued a formal apology to his widow and son.

Susan Bluman, a survivor, commented that "because of Sugihara, between the children and grandchildren [of those he saved], there are 40,000 people alive today. The most important lesson is that one man can make a difference."

Some people like to say that the Sugihara story is our own modern-day Hanukkah miracle. For it was on Hanukkah, the Festival of Lights—in Solly Ganor's home—that Sugihara's soul was first ignited, when his heart first flamed with compassion for the European Jews abandoned by the world. But while the Maccabees waged their battle with weaponry, Sugihara fought back with visas. And with this bold action, he brought light to generations.

In a tearful ceremony in the land of Israel, sixty years after the war, Solly Ganor met again with Clarence Matsumura, the Japanese-American soldier from the 522nd Field Artillery Battalion who had saved his life.

THE SEARCH FOR REB BURECHL

There are places engraved in our personal histories where monumental events, even miracles, have occurred. These physical places can alternately be bustling cities—meccas of culture, commerce, and wealth—or sleepy villages barely discernible on the map. Who has even heard of Yaklichi (Yagalizia)? An obscure little town in Poland, with no distinguishing features, no prominent personalities, no reason to emerge into public consciousness. Yet it was here that a major miracle unfolded for an aristocrat of a great Chasidic line: Munkatch.

Avid students of Chasidic dynasties will surely recognize the name: Rabbi Burech Rabinowitz, son-in-law of the legendary Minchas Elazar and father of the current-day Munkatcher Rebbe. In August 1941, he had been snatched off the streets of Munkatch (Munkacz) during a blitzkrieg *Aktion*, targeting foreign nationals. Hungarian Jews were still being protected by their government, but foreign Jews were fair prey. Reb Burechl had a Polish passport, so when the Nazis went hunting, his fate was sealed.

In the cattle cars, the Jews reeled from the stench, from the crush of bodies, from the lack of air. They had been transported over the border past Yasin and the Dnenster River in a long, torturous journey, and when they reached their final destination, they tumbled out, half-crazed with hunger, thirst, and fear. Someone whispered to Reb Burechl that they were in a place called Yaklichi.

The Jews were marched to a huge barn where they were corralled with no food, no drink, no explanations. They pressed against each other in the dark, a mass of human misery, wondering what was next. Outside, Nazi guards ringed the barn, standing sentry. No one even contemplated the possibility of escape; any such effort was clearly doomed.

Reb Burechl sat crouched in a dark corner, his thick brows furrowed, his mind racing. *Yaklichi, Yaklichi . . .* why did the name of this town sound so familiar? The name teased him, beckoned him, stirred within him old, dormant memories. Where had he heard this name before? And then he remembered a mysterious, almost supernatural story he had once been told . . . a story whose centerpiece was a town named Yaklichi.

Your great-grandfather, the Heilege (holy) Sassover, was a famous Chasidic Rebbe who—during his sojourns throughout Poland— once happened to travel past a little town named Yaklichi, where his carriage driver suggested they take shelter for the night. Yaklichi boasted a small community of simple, hardworking Jews, who were honored to have the great Rebbe in their midst. Not only were the living enthralled by his presence, so, too, apparently were the dead. At night, while he slept, the souls of the departed whose bones lay buried in the Jewish graveyard of Yaklichi visited the Rebbe and presented him with this petition:

"We are simple folk who are buried here, and do not boast a single luminary, not one great master, among us. Please, can you do us the great honor of joining us here, and keeping us company?"

The Rebbe murmured sincere words of regret, explaining that he had already promised his presence to a cemetery in a different town. "However," he consoled them, "I give you my word that some other member of my family will come to join you." Reassured by his pledge, the departed slipped out of his dream and back into their respective graves.

Many years later, the Rebbe's son, Reb Shmelke—who had heard the story recounted several times before—was traveling to a large city, when his horse-drawn carriage broke down along the way. He had been immersed in Torah study throughout the journey, and had been oblivious of his surroundings, until the driver apologetically tapped on the carriage door.

"Sorry, Reb Shmelke," he said, "but we'll need to be here for a while until the wheel is replaced."

"Where are we?" the Rebbe asked.

"A small town called Yaklichi."

"Yaklichi?!" The Rebbe looked up, startled, consternation spreading over his face. "No, no, we can't stay here for any length of time. Please, hurry and get it fixed as quickly as possible." The Rebbe hoped that his father's story was apocryphal, but he didn't want to wait to find out.

News spreads fast in Jewish communities—especially small ones—and soon the entire populace had streamed to the Rebbe's carriage, welcoming him warmly to their humble town and pleading with him to stay for the Shabbos.

"Please," they begged him, "we are simple, uneducated folk whose town is always bypassed for the larger ones. We have no masters here, no one to teach us, no one to inspire us with their leadership. We desperately need the spiritual infusion your presence can lend us; no Jewish sage or master has ever joined us for Shabbos; please, can you do us the biggest mitzvah, and give us the honor of your illustrious company?"

Reb Shmelke was torn. On the one hand, his father had volunteered a member of his family for the graveyard slot in Yaklichi, yet he certainly did not want to be the one to fill it. On the other hand, these sweet Jews seemed so lonely, so hungry for his companionship, how could he deny them? And maybe, after all, his father had lent too much significance to the dream. Maybe that was all it was—just a dream. He could not find it in his heart to turn them down. He agreed to stay with them as they requested. It was on that Shabbos that the great Rebbe *died and was buried . . . in Yaklichi.*

As Reb Burechl—grandson of the famous Reb Shmelke who was buried in Yaklichi, and now a prisoner in one of its barns—recalled the exact details of the story he had been told so long ago, he became electrified with excitement. *Can it be by chance that I am here?* he asked himself. *My own holy grandfather is buried here. I must slip away to the cemetery and pray for help at his graveside.*

Reb Burechl's determination became greater than the Nazi guards' vigilance, and he somehow managed to escape the barn and steal away to the Jewish cemetery. Despite the darkness, he found his grandfather's tombstone, larger and more majestic than any of the others, and flung himself on the grave, praying for his divine intercession. Later in the night, after Reb Burechl had wept and prayed until he was faint with exhaustion, something flickering in the inky night drew his attention. He raised his face from the muddy earth upon which he had flung his body and stared into the darkness. There it was again. It was not some random spark, but a great tongue of flame spurting out of the . . . the barn! Reb Burechl screamed in horror as he watched a small pinpoint of fire turn into a raging inferno, blazing across the sky and engulfing the barn. Later, he would learn that the Nazis had poured gasoline around the barn, tossed in a match, and burned the Jews alive. He was the sole survivor of the original transport.

Meanwhile, back in Munkatch, Reb Burechl's mother-in-law (the Minchas Elazar's wife) became frantic when she was informed that her son-in-law had been snatched off the streets and deported to Poland. A strong-willed woman of great strength and determination, she called one of her husband's devoted *Chasidim* to her side—a man named Avrum Mann—and instructed him to smuggle over the border to Poland and hunt for Reb Burechl.

"But *Rebbetzin*," Avrum Mann protested, "with all due respect, what you are asking is dangerous, impossible. I will be caught and arrested myself. And even if I did manage to make it to Poland, where would I go to find Reb Burechl? All we know is that he was deported to Poland; we don't have any other information. It's like looking for a needle in a haystack. Poland is a big country, with hundreds of villages, dozens of cities . . . I can't even begin to imagine how I would search for him. . . ."

The *Rebbetzin* looked at him with steely resolve. "Reb Avrum, I promise you that you will *not* be caught. I promise you that you will return home alive and well. I promise you that you will survive this war. And I promise that you will find my son-in-law. Go."

"One more thing," the *Rebbetzin* called after Avrum Mann, as he turned to leave. "I have one idea that might help you. Knowing my son-in-law, I assume that some way or another, he'll try to get to Yaklichi to *daven* (pray) at his grandfather's *kever* (grave). I strongly suggest that you start there."

Avrum Mann disguised himself as a gentile nobleman and hired a Christian driver to smuggle him across the border to Poland. His first days were spent in a town called Kolimei , where he lay the groundwork for a daring scheme to rescue Reb Burechl. Avrum enlisted the aid of a doctor from Rachav (a large bribe also helped) associated with the military hospital in Kolimei, as well as several well-placed Hungarian government officials who were also handsomely paid. It was arranged that Kolimei would be their designated meeting place, where they would all rendezvous once Reb Burechl was hopefully found. In Kolimei, Avrum was given an army car and donned a new disguise as a Hungarian officer. Then he set off to find Reb Burechl.

Everything went well, until Avrum's car ran out of gas. Pulling into a local gas station to refuel, he saw a group of Russian Jewish prisoners—guarded by a few insouciant soldiers idly smoking—standing miserably to the side. As he stared at them in anguish, his heart hammering wildly, they stretched out their hands to him and beseeched him for food. He knew that he was making a mistake, but how could he not respond? Avrum walked trancelike towards them, pulling pieces of bread from his pockets, and tossed them to his brethren, until there was no more. His action did not go unnoticed.

"You must be Jewish yourself," a soldier mocked him. "Why else would you care?"

"Don't be ridiculous," Avrum dissembled. "Why are you insulting me like that?"

"No one but a Jew would have mercy on those people. I saw you tossing them bread. You can't fool me."

"You are offending me deeply," Avrum said calmly. But inside, he was so deeply shaken by having his cover blown, that he abandoned the car and walked away with a slow, deliberate gait. When he was beyond the soldier's range of vision, he picked up his pace and fled. *He could have killed me*, Avrum thought with relief as the distance between them widened. *But where am I?* he wondered. *I have absolutely no idea where I am now. And how am I ever going to find Reb Burechl without a car?* It was then that he first noticed a small sign that proclaimed: Yaklichi.

Yaklichi! Wasn't Reb Shmelke buried in Yaklichi? Hadn't the Rebbetzin *suggested that he start his search for Reb Burechl here? What a coincidence that he should find himself in Yaklichi . . . of all places!* But the waves of hope

that initially engulfed him were soon enough dispelled. Only minutes later, Avrum realized with a sickening thud that he was being
followed—he heard soft footfalls, quite clearly, right behind him.

This is it! he thought despairingly. *I'm finished. I knew it was only a
matter of time before I would be snatched up myself. How did I allow the* Rebbetzin
to talk me into such an insane business?

"Reb Yid, Reb Yid!" a voice called after him.

Relief washed over Avrum. It was *not* a soldier who was pursu-
ing him, but one of the Jews from the gas station—an elderly man in
tatters—who had apparently detached himself from his transport.

"I'm sorry," Avrum said politely, "but I'm not a Yid." He picked up
speed to put distance between him and strange man.

The man was not shaken off so easily. "Reb Yid," he said creeping
up on Avrum Mann. "Why are you here? What's your mission?"

"I'm so sorry, I don't have any more bread," Avrum apologized.
He did have some food on him that he was saving for Reb Burechl, in
the event that he found him, and which he felt he couldn't spare.

"Why are you here? What's your mission?" the Jew asked again.

Avrum felt it wouldn't be prudent to answer. He didn't know this
man. *Maybe he wasn't really a Jew? Maybe it was some kind of trap?*

But the man continued to shadow him, pestering him with more
and more questions.

"I am *sure* you are Jewish. Aren't you?" the man harangued him.
"Just say one word of Yiddish to me, and I'll tell you something very
important."

Avrum was too frightened to respond. He continued walking
at a rapid clip, unable to lose the man, whose manner was becoming
increasingly worrisome.

"Okay, you don't want to identify yourself to me; you don't trust
me," the Jew said in exasperation. "Please...do not be scared, and do

not disregard me. I know why you are here. You are looking for Reb Burechl, aren't you? He is here, in this very town, hiding. I can lead you to him."

Avrum began to tremble violently. *Who was this man? This whole thing doesn't make any sense,* he thought. *Even if he suspects that I'm Jewish, how could he possibly know that I am here to find Reb Burechl?* It was all very strange, but the *Rebbetzin* had pledged that he would find Reb Burechl. *She comes from such a holy family. I must have faith. I should go with him. What do I have to lose?*

"I have food and medicine on me," Avrum Mann finally responded to the elderly Jew. "If you take me to Reb Burechl, I'll give you half of everything."

"Follow me," the mysterious stranger said, leading Avrum to a small abandoned hut deep in the woods. "I'll wait outside."

"Reb Burechl, Reb Burechl!" Avrum shrieked in joy and excitement and utter disbelief as he stumbled across the sleeping figure of his friend, stretched across the floor. Their reunion was tearful and joyous, and the two embraced and wept, exchanging their respective stories. Finally, Avrum remembered the stranger who waited patiently outside. "Excuse me, Reb Burechl," he apologized, "but it was a stranger who brought me to you, and he is waiting outside for the food that I promised him. Let me go outside to thank him and keep my part of the bargain."

But when Avrum went outside to pay him, the mysterious stranger was gone.

He walked though the woods, calling for him, even retracing some of his steps on the old dusty road that they had traversed together, but there was no sign of the stranger anywhere.

"I don't understand," Reb Burechl told Avrum. "This doesn't make sense. If the man desperately needed food, wouldn't he have waited a few minutes to claim his reward? Where could he have gone?"

"I don't understand it myself, Reb Burechl," Avrum answered, shaking his head in awe and something akin to fear. "I don't understand it myself."

Postscript: From Yaklichi, Avrum Mann and Reb Burechl took a boat down the Dnester River to Kolimei. There, the doctor from Rachav bandaged him up so that Reb Burechl was unrecognizable and placed him in an ambulance "borrowed" from the Red Cross. When the ambulance reached the border, the Hungarian soldiers (who had been bribed in advance) were told that the patient inside was a high government official, and they obligingly waved it through. From the border, Reb Burechl was taken to the town of Sighet/Mamorosh where he stayed for a while with Mordechai and Chaya Perlstein, grandparents of Yitta Halberstam's husband, Mordechai Mandelbaum.

Reb Burechl survived the war and helped to rebuild the shattered Munkatch dynasty in New York. As the *Rebbetzin* had promised, the faithful *Chasid*, Reb Avrum Mann, survived as well and fathered generations of illustrious children and grandchildren. The mysterious stranger was never found, and, to this day, remains the subject of much speculation. Many who have heard the story insist that he could surely be none other than Elijah the Prophet, who is said to don different disguises while he roams the world, aiding Jews in distress.

This story was told by the current Munkatcher Rebbe, Reb Burechl's son, who resides in Brooklyn, New York.

THE PHILOSOPHER

Yisroel Besser

Victor Frankl was a young man of spirit and culture, a penetrating thinker who had distinguished himself through his innovative ideas. He was a gifted writer, and among his most precious possessions was the manuscript he was working on—a brilliant thesis that elaborated upon his own personal philosophy.

The Nazi guard who "welcomed" him to Auschwitz cared nothing about who he was or what ideas he harbored. They knew that he was a Jew, and thus deserving of the most dehumanizing treatment possible. They stripped him of his clothing and possessions, shaved his head, and reminded him that the term *human being* was reserved for a particular race—and certainly not for Jews.

Although they took so much from him, they could not take his greatest resource—his ability to contemplate, to question, to probe. So as they pushed and kicked at him, as they cursed and spat at him, he was traveling in another realm. He believed that man should only live a life filled with meaning, with significance and goals. To merely "survive," to simply avoid the pitfalls of the camps—he did not consider this to be a life filled with meaning, for that would be mere coincidence and nothing more. True *meaning* would indicate that the actual experience of suffering through the camps also had a deeper dimension, answers that only a discerning questioner would be able to discover.

These were the thoughts in Victor Frankl's head as the beasts took away the physical representation of his philosophy—the manuscript he had been hiding under his shirt. This was his lowest point. His mental "child," the product of his toil and determination, was being taken from him. He felt like his life had lost its meaning; it was worthless.

He shuffled along in the camp where he was handed a tattered uniform, one whose previous owner had long since been led to the place of no return. He donned the striped rags, resigning himself to this new existence, to this nightmarish world without hope, without meaning, and without his precious manuscript. This loss left a gaping void in Victor Frankl's heart, where he had carried his life's work. Then, his fingers felt something. There was a tiny scrap of paper in a pocket, left over from the poor inmate who had worn these clothes before him. He opened up the small paper and tried to make out the words written on it: *Shema Yisrael, Hashem Elokeinu, Hashem Echad* . . . Hear, O Israel, the Lord is our G-d; the Lord is One . . .

He is one. He is in control. He is leading us through the depths of despair. He is expecting great things from us, wherever we may be.

Victor Frankl had his meaning, and he had his manuscript.

BUSINESS PARTNERS

Isser Handler grew up in the town of Satmar, Romania. A quick learner with a keen eye, Isser carefully observed his father as he conducted a successful textile business, and when his father fell ill, Isser took over the business at the age of seventeen. Despite his youth, Isser proved to be very capable in his newfound role. He carried on the lucrative business until the spring of 1943, when history intervened. The Germans had issued an edict that stated that Jews could no longer engage in business.

Since the company was the sole source of revenue for the family, Isser conceived a plan that would allow him to subvert the Nazi decree. He approached a middle-aged woman of Roman Catholic descent, Vargo Razilia, with whom he'd had previous dealings.

"Vargo," Isser asked, "since the business can't be under my name, would you be willing to keep it going under your name? You would sign your name on all the official documents and you would be the one to meet with everyone, face-to-face. Meanwhile, I'll actually continue to conduct the textile business from behind the scenes."

Vargo had watched the Nazis' oppressive restrictions strangulate the people whom she affectionally called friends. To her, these new edicts were evil. Without hesitation, Vargo responded: "Of course I'll do it." Isser felt deeply relieved. For the next year and a half, both Isser and Vargo benefited substantially from their arrangement.

By 1944, the situation had become hopeless. Isser's family, along with the Jews in Hungary and Romania, were rounded up from their homes and sent off in cattle cars to the concentration camps and the Nazi killing machines. The few who managed to escape sought refuge wherever they could, Isser amongst them.

Isser's nature was one of optimism. Despite the dire circumstances, Isser would not give up hope. Since Vargo was the only non-Jewish person whom he could trust, Isser turned to her for help. Trembling for his life, his voice barely audible, he posed a question to her that might save his life while simultaneously threatening hers: "Vargo, would you let me hide out in your house for the duration of the war?"

Once again, without hesitation, Vargo replied with a resounding: "Yes!"

Isser was overcome with gratitude, but he was also concerned about her welfare. "Vargo," he said, "do you realize that if the Germans find me in your house, they will kill both of us?"

"For so many years, you have proven yourself to be kind and trustworthy," Vargo said. "You have treated me so well in all of our business affairs, Isser, that I can only say this—for you, I am willing to risk my life."

True to her word, Vargo hid Isser in a back room on the second floor of her home. Anticipating the worst, both took great precautions. But one night, their worst fears became a reality when Vargo urgently conveyed a piece of bad news. "Isser," she said, "my uncle is a police officer, and he just told me that someone has found out about your living here. They reported it to the police! My uncle is trying to protect me, so he let me know that tonight there will be a raid on my house." Vargo was overcome with compassion for Isser, but she knew that what she was about to say was as much for *his* good as it was for *hers*. "Please, *Isserke*, run, go and hide somewhere—save your life. I only wish I knew where to send you, but I don't know where it would be safe. Tomorrow, come back. I'll be waiting."

Isser and Vargo said their farewells, not knowing if this would be the last time they would see each other. Just before he was about to leave, Vargo looked at the young, vulnerable man who stood before her and said, "May G-d watch over you tonight."

Isser went out into the cold, dark night, nervously searching for a place to hide. He was ridden with terror because he knew that Nazis still roamed the city searching for stray Jews who had eluded capture. He knew that if they found him, they would shoot him dead on the spot.

After several hours of walking, Isser began to suffer from hypothermia. His feet could no longer carry him. He had to stop and rest. It was midnight when Isser found his way into a Christian cemetery, where he lay down upon a gravestone. He shut his eyes and fell asleep, but within moments, he heard the sound of dogs barking. Instinctively he knew that these dogs were on the hunt for him. As he struggled to his feet, Isser fancied that he saw the bodies of the dead jumping over the graveyard's fence and running in a specific direction.

Is this my imagination? he asked himself. *Am I dreaming—or have I gone mad?*

Isser couldn't figure out what was happening, but he took the image of the ghosts vaulting over the fence as a message for him to do the same. And so he did. He clambered up the rails of the fence, hoisted himself up on the pointy spindles of the gate, and threw himself over to the other side where he stood, once again, out in the open street, with no cover in sight. *Out here,* Isser thought, *I will definitely be caught. I have nothing to lose by taking a chance on strangers.*

Isser decided to knock on the door of the first house he saw that had a light on. He reached the doorway of a house, raised his hand to knock, and then lowered it right before knocking, repeating this action several times over.

Finally, he knocked, waited, then knocked again. The door opened. Under the faint glow of the streetlamp, Isser tried to make out the features of the tall, broad-shouldered man who stood before him. At first glance, Isser thought he might be hallucinating. He squinted and looked again. The fear and dread that had consumed him melted into excitement. In disbelief, Isser stammered: *"Frejocka Spivako?"*

Frejocka was just as stunned to see Isser. It wasn't long ago that he had been the chauffeur for Isser's family. He looked in all directions to make sure that no one was watching, then opened the door wide and ushered Isser into a safe haven for the night.

* * *

The next day, Isser returned to the home of Vargo Razilia who, as promised, was waiting for him. For the individual Jews who remained in hiding in Satmar, word got out that Vargo's home was a safe refuge. Throughout the course of the war, on any given day or night, there were anywhere from four to ten people seeking shelter there.

After the war, the homes to the left and to the right of Vargo's were completely destroyed by the bombings, while Vargo's home stood solid—a testament to the fact that her home was more than just a house. It was a sanctuary.

Shortly after the war, Isser fell in love with Malku Rosenbaum, one of the few young women who had survived and returned to the town of Satmar. At their wedding, Vargo sat next to the bride in the place of honor, since both Isser and Malku's parents had perished in the Holocaust.

In 1947, Isser and Malku Handler emigrated to America, where he took a job in a candy store. Isser's paycheck amounted to thirty-five dollars a week. He sent Vargo a portion of the money, and she in turn was able to buy and sell many kerchiefs, from which she made a comfortable income. Over the next thirty years, Isser's income grew, and he continued to send Vargo increasingly larger sums of money proportionate to his earnings. In 1953, he sent her a refrigerator, and soon after, a washing machine. Eventually, Isser purchased a condominium for Vargo so that she was able to live out her final years in comfort. Isser was like the child that Vargo never had, so it was only right that when Vargo passed away, it was Isser who bought her tombstone, which he had engraved, and the plot where she is buried. For the care and precaution that Vargo took, on behalf of all those she sought to protect, her name is inscribed at the Yad Vashem Holocaust Memorial Museum in Israel.

Note from Judith Leventhal: For those who love, for those who have so much to give, titles simply fall away. When "business partners" treat one another with boundless respect and care, willing to risk their lives for one another, then they have transcended. When an uncle takes care of his niece as though she were his daughter and when a niece thinks of her uncle like a father, then the two have transcended. I know that as a fact, for Isser is my uncle and I am his niece.

STRANGERS ON A TRAIN

Shoshana Goldwasser Schwartz and Azriela Jaffe

By the time he was liberated in 1945, Elias Goldwasser had been imprisoned in eleven different concentration camps, had watched his pregnant sister march off to the gas chambers, and had personally witnessed the death of his brother—killed in front of his eyes by an irate Nazi guard. As Elias was moved from camp to camp, he felt fortunate to cross paths with his three siblings at one time or another, but by war's end, he had no idea if any of them had survived. As Polish Jews, they had borne the brunt of the suffering, for their travails had begun with the onset of the Holocaust.

No language could rightfully capture the physical atrocities the survivors had endured, the anguish that had forever seared their souls. Even upon being liberated, their jubilation was short-lived, for now began the painful process of hunting down their families. Most would make the excruciating discovery that death had released their parents and siblings from the jaws of the Nazis, *not* the Allies. Ultimately, Elias would learn that everyone in his family had been killed, with the sole exception of one brother named Peretz. There was no news about him at all, either way. Elias had no idea what his brother's fate had been, but he was determined to find out.

In postwar Europe, the trains were packed with survivors criss-crossing the continent, searching for pieces—and people—from their past. During that chaotic time, crossing borders was relatively easy, as no one was being picky about documents and visas. Elias made many such trips out of Germany (where he was interned in a DP camp) to scour neighboring countries for his missing brother. Each time he came up empty.

Elias was returning to Germany from one of these unsuccessful trips, this time, to Austria; his despair at being unable to find his brother was growing progressively greater with each failed mission. Even though he was discouraged, Elias was delighted to find himself seated next to an attractive young woman. The Holocaust had done little to dampen his flirtatious nature. He attempted to strike up a conversation with her:

"So, where are you coming from?" he asked her affably.

"My brother is in a TB sanatorium in Austria," she replied. "And you?"

A friendly conversation ensued, during which she rummaged in her handbag for something, eventually pulling out her wallet. For some reason that he couldn't explain, Elias playfully grabbed the wallet from her hand, and as he did so, a picture fell out.

"So, who are these people?" he asked boldly, retrieving the photo from the floor and trying to prolong their conversation.

"Oh, this is actually a picture of the brother I just told you about—the one who's in the sanatorium in Austria. The people with him are his roommates there." Elias took a peek at the photo, just to be polite, and then he took a second look. Then he took a third and a fourth, his eyes fixated on one particular man in the picture. Although it scarcely resembled the brother he had last seen in 1939, there was no mistaking it: This was Peretz, the sibling he had almost given up on. His brother was rooming with this young woman's brother at the sanatorium! Since she had just returned from that very institution, she was able to give him the address and precise directions.

Delirious with joy, Elias bid farewell to the lovely lady at the next train stop, making a U-turn right back to Austria. This was one time, he was sure, that his brother wouldn't scold him for being a flirt!

MELVINA'S DREAM

As told by Bailey Lustig and Breindy Muller

The morning after her mother and father had been rounded up by the Nazis and deported to G-d-knows-where, twenty-one-year-old Melvina Muller woke up and discovered that her hair had changed color. The jet-black tresses that had covered her head the day before had turned completely white overnight—such was the great impact the loss of her parents had on her very being.

Even though she had lost them, Melvina's parents continued to safeguard her long after they were gone. The first time occurred shortly after she fled from her hometown of Presov, Czechoslovakia, to the village of Jaline. Melvina had dyed her hair blond and was carrying the false papers of a non-Jew named Helena Kumava. Disguised as a gentile in a town where she knew no one and no one knew her, she ventured out of the small room in which she lived to work at various jobs to pay for food and rent. Her fluent German helped with her new persona—a persona she was convinced no one would be able to penetrate since she had totally altered her appearance. She kept to herself, speaking to no one, trusting nobody. Despite all the precautions she took, however, someone betrayed her. She was arrested and hauled off to a German courtroom, where she was told she would stand trial.

"Approach the bench," the judge ordered. He gave her a cursory glance as she stepped forward. For a moment, she fancied that his expression flickered with something other than the boredom she had first seen in his eyes. He looked down at the papers spread before him. "You are Helena Kumava?" he asked.

"Yes," she answered in a small voice.

He studied her features with what seemed to be more than normal interest. "Clear the courtroom," he commanded the bailiff. "Everyone leave except the defendant. I want to talk to her alone."

What was going on? Melvina wondered.

When the courtroom had emptied, the judge turned to her again, his harsh countenance softening.

"Young lady," he said, "I happen to know that you are *not* who you say you are. You are *not* Helena Kumava as you claim, but Melvina Muller from Presov. You may not recognize me, but I certainly recognize *you*. Your father's memorable face is stamped in yours; I knew it the moment you entered the courtroom. I went to school with your father, and we were good friends. He was always very kind to me. I've never forgotten all the things he did for me. When your parents got married, I used to visit them at their home in Presov; and when you were a baby, I held you in my arms. I even remember what corner of the room held your crib. Don't worry . . . I will not forsake you.

"I have to mete out a sentence to you, or else suspicions will be aroused. But *where* I send you can make a huge difference in your destiny. Instead of a labor or a transport camp, I will send you to a jail in Novoki instead. Here the conditions are less harsh. You will be given ample food and more comfortable shelter than you would find in the camps. This is the best I can do, and I hope it saves your life. It is my way of repaying the many kindnesses your father showed me throughout his life."

This was the first time that Melvina's father would save her life— but it wouldn't be the last.

Melvina was remanded to a medieval castle in Novoki that had been expropriated by the Nazis and turned into a prison. Here, the conditions were tolerable, as the judge had predicted, and once again, her fluent German gave her an edge in finding employment and relative safety in the commandant's administrative office.

One night, Melvina awoke with a start. Her beloved father had come to her in a dream, the first time he had made such an appearance. He did not tell her that he loved her, or that he and her mother were in a better place, or any of the other comforting words she longed to hear. She yearned for reassurance, for pledges of love. Instead her father said with intensity, "Mirchu, my darling daughter, tomorrow you must *not* wear a coat—no matter how cold it is. I want you to listen to what I am saying. It is important that you do *not* wear a coat tomorrow. Remember." And then he disappeared.

So they are both dead, then, Melvina sadly concluded as she considered the dream. *How else could he come to me in a dream? I knew they were in all likelihood gone, but this dream confirms it.* She had been gnawed by uncertainty throughout the war, her hopes rising and falling in a wild roller-coaster ride, her emotions in a constant state of flux. Now she knew. It was ironic, perverse, really, but somehow absolute knowledge of the worst possible information was better than no knowledge at all.

She went back to sleep and again her father appeared to her—with the same exact message. She awoke, and after a short while, returned to sleep. The vision returned a third time with the same instructions: "Whatever you do, don't wear a coat tomorrow morning. No matter how cold, don't take your coat." By now she had ascribed a great deal of significance to her father's warning: It couldn't be a fluke.

In the morning, Melvina awoke to find that the windows of her barracks were covered with frost. A shivering woman told her that the temperature had plummeted to below zero that day, not uncommon for the harsh Eastern European winters. So when a Nazi guard strode into the women's quarters and randomly chose Melvina and another girl to clean the commandant's personal office, everyone was startled when Melvina left without her coat.

"Melvina," a friend called after her sharply. "You forgot to take your coat!"

Melvina knew they would think she was mad, but her father's instructions—as incomprehensible as they seemed—were engraved on her heart.

"The commandant's office is only across the courtyard," she said. "It's just a short walk."

The women in her barracks—even the Nazi guard himself—looked at her in astonishment. Had she gone insane?

"Have you lost your mind?" another bunkmate shouted. "It's *freezing* outside."

"No, I don't need it," she said, heading out the door and braving the frigid weather without any protection.

In another wing of the unheated medieval castle, Melvina and the other girl worked diligently in the commandant's office on the second floor—dusting, scrubbing, polishing, sweeping, mopping—under the vigilant eyes of the Nazi guard assigned to keep them under surveillance. At twelve noon, the guard began to impatiently tap at his wristwatch and pace the floor. His shift was over, and his stomach was growling; it was time for lunch. With two long strides, he crossed the room and stood at the threshold, peering out the door in search of his replacement, who was late. Where could he be?

It was at this precise moment that Melvina turned to clean the windows of the commandant's room. These windows were extremely tall but unusually narrow, in keeping with the architecture of medieval times. As she stooped for her bucket, a slight movement on the ground below caught her attention. The tallest man she had ever seen in her life—well over six-five—stood underneath her window and beckoned her. *"Möchtest du entgehen?"* (Do you want to escape?) he mouthed to her in German. *"Sprung vom Fenster und von mir verfängt dich."* (Jump from the window and I'll catch you.)

Melvina spun around. The Nazi guard was still peering down the hallway. She had no time to think, to consider. She paused for only a moment before leaping through the window into the safety of the man's arms. A jump that would normally have been suicidal was made possible by the man's unnatural height. Melvina thanked him and bolted to the forest nearby. She was the only person ever known to successfully escape from the medieval castle of Novoki.

The narrow castle windows had never once been considered a viable escape route by the compulsively cautious Nazis. A child could hardly wiggle through them, let alone a full-grown adult. And they were too high up; a jump to the ground two stories below could have meant serious injury, if not death. If Melvina had been wearing her bulky coat, she would not have been able to squeeze through the aperture. And if she had taken the time to remove her coat, precious seconds would have been wasted and the Nazi guard would have wheeled around to intercept her. Her split-second decision was only made possible because she had listened to her father. Once again, he had saved her life.

COMRADES

In the trenches, there are no enemies, only comrades. This is true for every war and every skirmish, no matter the location of the battlefield. Despite differences in age, rank, religion, class, and ethnic group, soldiers in the combat zone unite and bond. Fury and hatred (if any lurk beneath the surface) are directed at the other side; what matters most to men on the front are their fellow soldiers . . . their brothers.

Solomon Geier didn't know the name of the German soldier, just twenty yards away from him, who had screamed out in pain when the bullet hit. He didn't care. He heard the moans, and his instincts took over. While bullets whizzed above his head, Geier kept low to the ground as he crept toward the writhing figure. It was the longest twenty yards he had ever traveled in his life. When he reached the bleeding man, Geier whispered tender words of reassurance: "Don't worry, buddy, you'll be fine." Then he dragged the wounded man by his belt to the medics in the rear. Gripping the soldier's hand with compassion, Geier continued to murmur encouragement until the medics loaded him onto a canvas stretcher and took him away. Right before they did, the man's eyes flew open for a second and flickered; it was like the soldier was trying to communicate something to Geier. *What is he trying to say?* Geier wondered. *Thanks? You're a good man?*

Geier shrugged his shoulders and hastened back to the front. It was World War I, and Geier, a loyal German citizen, had a battle to win. The episode soon faded from his mind, and he never did have a chance to learn the identity of the man whose life he had saved.

* * *

Geier, like hundreds of thousands of his Jewish compatriots, never conceived that one day, this deep and abiding loyalty would be betrayed. To him—and to so many other naive, flag-waving German Jews—Germany, not America, was the true "golden land," where Jews could fully participate in and significantly contribute to the country's rich economic, political, and cultural life, heading up some of its most elite institutions. It was utterly unthinkable that one day those in the vanguard would be unseated, and that the once vaunted would become despised pariahs, *persona non grata*.

The German attitude toward Jews changed radically once Hitler rose to power. Almost every week, new decrees and anti-Jewish legislation were handed down at a faster and faster clip, and the parameters of Jewish existence became increasingly smaller and ever more threatened.

Jews made up only one percent of the German population, but according to Nazi propaganda, Jews were responsible for anything and everything bad that had ever happened in the Teutonic State. Well over one hundred thousand Jews left Germany in the early 1930s, but the rest stayed on, determined to ride out the storm. Many were convinced that Hitler's rule could not last—that the good German citizenry wouldn't tolerate his campaign of terror against the Jews. Others were in full-blown denial.

In 1933, Germany enforced a series of ordinances designed to segregate the Jews. A nationwide boycott of Jewish businesses, professional services, factories, and shops was implemented, with storm troopers stationed menacingly in front of these establishments to prevent anyone from entering. Yellow Stars of David were painted across their windows and doors, and signs were posted that proclaimed JUDE—DON'T BUY FROM JEWS.

Jews were banned from holding public office; participating in artistic, literary, dramatic, or film enterprises; and working for any state-affiliated agencies. Their bank accounts were confiscated, their properties taken away. Beginning in 1938, all Jews were forced to wear the infamous Yellow Star on their clothing, to make them easier to identify—and to persecute. Books written by Jews were removed from public libraries and burned in public autos-da-fé. Among these were the poetry books of Heinrich Heine, the great nineteenth-century German-Jewish poet, who chillingly prophesied in one his poems: "Those who begin by burning books end by burning people." Every day, newer and harsher draconian measures were announced, until German Jewry was asphyxiated.

It was in this atmosphere of terror and oppression that Solomon Geier, decorated German war veteran, now lived, together with his wife and daughter, his son, daughter-in-law, and grandchildren. It was 1938, and the myth that the Jews had clung to for so long—that a civilized nation like Germany would never succumb to the demonic demagoguery of a nondescript artist, especially in the twentieth century—had finally shattered. The Geiers applied for visas to emigrate to the United States, and they were waiting for appointments with the American embassy. They assumed that their departure from their beloved country—though filled with pathos—would be orderly, methodical, and mundane. But on the night of November 8, 1938, an unexpected, forceful knock on the front door of their Berlin home changed their well-laid plans.

The Geiers exchanged frightened looks. Knocks on the door, especially late at night, were not welcomed by Jewish residents. After such visits, men had been known to suddenly vanish from their apartments, never to be seen again. When the patriarch of the family, Grandpa Geier, opened the door and beheld a tall man with strong Germanic features standing on the threshold, his heart sank. The two were approximately the same age, but in every other respect, they were diametrically different. One was oppressor, the other oppressed. One was stalker, the other his prey. They assessed each other warily, silently acknowledging the stand-off.

"May I come in, please?" the man asked. Geier bowed his head. There was nothing he could do. He stepped back and allowed the man to enter. He wondered where the man's pistol was, and when it would appear. Whom had he come to round up? *Please spare my children and grandchildren*, Geier prayed. *Take me. I'm old; I've already lived.*

"Are you Herr Solomon Geier?" the man asked.

Maybe it is only me they're after, Geier thought, almost jubilantly. He nodded affirmatively, bracing himself for the next words. He could not have anticipated what would follow.

"Herr Geier, do you remember that in 1915, you saved a soldier on the battlefield? Well, *I* am that soldier."

Geier had all but forgotten the incident that had occurred twenty-three years before. But for the man whose life he had saved, it was still vivid, emblazoned on his heart, seared on his soul.

"I always remembered what you did for me," the man said. "I never forgot. And I have been keeping track of you for a long time. Now listen to me: I work with the chief of police in Berlin, and tomorrow night, the police and the SS will round up adult male Jews from all over Germany. I have seen the list, and you and your son are on it. Do whatever you wish with this information."

The man turned to leave, then paused and said: "My debt to you is now repaid. *Auf Wiedersehen!*"

All night long, Solomon Geier and his son were on the telephone, warning the Jews of Berlin that *Mr. Malach Hamoves* (code word in Hebrew for the "Angel of Death," just in case the phones were tapped) would be coming to town the following evening. Everyone should call their friends and relatives with news of his arrival, so that he could be "properly welcomed." Acting upon this information, hundreds of Jews dropped out of sight, among them Geier's son, who hid in the home of a Christian friend.

On November 9, 1938, tens of thousands of Jewish homes, synagogues, businesses, and schools were attacked and burned, officially launching Hitler's full-blown campaign of terror against the Jews. Because so many windows of shops and buildings were smashed during the night of wanton destruction that followed—splintering shards breaking everywhere—that evening would later come to be known as *Kristallnacht*, The Night of Broken Glass. It was a horrific beginning to an incomprehensible end.

But because of one soldier's good deed during World War I, hundreds of Jews, including the Geier family, were saved at the outset of World War II. Solomon's grandson, Arnold Geier, now in his nineties, still lives to tell the story today.

A PROMISE TO FATHER

As told to Tamar Snyder by Frank Hershkowitz

It was the middle of the night when the stench-filled cattle car finally ground to a halt. The doors snapped open, and seventeen-year-old Frank Hershkowitz and the people crammed in with him were thrust into the dark world of Auschwitz.

"Out!" screamed the German officers as their dogs growled.

The Nazis began to rip the children away from their mothers. Frank's mother grabbed one of her grandchildren and held the child close. A Nazi soldier spotted her. He smacked her face with a rifle, crushing her nose. "Let it go," he snarled. She clenched the child to her breast, tightening her grip. Suddenly, two soldiers appeared and grabbed her thin frame, spilling blood across her face.

"*Tatte*, look at what they did to Mother!" Frank cried to his father, visibly shocked.

His father grabbed his hand. "You're imagining things," the father said. He struggled for comforting words.

"*Freimele*, don't worry," he said, his voice unwavering and confident. "Remember, G-d is our father, we are His children. Would a father harm his children?"

Frank glanced back at his father, whose face was lit up with his trademark smile. Father and son recited *Viduy*, the confessional prayer, together. Then his father spoke again, his words as binding to him as those of the Almighty. "Promise me that you'll be a good Jew, that you'll observe G-d's laws with a full heart. Never forget that we have a G-d in heaven. If you do that, I promise you, nothing bad will happen to you. Promise me," his father said again, shaking him.

"I promise," Frank said.

As his father began to recite the holy *Shema Yisrael* prayer, a Nazi grabbed him by the neck, dragged him to the side of a ditch, and shot him.

Frank wept. His father had been shot, and his mother was sent to the gas chamber. He was now an orphan.

* * *

Time passed. Frank had managed to (just barely) survive Auschwitz, Buchenwald, and Mittelbau-Dora concentration camps, and was now in Bergen-Belsen. The Allies were getting closer, and the resounding boom of bombs began to fill the air.

One of the Nazis commanded Frank and another young man to clean the floors and windows of an administrative building. When a siren pierced the quiet, the Nazi raced out of the room. Hours later, after scrubbing the floors to perfection, Frank and the other boy grew tired, so they lay down on the floor and fell asleep. When the Nazi returned, he found them sleeping. "You stinking Jews!" he shouted. He waved his gun in their faces, and pulled some ammunition out of his pocket. "You see this bullet? It costs five cents," he said. "But you're not even worth that much." He grabbed the leash from his dog. "I can hang both of you and still have this rope," he said.

The Nazi grabbed a stool and ordered Frank to stand on it. He took the leash and tied him up by the neck. Then he turned to the other boy. "Kick the stool," he commanded.

"I can't," the boy lied. "He's my brother."

The Nazi, ever persistent, tried the same thing in reverse. He tied the other boy up and ordered Frank to kick the stool. He also refused. The Nazi then grabbed both of them, pushed them onto the stool, and tied the dog leash tightly around both of their necks. The boys stood on their tiptoes, eyes closed, gasping for air. They knew that in another moment, they'd be dead.

"*Tatte*, you promised me," Frank cried out. "You promised me I wouldn't get killed." A vision of his father flooded his mind's eye.

A split second later, another SS officer barged into the room. He took a knife and cut the leash, freeing the two boys. Then he stormed out of the room with his fellow officer in tow, offering no explanation, and leaving the two boys visibly shaken.

His father had intervened, Frank was sure. And he had kept his promise.

Postscript: Frank Hershkowitz survived the war, and was brought to America by Yeshiva Chaim Berlin. He has been happily married to Rebecca (née Stein) for over 50 years and is the father of three, grandfather of twelve, and great-grandfather of three. Frank was a co-founder of the first Glatt Kosher self-service butcher store, "Glatt Pack," in Borough Park, Brooklyn.

SUBWAY REUNION
As told by Ruth Fisher

Late one night in 1947, I was riding the BMT line of the New York subway, going home after an evening session at Hunter College. A man chose to take the seat adjoining mine. *Now why did he do that?* I wondered. *The entire subway car is practically empty, and yet he decides to sit right next to me. How strange!* I peered into his face and was reassured to see a mild-mannered man with a pleasant countenance. Rather than appearing threatening, he seemed merely meek and timid. *Ah, that's it—he's scared of the empty subway car himself! He's huddling close to me for comfort.*

A few seconds later, he took out a foreign-language newspaper and spread it on his lap.

That's it, then, I reassured myself. *No need to worry; he's a harmless foreigner.* I settled back into my seat and returned to my book.

At the next stop, a middle-aged woman boarded the train. Her head swiveled around the nearly empty subway car and then she started moving in our direction. To my surprise, the woman eased herself onto the same bench as the foreign gentleman.

Now that's peculiar, I thought. *The whole car is practically empty and she has to sit right next to a strange man, and real close at that.* I watched the woman with interest. First, she peered over the man's shoulder to see what he was reading. Then she began to address him in Yiddish—a language in which I was not fluent, but could certainly follow as I had an excellent command of German, which is very similar.

"Where are you from . . . originally?" she inquired.

The man named a country in Eastern Europe.

"What city?" she asked.

He answered again, noncommittally. He seemed confused by the interrogation, and barely looked up from his newspaper.

"What did you do before the war?"

He named his profession.

"Look at me. *Look at me!*" she commanded. "Don't you recognize me anymore?"

They were husband and wife.

They had been separated in 1938 at the outset of World War II. Each had endured the horrors of different concentration camps and, at war's end, each had assumed that the other was dead. Both went to New York City to begin a new life. Now they had found each other, nine years later, on the BMT line.

The story would be reported in all of the local papers—but I could say that I had witnessed this incredible reunion from the best seat in the New York subway system.

DANCING WITH G-D

They were mere boys—all under the age of eighteen—but in this particular case, their youth proved to be a liability, not the asset it had been under other circumstances. It was puzzling, really: Most camp commandants consigned teenagers sixteen and older to life, since they were deemed hardy enough for the slave labor force into which they were conscripted. But this camp commandant had drawn the line at eighteen instead, decreeing that all those who were younger be sent to certain death. His orders for additional selections grew more shrill and fevered with each passing day, multiplying the numbers that were fed into the furnaces. Perhaps it was the advent of the Jewish High Holidays that had unleashed his fury, or, in perverse irony, his own heinous way of celebrating.

It was the fall of 1944 at Auschwitz, and Hungarian Jews—the last nationality to be transported to the camp—had arrived in massive numbers. The furnaces worked overtime as the inmates were sped to their inexorable fate. Everything about the camp seemed so surreal—the perpetual fog cover of smoke and ash, the barren landscape of barbed wire and slime—that it served to mirror the prisoners' own profound sense of displacement and disorientation. Everything had happened *so* fast: being crammed into the cattle cars that had disgorged them at Auschwitz; the quick, merciless dismemberment of families as spouses, children, parents, and siblings were torn apart from one another during selection; being dispassionately stripped of the clothing and personal belongings that made them human; and the freezing-cold showers and assembly-line delousing that had followed. In the course of only minutes, the new inmates had lost everything they owned, everyone they loved.

Already, some were so engulfed by the horror, so stunned by their sudden plunge into hell, so mummified into *Muselmann* (the walking dead), that they could barely remember their own names, let alone the religious holidays. But there were those remnants, those few who still cared about observing the Jewish holidays; among them were fifty religious boys who had just been selected for the gas chamber and were now being herded into a bathhouse, ostensibly to take "showers." It was late enough in concentration camp history that the boys knew the truth. Gas would pour through the pipes, not water. It was a ruse that the Nazis used to disarm the inmates, to ensure their cooperation. But these spiritual heroes made a conscious decision *not* to give it to them, choosing defiance instead.

Amid the tumult in the bathhouse, one boy sprang up and shouted: "Brothers! Today is the holiday of Simchat Torah, when the Jewish world rejoices, having concluded the reading of the Torah over the past year, followed directly with the commencement of the new cycle of Torah reading. During our short lives, we have tried to uphold the Torah to the best of our ability, and now we have one last chance to do so. Before we die, let us celebrate Simchat Torah one last time.

"We do not possess anything anymore," the boy continued. "We have nothing. We do not have clothes to cover us, nor a *sefer Torah* (Torah scroll) with which to dance. So let us dance with G-d Himself—who is surely here among us—before we return our souls to him."

Since it had first been erected and used, the gas chamber had absorbed a cacophony of human sounds—screams, cries, moans, benedictions—that would forever reside within its cold earthen stone walls. But never before had its rafters trembled with the pure, sweet strains of fifty young voices raised in fervent song; never before had its concrete floor shaken under the pounding of fifty pairs of feet stamping in unbridled joy. The boys pierced the heavens with their song: *"Ashreinu mah tov chelkeinu u'mah nayim goraleinu umah yafah yerush-ateinu. . ."* (How fortunate we are and how wonderful is our portion; and how beautiful is our heritage.)

"What is going on in there?" one scowling Nazi guard asked his comrade as they waited outside. "Why hasn't the gas been turned on yet?"

"It sounds like they're singing . . . and *dancing*. Are they *crazy?*" another guard said in disbelief.

"Go find out what's causing the delay," an officer commanded. "And get the commandant."

Summoned to the doors of the gas chamber, the commandant listened with growing fury to the incongruous revelry inside. He had watched Jews marching to their deaths hundreds of times before— some weeping softly, others reciting prayers—and he had relished these scenes. But *this*—this singing and dancing—*this* was unacceptable. He flung open the gas chamber doors and pulled one boy toward him.

"You!" he shouted. "Tell me why you are all singing and dancing now."

"Because leaving a world where Nazi beasts reign is cause for celebration," the boy sneered. "And because we are overjoyed at the prospect of reuniting with our beloved parents, whom you murdered so viciously."

The commandant became enraged at the boy's contemptuous words. Obsequiousness . . . fear . . . last-ditch attempts to ingratiate one's self into his favor—those were acceptable modes of behavior. Insolence was not.

"I'll teach you a lesson," he screamed as the boys continued to dance and sing, heedless of his presence. "You thought that the gas chamber would be your last stop. You'll find out otherwise. The gas chamber would have been easy and painless compared to what awaits you now. I will torture each one of you with unbearable suffering. I will slice your flesh till you expire." The commandant ordered the guards to remove the boys from the gas chamber and place them in a holding block overnight. He planned to begin the torture sessions the following day.

But the next morning, his plans again went awry. A high-ranking Nazi officer had traveled to Auschwitz to round up slave labor for a work camp that lacked sufficient help. He needed to find several hundred young, able-bodied men capable of performing grueling work under barbarous conditions. As he strode through the camp looking for prospects, the Nazi officer just happened to pass by the barracks in which the fifty religious boys had been temporarily housed. Their vitality undiminished by their overnight stay, the boys still radiated strength and good health. "Excellent," the Nazi officer smiled in satisfaction. "Exactly the type of boys I need."

The Nazi officer pulled rank on the camp commandant, who revealed nothing about *his* original plans for the boys' fate. He stood silently as the Nazi officer ordered the boys—and several hundred other inmates—to board the trucks that rolled out of Auschwitz into safer climes. Some say that the boys left the grounds singing.

Postscript: Survivors of Auschwitz report that all fifty boys survived the war.

THE FREQUENT FLYER

Shlomo Carlebach, the late "singing Rabbi," probably amassed more frequent-flyer miles in his lifetime than anyone in history; in his travels to Jewish communities across the world, he crisscrossed the globe several times a year. He was a familiar and beloved figure to flight attendants and pilots on almost every major airline in the United States, and he knew many of them by name.

On one such flight, Shlomo was attended to by a blond, blue-eyed stewardess named Kathy who piqued his curiosity because she radiated such an unusual purity. He was impressed by her sweetness and wanted to find out more about her. An hour into the flight, Shlomo rose to stretch his legs and passed the galley, where, to his shock and amazement, he saw Kathy *davening* (praying) from a *siddur* (prayer book). He waited quietly until she had completed her prayers, and then approached her.

"Holy sister!" he exclaimed, typical of how he greeted people. "You're an angel from heaven! What are you doing?"

Kathy explained that although her parents weren't Jewish, she had been drawn to Judaism for a long time. "I really have no idea where this love comes from," she told Shlomo, "but it has been such a compelling force in my life that I recently decided to convert." Kathy told Shlomo that she had studied for years with an Orthodox Jewish rabbi, had undergone a thoroughly *halachic* (according to Orthodox Jewish Law) conversion, and was now a practicing Jew. Shlomo and

Kathy conversed at length until a passenger called for her assistance and Shlomo returned to his seat.

Several minutes later, Kathy reappeared at his side, approaching Shlomo tentatively. "You know, because you're a Rabbi, maybe you can help me with a pressing problem that I have?"

"It will be my honor and privilege to be of service to you, holy sister," Shlomo rejoined immediately.

"Well, here's my problem," Kathy said, launching into her account. "You see, I'm in love with a Jewish man whose parents—although not religious in the slightest—strenuously object to him marrying a convert. They've been carrying on something terrible, screaming and crying and threatening to disown him should we in fact marry. We love each other very much, but he is also equally devoted to his parents, and doesn't want to cause them grief. As a result, he's terribly torn. The whole thing's incredibly ironic because I'm much more of a Jew than his parents are! Nonetheless, I'm fearful that he's going to cave in under the pressure and call the engagement off. Can you help me?"

"I will indeed try my best to help you," Shlomo promised. "Give me the phone number of your fiancé's parents, and I'll call them as soon as I get into my hotel. I will do my utmost to convince them not to oppose your marriage."

When Shlomo reached the father of Kathy's fiancé, he found him hostile and unreceptive. Despite his best attempts to make the father listen to reason, Shlomo made little headway. As Shlomo persisted, the man grew irate. Finally, he snapped. "Listen here—I'm a Holocaust survivor, and because of what G-d did to the Jews, I hate *Yiddishkeit* (Judaism), but still, if my son marries a *shiksa* (non-Jewish woman), I'll kill him!"

Shlomo realized that meaningful dialogue with the father was impossible and bade him good-bye. He then reached for the phone to call Kathy and report, regretfully, on his lack of success.

It was Kathy's father, however, who answered the phone, and he too was antagonistic and contentious. He was angry at Shlomo for attempting to mediate between the two families and castigated him for his "interference." Silently absorbing the torrent of abuse, Shlomo responded with a Talmudic tale. "Now that G-d has finished creating the world, the Talmud asks, what does He do all day? The Talmud answers that G-d spends one-third of his time making *shidduchim* (matches). So," Shlomo said humorously, "I'm just trying to give G-d a little help! Obviously, your daughter and her fiancé love each other very much. Wouldn't it be a terrible shame if they did not get married?"

Something in Shlomo's voice must have touched the man, because he began to cry. "I will tell you a secret that nobody else knows," he told Shlomo, "and until your call came, I thought I would never share it in my lifetime. My wife and I are not really Christians; we are Jews. We are, in fact, Holocaust survivors, and because of what G-d did to the Jews, we came to hate *Yiddishkeit* and renounced our heritage. We never officially converted, but we pretended we were Christians and raised our children as secularists. To this day, they don't know the truth about who they really are."

"But if this is the case," Shlomo responded, "and Kathy is in fact Jewish by birth, then there is no problem. Her fiancé's father objects to her non-Jewish parentage. If you will tell her the truth, the obstacles barring the way to her *bashert* (destined one) will be removed."

Kathy's father tearfully agreed. Shlomo spent the next few hours on the phone, making a flurry of phone calls between the two sets of parents. Finally, he arranged for them to meet in his hotel room the next day.

When the two fathers were formally introduced and rose to shake hands, they both blanched in shock and recognition. A series of varying emotions—confusion, astonishment, pain, and awe—flitted across their faces in rapid succession.

"Herschel!" shouted one in jubilation.

"Yankel!" shrieked the other in joy.

To the bewilderment of everyone present, they fell into each other's arms and cried.

"We were *chavrusahs* (learning partners) in yeshiva together before the Holocaust!" they cried out in explanation to their wives and children.

"We were best friends."

"But I thought you were dead!" they simultaneously exclaimed.

The tearful reunion brought back memories of a long-lost era, forever gone. Finally, one looked at the other and said with a crooked smile: "Do you remember the fanciful pact we once made, as we dreamed about the future?"

The other laughed delightedly in remembrance. "Why yes, I do! How strange, how very strange!" he murmured and turned to Kathy and her fiancé to elaborate.

"This is indeed curious, but I promise it is true. When we were yeshiva *bochurim* (boys) together, we promised we would forever be friends. And to solidify our friendship, we pledged that when we would marry and have children, we would betroth them to one another. It seems that even though *we* forgot this pledge, G-d did not. Against all odds, you met each other and fell in love—and reunited two best friends who never knew they had both survived the flames of the *Shoah*. I ask you, Rabbi Carlebach, how do you explain this? Is this coincidence or is this providence?"

And Shlomo, who hadn't said a single word while the reunion was taking place, leaned back in his chair and beamed.

SEDER

As told to Tania Hammer by her Father

My fondest memory of our community rabbi was when we, as children, would line up on the eve of Rosh Hashanah to receive *lekakh* (honey cake) from him. Rabbi Tzvi Hersh Rabinowitz* came from a rabbinic dynasty that traced its *yichus* (lineage) all the way back to the great sage, the Mahral of Prague. In my little village of Hodu Nanash, north of Debrecen, Hungary, the honor of knowing such a majestic figure was not lost on us youth, the children of the community. We collected our *lekakh* dressed in our Shabbos finery, and the rabbi would bend down to each of us and wish us a *gut yontif* (good holiday). His beatific smile would reassure all of us that indeed, it would be a good holiday and a sweet new year.

I also remember standing on line once when my father wanted to speak with the rabbi. He had certain hours when he received people, and my father brought me along to get a *bracha* (blessing). I must have been about ten years old at the time. We were waiting in the room next to the rabbi's office and my father was learning from a *sefer* (holy book) he had brought with him. I was keeping myself amused with my shoelaces. (My shoes were polished to perfection for this special evening, and I remember thinking it would seem strange to have perfectly polished shoes with untied shoelaces!) Finally, we were called in, and after warm greetings between my father and the rabbi, he shook my hand and greeted me by name. To this day, I can still remember the regal clothes he wore that night: a beautiful, dark silver brocade *bekeshe* (a long coat with two columns of black velvet trimming edged around the collar and then going down to the bottom). His cuffs were also trimmed in velvet, and the perfect *streimel* on top of his head made him look like a king.

The war broke out shortly after this, and our community was dispersed. My parents and six brothers and sisters tried to stay together, but inevitably, our family was torn apart. Two of my brothers disappeared, but the rest of us were assigned to the same labor camp, where my mother took ill. Our rations were meager, so my younger brother and I volunteered to try to supplement them by scrounging around for food that had fallen from the garbage, or rotten fruit that had dropped from the trees. It was during one of these expeditions that we first encountered a frightening apparition: a bedraggled old man dressed in filthy tatters, his beard in dreadlocks. He walked around the camp, feverishly muttering all kinds of strange things to himself. He never tried to hurt us, but still, we wanted to avoid him at all costs. There was something terribly wrong with him, and we kept our distance.

One day, my father came with us to see where we got our "food," and we pointed to the strange man who was pacing nearby. My father did not share our terror. A kindhearted, compassionate person, my father approached the man and offered him a crust of old bread. He started speaking to him. Socializing in the camp was risky, but my father wouldn't stop. He eventually called us over to where they both stood and asked us: "Don't you *kinderlach* (children) recognize Rabbi Rabinowitz?" When my father told us that this unkempt, wild-looking man was Rabbi Rabinowitz, I was close to tears. How could someone so regal, so majestic, end up looking like this? He was unrecognizable. I held my questions for a different time. Before we parted, my father promised to help him.

Even though we now knew that this terrifying specter was our rabbi, my brother and I remained afraid of him. He was badly in need of medical attention, and yet our father insisted that we aid him in any way we could.

At midnight one spring evening, a man came looking for my father and took him away. My father was shaken to the core, and we were all trembling with fear. We had no idea who this man was, where he was taking our father, or why. Had the Nazis discovered that we were pilfering food? Was our family group going to be split up? My father was gone for an hour and a half, during which time my mother and my siblings kept vigil, chanting *Tehillim* (Psalms), *davening* (praying), and watching for my father's return. We had heard many stories like this, where people were torn out of their homes, never to be seen again.

My father came back at about 2:00 A.M. with an ethereal smile on his face. It was a glow of *kedushah* (holiness) that couldn't be mistaken for anything but an experience that was not of this world. Here is what he said to us as we looked at him, stupefied.

"*Kinderlach* (children), these times are so hard for all of us. Who knows where your two brothers are—may they live and be well. We have seen many things that we will not soon forget, some too painful to bear; may Hashem (G-d) avenge the blood of our enemies. Tonight, however, is different. Tonight is the first night of *Pesach*. Tonight, for a short time, I redeemed all of you, like our rabbi redeemed us. Our rabbi has seen so much horror—he watched his wife and all his children killed in front of him. He became crazy after that. We have helped him these past few months, as hard as that was for us, but tonight, *kinderlach*, he gave back something that I will spend the rest of my life repaying.

"Rabbi Rabinowitz, the person you are so afraid of because he hasn't spoken a single lucid sentence since we found him, recited the whole *haggadah* (the story of Passover) *by heart*, from *Kaddesh* (the beginning of the *haggadah*) to *Nirtza* (the end). Somehow, someone got wine and a potato that we divided up, and Hashem gave Rabbi Rabinowitz his speech back long enough to tell us the story of *Yetzias Mitzrayim* (the Exodus), even in these dark times. I brought you back the piece of potato that was mine, and because it's *Pesach*, I would like to repeat for you everything that the rabbi said."

That night, we had a seder like no other seder. We sang softly and we each ate a tiny piece of raw potato. We felt grateful to the rabbi for giving us the opportunity to remember that as bad as we had it in the camp, our brethren in *Mitzraim* (Egypt) had it so much worse. And we were grateful too, that the rabbi had regained his lucidity and dignity, if only for a short while. Almost immediately afterward, he relapsed back to his former state.

A few weeks later, we were liberated, and we went back to Hodu Nanash. We took the rabbi with us. Although his entire immediate family had been wiped out, his sister had survived the war, and she brought him to her house in Budapest. My father visited him frequently. The rabbi died a few years after the war, never regaining his health. In an uncommon twist of the human condition, our holy rabbi was able to bring redemption to us in a place of darkness. Through the story of *Pesach*, he perpetuated our identity both as Jews and as human beings. It remains the story that we continue to tell.

SHOCKING DISCOVERY
As told by Raquel Schraub

It was 1946, one year after the Holocaust's end, and life was *not* back to normal. Many survivors were feverishly crisscrossing the continent in frantic pursuit of lost relatives and loved ones. Others had returned to their original hometowns, hoping to find family members—and some semblance of normalcy. Some had already left for Israel or the United States, desperate to flee the countries so drenched in Jewish blood. But for the bulk of the remnants, the first years were spent interned in what were commonly known as "DP" (displaced persons) camps, way stations for those in limbo, those who had nowhere to go as they waited for visas, passports, destiny.

Jews were not prisoners in the DP camps, but it was where they did most of their living. Self-contained, the DP camps met most of their residents' myriad needs, and there was little reason for the Jews to wander "outside," unless they were seeking adventure or certain specific items the DP camp could not provide. As it so happened, one day, a young man in the Foehrenwald DP Camp in Munich could not obtain a particular medicine (the name of which has been lost to history) that his newly pregnant wife desperately needed, and so he left the camp's confines to hunt for it. Yehoshua Heschel Deutsch (who later came to be popularly known as the *Freymanner Rav*), a twenty-five-year-old newlywed, was determined to find a pharmacy that stocked the medicine that might help his wife.This unremarkable errand would spawn an extraordinary moment in post-Holocaust history.

The language barrier was an obstacle for Yehoshua. He politely named the drug he sought, but the proprietor of one store shook his head and vaguely gesticulated toward the back. Yehoshua scoured the open shelves where over-the-counter medicines were displayed, but he could not locate the pills. He looked helplessly at the pharmacist at the front of the store, but several customers standing in line occupied his attention. Yehoshua decided to broaden the hunt on his own. He drifted toward a different part of the store and began foraging through the piles of bottles and jars that spilled from a musty cabinet in a long-forgotten corner. Mildew and spiderwebs clung to some of them, but Yehoshua soldiered on, undeterred. His wife needed the medicine, and he was not going back to the camp without it.

Yehoshua's hand grazed the object before it registered in his eyes, mind, and heart. Firm . . . solid . . . rectangular in shape; what kind of strange container was this? Yehoshua pulled it out from the heap of objects and examined it in the dim light. His heart skipped a beat. YIDDISHE SEIF, he read on the packaging; JEWISH SOAP.

Was it the economical impulse of the Nazis, the demonic one, or both? Everyone knew that the Nazis had plundered Jewish bodies before tossing them into the furnaces or gassing them into extinction. Gold fillings were extracted from teeth, or the teeth themselves were pulled out of the mouths of corpses to make jewelry; clothes were peeled off dead bodies, then recycled and shipped back to German stores; hair was ripped from scalps and stuffed into quilts or woven into blankets for Aryans suffering from fuel shortages. *And the fat from Jewish bodies was made into soap.* Yehoshua had heard the whispers long ago, and now he held the evidence in his hands. His face blanched white. He clawed through the rest of the cabinets in the back and found about a dozen more, all labeled JEWISH SOAP.

"They didn't even try to hide it," he thought.

Yehoshua checked his pockets for money, even though he knew what they contained: a pittance. Not enough for what he wanted to do. He staggered out of the store, ran back to the DP camp, and went from room to room, collecting coins. When he told everyone what the money was for, no one hesitated. Yehoshua returned to the pharmacy, gathered up the bars of soap he had found, brought them to the counter, and told the proprietor he wanted to buy them all. The pharmacist—a harsh line replacing the jovial smile he had flashed at Yehoshua only moments before—looked aghast at his customer's grisly discovery. He started to say something, but checked himself and fell silent. Yehoshua, trembling, was silent, too.

Back in the camp, Yehoshua consulted with some of the renowned rabbis who were also interned at Foehrenwald and then, with their blessings, rounded up everyone—men, women, and the few children still alive. "We are assembling outside for a mass *levaya* (funeral)," he said. "Who died now?" they asked in distress. "Come quickly," he urged.

Outside, in the courtyard, the bars of soap were lined up in neat columns, as was only fitting. For it was in columns that the dead had been "selected" and torn from their families; in columns that they had been marched to their deaths; in columns that they had been machine-gunned or pushed into the gas chambers. No one knew how these people had died, these people whose body fat had been boiled into oil for soap so the Germans could be clean, but surely they had once been part of a neat column, just like they were now.

One of the rabbis stepped forward and intoned the *Kel Molei Rachamim*, while another rabbi chanted the *Kaddish*, the traditional

Jewish prayers chanted at funerals. The assembled Jews recited *Tehillim* (Psalms). No one remembers if the bars of soap were eulogized. What could the rabbis have said?

"We do not know your names, you who were once human, now bars of soap. We do not know who you were in your lifetimes, where you lived, what you did, what kind of Jew you were. All we know; all we care about is that you are Jews; our brothers and sisters. We cannot bury your bones, not even your ashes, everything is gone save these bars of soap in which you are contained. There is no gravesite where your bereaved can gather and mourn; they do not even know with certainty that they should mourn. We mourn for them; we mourn for you. We do not know your names, so we will simply call you the most apt name we know: Tehorim, the pure ones. Whatever spark still remains in these bars of soap, we honor here today. You are still precious, you are still sacred. Your essence lives on."

And then the men dug a shallow grave and buried the bars of soap. Each man walked past the hollowed-out ground and threw a little dirt into it, until the cavity was filled.

"*Yidden*," proclaimed Yehoshua as they stared mutely at the mound of earth that swelled heavenward. "Today we have honored our fellow Jews in death, as they were not honored in life. May their memory be a blessing."

GETTING TO KNOW GERMAINE

Gerda Bikales

For sixty years, I knew nothing about the woman who had saved my life on that cold February morning in 1943. Not her name, not how she came to be there, not what happened to her afterwards.

At the height of Nazi persecution, my mother and I were Jewish refugees from Germany trying to survive illegally in Lyon, France. Though we tried to be inconspicuous and avoided official premises of any kind, we nevertheless had to appear periodically at the headquarters of the UGIF (*Union Genérale des Israélites de France*) on Rue Ste. Catherine. This was where the "Jewish Council" was located, and where Jews had to report every so often to receive their ration coupons.

The UGIF was an instrument of the occupying Nazi bureaucracy, which appointed such councils in all the occupied territories and forced them to cooperate in rounding up their fellow Jews. At the time, we did not fully grasp the nefarious role of the Council, but we always feared potential trouble in a place where only Jews congregated.

That morning, I accompanied my mother as she went to collect food stamps. I had stopped going to school because people were arrested at all hours, in their homes and on the street, and I was afraid to separate from my mother for even a short time. We had learned to look for signs of danger everywhere, and as we neared our destination, we cased the surroundings. All seemed normal, so we entered the building and started up the flight of stairs. Halfway up we noticed that the woman who was busy cleaning the first-floor landing was waving her hand at us, discreetly signaling us to leave. We didn't ask any questions, just turned around and left.

Later that day we learned that the Gestapo had taken over the UGIF office that morning, without betraying any hint of their presence. For several hours, they had trapped unsuspecting people as they entered the office. Over ninety people were arrested in that raid, and eighty-four were deported.

Since that day, I have often wondered about the woman who saved our lives. Was she the janitor, who had observed the Germans enter but not leave? Was she an office worker somewhere in the building? Or maybe a tenant in one of the apartments? One thing I knew for sure: She had risked her life to warn Jews of the danger awaiting them. Had she not been there that morning, I would not be here now to tell the story.

* * *

Many years later, my husband was vaguely talking about retirement when he received an invitation to take a new post in Paris. Without hesitation, we moved to France. I visited Lyon, and found myself in front of 12 Rue Ste. Catherine. The 1943 Gestapo raid that had nearly ensnared me was memorialized with a modest plaque affixed at the building's entrance, placed there by the Jewish community of Lyon.

In Paris, I attended a lecture and book signing by Germaine Ribière, the author of a newly published memoir about the Finaly affair, which had gripped French society for eight years immediately following the war. At the center of the drama was the fate of two young boys, Robert, born in 1941, and Gerald, born in 1942. Their parents, Fritz and Annie Finaly, had sought refuge in France after their native Austria was annexed to Nazi Germany—to little avail. They were deported from Nazi-occupied France in 1944. Before their arrest, the parents had found shelter for their children in a convent, from which they were later transferred to a municipal nursery run by a devout Catholic woman who had them baptized.

After the war, when it was determined that the boys' parents had been killed in Auschwitz, the Church refused to release the children to their surviving aunt, who lived in Israel. At issue was the assertion by the Vatican that no child baptized in the Catholic Church could be allowed to grow up in a Jewish home. A long and bitter custody battle ensued. The French court's final ruling favored the aunt. Ignoring the verdict, the church had whisked away the children to a convent in Spain. Germaine Ribière played a pivotal role in negotiating their eventual release and their safe return to their Israeli aunt.

Germaine Ribière was by now very elderly, her voice barely audible. I bought the book and asked her to inscribe it to me, which she graciously agreed to do despite an unsteady hand. I slowly spelled my unusual name for her, and thanked her.

* * *

After some interesting years in Paris, my newly retired husband spent ample time reading a wide range of publications. One day, he called out excitedly, "You won't believe this! Here—read this!" He handed me a small French periodical, open to the obituary page. It announced the death, at an advanced age, of Germaine Ribière, a Catholic Resistance fighter who had rescued many Jews during the Holocaust years. Among her numerous exploits, mention was made of her presence during the UGIF raid in February 1943. Upon espying that the Gestapo had taken over the office in Lyon, she had dressed as a cleaning woman to warn Jews of lurking danger.

After the war, she resumed her career as a scientist and remained a devout member of her church. But she stayed close to the traumatized Jewish community, becoming its advocate in epic struggles for the custody of Jewish orphans hidden with Catholic families or in Catholic institutions. She had published a book about her role in recovering the Finaly children, who had been hidden in Spain to keep them away from their surviving Jewish relatives.

So, sixty years later I learned something about my rescuer. Sadly, I also discovered that our paths had crossed, without any awareness on either side of the bond between us.

Postscript: Coincidences don't always lead to happy endings. They sometimes leave us with deep regrets about what could have happened, but didn't. How satisfying it would have been to thank my rescuer for the gift of life, my own and my mother's! For Germaine, burdened by the infirmities of old age, it would have been a meaningful encounter, so many years later, with a child she had pulled back from the edge of catastrophe.

Still, I am pleased to know more about this courageous woman. In my travels, I have looked for her name on the Righteous Gentiles memorial at Yad Vashem in Jerusalem, in the United States Holocaust Memorial Museum in Washington, and just recently, on the new Wall of the Righteous in Paris. I think of her often, with affection and gratitude. She is no longer a vague, anonymous figure in my mind. Her country and the Jewish community have honored her, and honored themselves by doing so. And I take special pride in *my* heroine.

THE LAST JEW OF AUSCHWITZ

Over the years, sporadic stories have occasionally surfaced about the strange-but-true lives of people frozen in time and space. These are the media accounts about tragic figures for whom time stopped decades ago and has remained at a standstill ever since.

While little is actually known about the people who lived their lives trapped in a time warp, they seemed to have shared one common denominator: they were all casualties of World War II. A few years back, newspapers reported the sad tale of a Japanese soldier who had hidden in the forests for most of his life in the belief that World War II was still raging. When he finally emerged from the woods in which he was hiding, he was old, and he could not retrieve the lost years. Recently, a similar story has begun to be told about another individual whose entire existence was predicated on his unshakable conviction that the Holocaust had never ended; an individual known as "The Last Jew of Auschwitz."

The village of Oswiecem (that abutted the infamous camp of the same name) had once bustled with Jewish life, but after the war, it became *Judenrein* (completely cleansed of Jews.) Survivors retured briefly to Oswiecem (Auschwitz) to search for lost family members in the vain hope that they, too, would be searching for *them* in their old hometown, but all the Jews eventually left—except for one man named Shimshon Kluger, the "Last Jew of Auschwitz."

Perhaps his familiar childhood surroundings provided him with some small measure of comfort, or perhaps he hoped that other Jews would soon follow his lead, and resettle in their place of birth. No one quite understood his rationale, but in Shimshon Kluger's quest for normalcy, in his desire to reclaim his old life, he did something inexplicable: he remained in Auschwitz, the only Jew to do so. His devastated brother and sister begged him to leave, to join them in America, but Shimshon had withdrawn too deeply into himself and would not succumb to his siblings' pleas. They could not coax him to re-enter life. He was sure that the Nazi reign of terror continued on. And so, Shimshon Kluger lived in Auschwitz for an incredible fifty years, its only Jew.

He was visited every summer by his brother and his sister who respectively stayed with him a month at a time. But while their lives progressed with marriages, children, work, and other life milestones, Shimshon's had ground to a complete halt. Each time his siblings visited, they made sure that he was well taken care of: they paid for running water and electricity to be installed in his home, for meals to be cooked and delivered to him by the local townspeople. But as much as they tried, they could not persuade him to leave his ancestral home.

On May 26, 2000, the rabbi of Cracow, Poland, was notified of the death of Shimshon Kluger—the last living Jew in the town of Auschwitz. *How should he be buried?* the Christian townspeople wanted to know. A Jewish cemetery remained in Auschwitz, but there were no other Jews living in the town who could form a *minyan* (quorum of ten or more) or prepare his body for the funeral. To make matters more daunting, it was *Erev Shabbos* (Shabbos eve). Despite the formidable odds, the rabbi was determined to make this funeral happen. Certainly, Shimshon Kluger—a man who had lived such a sorrowful life—deserved, at the very least, dignity in death.

As the rabbi paced his study, nervously trying to solve the dilemma, he suddenly remembered a key piece of information, and an idea began to take shape. Each spring, a school group from the United States toured Jewish sites in Poland. The rabbi knew the guide. Were they in Poland right now, and if so, could they possibly be anywhere near the town of Auschwitz? The rabbi picked up his cell phone and called the guide.

For many years, Michael Berl, director of Heritage Seminars, had conducted Holocaust educational tours in Eastern Europe for American teenagers who wanted to explore their roots. He and Rabbi Yossi Weiser were on the road with a busload of seniors from Ramaz High School in Manhattan that very day when his cell phone rang.

"Michael, where do you happen to be right now?" the rabbi asked.

"We're on our way from Sandowicz to Kielce," Michael answered.

"Excellent!" the rabbi shouted in jubilation. "Would you mind doing a big *mitzvah* (good deed)?"

The bus wheeled around and changed direction, heading for the Jewish cemetery in Auschwitz. Coincidentally, one of the tour guides on board the bus, Rebbetzin Berglas, happened to be a member of the *chevrah kadishah* (burial society) of Neve Aliza in Israel, and she began to prepare the students for the funeral. For most, it would be their first encounter with death, their first attendance at a burial service. They came from sheltered lives and comfortable homes. But they had to do it. There were no other Jews within traveling distance of Auschwitz, and it almost seemed as if G-d had ordained them to be nearby.

When the students saw the casket, tears welled in many of their eyes. When they were called upon to shovel dirt into the grave, their hands shook. And their lips trembled as they recited the *Tehillim* (Psalms) for the last living Jew of Auschwitz.

Perhaps the soul of Shimshon Kluger would finally know in death the truth he had never grasped in life—that Hitler had failed in his mission to wipe out all the Jews, and from the ashes of the phoenix, new life had emerged. The proof was right at Shimshon's side even as he was gently laid to rest: the fresh young stalks, the brand-new buds, the tender shoots—the teenagers from Ramaz, whispering the triumphant message: *Hitler did not succeed. We are here.*

WHAT'S IN A NAME?

As told by Masha Leon

"What's in a name?" Shakespeare famously asked in *Romeo and Juliet*. His conclusion—"That which we call a rose by any other name would smell just as sweet"—suggests that names are essentially interchangeable, bearing no real impact on one's fate or fortune. With apologies to the great bard, Masha Leon respectfully disagrees.

Masha was eight years old when she and her mother, Zelda, fled Warsaw in 1939. Only three days after Hitler's bombardment of Warsaw, Masha's father, Matvey Bernstein, a journalist for one of Warsaw's leading Yiddish newspapers, was warned to leave the city posthaste: Members of the Polish intelligentsia—Poles and Jews alike—were going to be the first group to be rounded up and arrested when the Germans entered Warsaw.

Although Matvey wanted Zelda and Masha to accompany him, Zelda chose to stay behind to care for her pregnant sister.

"How can I leave her behind? No, you go ahead of us, and as soon as we can, we'll meet you in Byten," she said, naming their birthplace in then Soviet-occupied Poland (now Belarus.)

But a few months later, Zelda was forced to rescind her stoic decision. Under the harrowing circumstances of ghetto life—no food, heat, or water—Masha's health was rapidly deteriorating. She contracted mumps, and suffered from malnutrition. Meanwhile, Jews were being brutally assaulted on the street, randomly picked out, and rumors of even more drastic occupation orders circulated daily. "It's time for us to leave, too," Zelda told her daughter one day as she collected needles, matches, thread, salt, and sugar—the currency used to trade for food—and threw them into the rucksack on Masha's back. "I've found a Polish peasant who is going to take us and several other Jews to the other side. We leave tonight."

The Polish peasant was an opportunist: Without telling Zelda and Masha, he left them sitting in an open wagon for hours, exposed to sleet, snow, and rain, as he collected more Jews to fill it up. His "load" consisted of several unaccompanied children, a couple of women, and an elderly Jew. The peasant had insisted that the Jews—a total of eleven—pay him in advance. As he settled them into the back of the wagon, he carefully suggested that they also give him their valuables to safekeep, because the Germans would search them but not him. After he had stashed away their "loot," the peasant climbed into the wagon, and drove them straight to Gestapo headquarters. "I have a load of Jews for you," he bragged.

German soldiers lined them up and pinned numbers on their coats. They stood all night long against a wall. At dawn—on a whim—several soldiers arbitrarily shot the odd-numbered refugees... numbers 1, 3, 5, and 7... men, women, and children. Zelda and Masha had been pinned with numbers 4 and 6. They were free to go.

Zelda and Masha headed eastward towards the German-occupied Polish borders. At night, they knocked fearfully on doors of peasant huts, asking for food and shelter. Masha was blonde and blue-eyed, so she easily "passed" as a non-Jew. Zelda, dark-haired and brown-eyed, posed as her Italian nanny. "Whatever you do, don't call me Mama," she instructed her daughter. "And don't speak in Yiddish, either."

"And one more thing," she added as an afterthought. "If the Russians stop us, I want you to start crying, because the Russians have warm hearts."

A barren, snow-covered swath of land about three to four blocks in width separated the Russian- and German-occupied sectors of Poland. When mother and daughter reached the checkpoint and were waved across the barrier by the Germans, Zelda heaved a sigh of relief. But the ordeal was not over. As they hurried across the no-man's-land, Russians galloped out of the forest, bellowing, "Go back, or we'll shoot!"

Terrified, they raced back to the German side, but the soldiers there refused them reentry. "Go . . . go back to your Bolshevik friends!" they sneered. They dashed back to the Russian side, where again guns and bayonets were pointed threateningly at them, and once more, they were ordered to return to the German checkpoint. This tableau was repeated for three days, until the helpless Jews realized that they were truly trapped in a no-man's-land from which there appeared to be no exit.

After several days of shuttling back and forth between the two sides and constant exposure to freezing sleet without shelter or food, people began to get ill or die. "We have to get out of here!" Zelda told her daughter, heading to the Russian forest line. There they spotted a Polish woman with a wagon of hay crossing the neutral pass. The woman hid them in her horse-drawn cart, brought them to her home, and concealed them for three days. Then she told her son to lead Zelda and Masha past German patrols to the Russian tree line, where they slowly and calmly walked into the forest, pretending to be "locals." But their efforts were foiled again.

This time it was a lone, young Russian soldier with a bayonet who blocked their passage. "Go back or I shoot!" he cried. Zelda began to speak to him in flawless Russian, explaining that she had been born under Russian rule, and possessed a Russian-lettered birth certificate. The soldier was unimpressed. "Go back or I shoot!" he repeated angrily.

At that precise moment, Masha remembered her mother's instructions to cry whenever they encountered a Russian, and, on cue, began to weep loudly. *This is useless now*, Zelda thought. *He's definitely going to kill us. Masha doesn't realize there isn't any point to this ploy anymore.*

But Masha's sobbing increased in intensity.

"*Nie płakaj* (don't cry), Mashinka," Zelda told her daughter in Polish.

The soldier's scowl suddenly softened. "Since when do Poles give their children Russian names?" he asked with interest, lowering his gun.

This is your last chance, Zelda told herself.

"My daughter is named after Masha from the great Russian novels," she said. "Masha from Chekhov's *Cherry Orchard* and *Three Sisters*; Masha from Dostoyevsky's *Brothers Karamazov*; and Masha from Tolstoy's novels, too!"

The soldier picked up Zelda's birth certificate, turned it upside down, pretended to read it, and then handed it back to her. With a sickening thud, Zelda suddenly realized that the man was illiterate. "*Er iz a niekulturnik* (uneducated person)," she whispered to Masha. "He can't read!" Her literary references were meaningless to him.

Unexpectedly, the soldier smiled.

"I have a sister named Masha," he said. "Same age, same braids. If I shoot you, it's like I'm shooting my sister. Come with me." At Russian headquarters in the forest, the soldier announced to everyone: "*Eto Mashinka.*" (This little girl is named Masha.)

Masha, Russian for Mary, was a name that drew nostalgic sighs and sentimental smiles from the soldiers, as it conjured up images of beloved mothers, sisters, wives, left behind the front lines and sorely missed. As "Masha" was—and remains to this day—the most popular women's name in Russia, practically everyone inside the station had positive and heartwarming associations that were instantly transferred to the little girl and her mother.

As soon as her name was announced, they were given the royal treatment. Out came a samovar, and some bread and butter. At dawn they were driven to the train station in a Soviet military truck. They went by train to Byten where they were reunited with Masha's father, Matvey. Later, they were spirited out of Byten at night in an ambulance to avoid Matvey being arrested by the Communists. Eventually, they headed to Vilna and the next stage of their survival via Japan.

Of course, the little girl had never been named after any of the fictional heroines in the Russian literary canon. Nor had her parents meant to give her a Russian name to begin with, either.

As is the Jewish custom, Zelda and Matvey planned to name their baby after Matvey's deceased father, Moshe. When the child turned out to be a girl, the parents simply adapted the male name to a female one. Ultimately, all that was required was a simple two-vowel change—the "o" to an "a," and the "e" to another "a." The result was a name responsible not only for perpetuating the grandfather's memory, but also one that would save their own lives as well.

Postscript: Masha Leon writes a weekly column for the English *Forward* titled "On-The-Go," which focuses on the cultural, social, and communal doings in the Jewish social world. She is also a contributor to the Yiddish *Forward*. Masha and her parents were the only survivors of an extended family of nearly two hundred. Her parents lived long enough to enjoy three grandchildren.

THE HIDDEN CHILD

It is a startling fact that, of the 1.6 million Jewish children who lived in Europe before the Nazi apocalypse, 1.5 million perished. Since almost no children survived the concentration camps, the 100,000 who remained alive did so by either escaping to nonoccupied countries or by going into hiding. Robert Krell was one of these "hidden children," a little-known group bypassed by both journalists and historians in the first decades after the Holocaust, and whose stories have only recently begun to be told.

Born in 1940 in The Hague, Holland, Robert was two years old when his family received papers to report for "resettlement to the East." Friends, relatives, and acquaintances had been similarly summoned long before, and had never been heard from again. Robert's parents, Emily and Leo Krell, had never received a single promised postcard from *any* of them signaling that all was well.

"We have to leave immediately," Leo told his wife, as he scanned the papers that he knew, in essence, were death certificates.

"Can I have a few minutes to scoop up some things to take along?" his wife begged.

"We can't risk it," her husband answered. "Our lives are at stake. We must flee *now*." An hour after receiving the deportation papers, the Krells were gone.

The Krells were not unprepared for this critical moment. They had a plan already set in place when the deportation papers arrived:

The family would separate and hide with three different Christian neighbors. Robert was placed with an elderly Christian couple, the Hols, who had agreed to take him weeks earlier. But when the arrangement had originally been made, neither the Krells nor the Hols were aware that shortly thereafter all elderly Dutch would be moved to the countryside.

"What are we going to do with little Robbie?" the Hols asked one another in consternation, only a few weeks after his arrival. "It's one thing to hide him in our house, where no one can see him, but traveling to the countryside . . . he'll be exposed to public scrutiny. No one will believe that this dark-haired, dark-eyed child is our grandchild."

Once a year, like clockwork, a young Christian acquaintance by the name of Violette Munnik came to pay the Hols a social visit. Coincidentally, she happened to arrive at their doorstep shortly after they had received their orders to relocate to the country, and were in the midst of weighing their options. The Hols entrusted Violette with their secret and discussed their dilemma. "I'll take him," she instantly offered. Perhaps Violette didn't fully grasp the danger in which she was placing her family; or perhaps she naively miscalculated how long the war could last. There certainly was no way that Violette Munnik could have known that her impulsive act of generosity would lead to a three-year commitment, during which time she would come to love little Robbie as her own.

Violette Munnik, her husband, Albert, and her ten-year-old daughter, Nora, were good, decent people, who unrestrainedly lavished their love on Robert. Despite their kindness, however, life as a "hidden child" was taut with tension for Robbie, who was firmly instructed to stay away from the windows, refrain from talking loudly or laughing boisterously, and never, ever to venture out on the streets. The Hague was infested with traitors, and the Munniks trusted no one. Robert had to be rendered as invisible as possible, to make the possibility of betrayal remote.

During his three-year confinement in the Munniks' home, Robert never vented his emotions, not once. He never wept the normal tears of a child abandoned by his parents, and, over time, his reason for weeping ceased, too. As memories of his biological parents gradually receded over time, Robert no longer remembered Emily and Leo Krell. He lived with the Munniks during the critical childhood years, from the age of two until he was five, and soon came to regard them—not the Krells—as his "real" parents.

On May 5, 1945, Holland was liberated from Nazi occupation, and the scattered Jewish remnants that had survived the Holocaust started creeping out from the secret places in which they had been hiding all this time. Out of a prewar population of 140,000 Dutch Jews, only 35,000 survived; Emily and Leo Krell were among them, and Robert Krell was among the 3,500 Jewish children who remained alive.

But when the Krells came to retrieve him, Robert did something he hadn't done these last three years: He shrieked and cried, flailed his arms, kicked his legs, and refused to go with them. All this time little Robbie had not raised his voice, not even once, but now he was vocal—histrionic—in his protests and fury. "How can you say these are my parents?" the five-year-old screamed at the Munniks. "You are my parents! Why are you lying? I don't know these people; I know you."

These postwar scenes were not uncommon; in fact, they were taking place everywhere in Europe where there were hidden children and surviving parents who returned to claim them. Although they had tried to be realistic, the Krells had still hoped for a tender reunion, and they were crushed. How would they convince Robert that he was theirs?

Three years before, on that fateful day when the Krells had stared with horror at the deportation papers trembling in their hands, Leo had told his wife to leave everything and take flight. Leave *everything*? All the artifacts that made up the fabric of their life together . . . all the possessions and mementos that gave it meaning and bore it testimony? As she watched her husband walk out the door, Emily Krell had resolved to grab *something* that was truly meaningful. It so happened that what she took in that fleeting, frenzied moment was a single, wallet-size photograph of her family: Leo, Robert, and herself. And this photograph, too, had miraculously survived the war.

"Look," Emily said, gently beckoning to Robert as she pulled out the photograph from her pocket. It was creased and begrimed, but still clear enough to make out the figures. "This is a picture of our family before the war. Do you recognize the little boy in the photo?"

Robert's wild thrashing subsided as he stole over to Emily's side to inspect the photograph she held in her hands. Some children's appearances change over time, but as he examined the photo, Robert knew he was looking at a mirror image of himself. A precocious child of exceptional intelligence, he had always wondered why *he* had dark, curly hair while, in contrast, his "parents," Violette and Albert Munnik and "sister" Nora had silky, straight blond tresses; why his eyes were dark while theirs were light; and why his complexion was swarthy while they were so fair. Robert's thoughtful gaze compared the people in the photo against the Krells and the Munniks standing nearby—the former, who resembled him, and the latter, who did not—and he became convinced. It would be a long and painful adjustment, but thanks to the one item his mother had salvaged from their old life together, and lovingly preserved during the turbulent war years, Robert Krell knew who he was, and to whom he belonged.

Postscript: After the war, the Krells eventually emigrated to Vancouver, British Columbia, where Robert Krell continues to live to this day as an eminent psychiatrist, professor, writer, and lecturer. He has written extensively about the "Hidden Children" experience. Over the years, he maintained constant contact with the Munniks, sending them gifts and money, visiting often at their home in Holland, and paying for their visits to his home in British Columbia. He flew them into Vancouver for his graduation from medical school in 1965, and for his wedding in 1971. Robert Krell had all three Munniks—Albert, Violette, and daughter Nora—inscribed as Righteous Gentiles in Yad Vashem in 1981. Albert Munnik died in 1972, and Violette Munnik, in 1985. Robert flew to Holland for her funeral, where he said *Kaddish* for her. When someone asked him if it is permissible to say *Kaddish* for a Christian, Robert answered, "I determined for myself that she deserves it." He maintains an ongoing and close relationship with "sister" Nora Munnik, who continues to reside in Holland.

TRUNKFUL OF LETTERS

The place: 2107 Van Ness Avenue, a nondescript office building in the heart of San Francisco's bustling business district. The time: the year 2000, fifty-five years after the Holocaust. The principal characters: a wealthy and successful attorney, a hardworking Russian immigrant, a bedraggled vagrant roaming the streets, and a standard, unexceptional steamer trunk. The story belongs to many people, but in the beginning it belonged to author/lawyer Al Anolik, the landlord of the unprepossessing property on Van Ness. In 1977, Al traveled to New York to tie up loose ends left in the wake of his father's recent death. There were papers to organize and possessions to sort out, the irony not being lost on Al that while men die, their stuff survives.

Al's father Morris Anolik had been a man of humble means, leaving little of monetary value. But in the attic of his father's home, Al was not hunting for precious gems or priceless paintings, or anything else that could be turned into liquid cash. He was searching for treasures of a different kind: sentimental mementos that connected him to his father's being, to his essence, little knickknacks that would stir up memories. As Al foraged through the heaps and piles of mostly useless junk that tend to clutter most people's attics, he plucked out little trinkets that reminded him of special occasions, such as old birthday presents he had sent his father. None of the items elicited any surprise on his part, just rueful smiles and tender expressions—

until he stumbled upon a stack of old, yellowing envelopes, many of them postmarked 1945, 1946, 1947—postmarked from Germany.

Morris Anolik had emigrated to the United States from Kovno, Russia, in 1918, the sole member of his family to do so. He had left behind his parents and his sister, Reva. His was a trajectory typical of the times, as most families could not afford to emigrate en masse. Fathers, or their pioneering sons, commonly went first, blazing their brave trail into the Promised Land, working hard, saving their pennies, and then extricating their loved ones one by one from the countries where pogroms and poverty ran rampant. Eventually, many families made it intact to these shores, reuniting with their loved ones. But often, plans went awry; money was not plentiful, and family members remained stranded on "the other side." The pain of separation was intensified by fears of extinction once Hitler rose to power in the 1930s. Family members in the United States were mostly helpless when it came to saving those ensnared by the Nazis' far-reaching web.

Al Anolik sat down in the musty attic, painstakingly poring over every page, frustration mounting with his realization that practically every letter was written in a foreign language he could not decipher. In spite of this, he was able to piece together that his father's sister, Reva, had survived the concentration camps and that Morris had attempted to free her from a displaced persons (DP) camp. But the rest was unintelligible to him.

"I'll wait until my children are older," Al vowed to himself, *"and then I'll get a translator and we'll open these letters and read them together. 'This is your family history,' I'll tell them. These are my father's words . . . my aunt's words . . . and the only real connection I have left to my father. These letters are invaluable."*

Al tenderly placed the letters in an old steamer trunk he found in the attic, together with the little mementos he had unearthed. He shipped the trunk to San Francisco, where it was ultimately deposited in a storage room in the office building that he owned on Van Ness Avenue. He often thought about the steamer trunk and its contents over the years, but somehow he got swept up in the busy-ness of daily life and never got around to reading the letters as he had pledged. He did gain a measure of comfort, knowing the trunk was in a room nearby, waiting. Decades passed. Al's practice flourished while the letters inside the steamer trunk withered, growing increasingly more yellowed with age.

* * *

The office building which Al owned was, by all respects, commonplace. The ground floor housed six small retail shops, among them Mike Brod's VCR and wide-screen television repair shop. A recent immigrant to the United States from Russia, Mike was a bighearted man who took in strays and shepherded other Russian newcomers. He was a fount of information, a one-man referral and networking agency, and his store had become a mecca and gathering place for new settlers passing through. Mike Brod's generosity, however, extended well beyond his fellow expatriates. Local panhandlers and the itinerant homeless knew he could be counted upon for a sizable handout. He never turned anyone away, and soon a steady stream of regulars wended their way to him whenever they were in need.

The third floor of 2107 Van Ness Avenue was occupied by the law offices of Al Anolik, where loving-kindness was practiced on a completely different level. In his employ was an AIDS patient, Johnny Bertolucci,* a man for whom death was imminent, but who had no financial resources to pay for the medicine, food, and shelter he needed to live out his last pitiful months.

Al had met Johnny thirty years before when both were law students, and Johnny had been a brilliant and ambitious man. Although their paths had diverged after law school, Al had heard through the grapevine that Johnny had become a wealthy entrepreneur and, later, mayor of a small town in Indiana. By all accounts, Johnny had been extremely successful. Al never learned exactly how Johnny's fortunes had spiraled downward, when he had hit skid row, become an alcoholic, and gotten infected with AIDS. When Johnny Bertolucci unexpectedly showed up one day, Al was shocked by his graying visage and haggard appearance. Al had taken pity on his old friend and hired him as the firm's janitor and clerk. It was a way of restoring some dignity to the man and giving him money on which to live.

Meanwhile, Al continued to chide himself for failing to have the time to properly inspect his inheritance—the stack of letters in the old steamer trunk, the invaluable spiritual legacy from his father. Although he neglected them, he still drew comfort from the knowledge that they were safe in the storage room on his office floor.

One day, Johnny approached Al and muttered that he had nothing to do. To give him some busy work, Al suggested that he organize the storage room. As Al would later learn, Johnny's idea of "organizing" the storage room was to throw out everything that was inside it—including the old steamer trunk.

* * *

Skipper* was an elderly vagrant whose turf was Van Ness Avenue and its immediate environs. He could often be seen frequenting the local donut shop that abutted Al's office building, or the church next door that allowed the dispossessed a place to rest their weary bodies. His route also included customary stops at Mike Brod's VCR repair shop, where the affable Russian could always be counted upon for a kind word, a ready smile, and a generous handout. The handouts couldn't sustain Skipper, so to supplement them, he took to foraging through the Dumpsters that stood in the alleys behind the office buildings. It was here that he found a stack of old letters.

For some reason, Skipper picked them up. Clearly, they weren't marketable commodities. Skipper couldn't sell or barter them, but something made him go through them, right there inside the Dumpster. He realized that they were written in a foreign language he didn't know. *Maybe somebody needs these letters—maybe they're important,* he thought. *But what language are they in?* A lightbulb went off in his mind. "Maybe Mike would know."

Mike Brod *did* know, because the letters had been written in Russian and Yiddish, and they were signed by both a man and a woman whose last name he knew as well: *Anolik*. It was an uncommon name, but it just so happened to belong to his landlord on the third floor—Al Anolik. Surely, there had to be a connection?

For Al, the return of the letters was nothing short of a miracle, and a wake-up call to finally read them. He asked Mike to translate the letters, which he did. Al learned that much of the correspondence centered around his aunt's descriptions of her Holocaust experiences, her post-Holocaust trauma, and the harrowing conditions of the DP camp in which she was interned. The letters did, indeed, represent a major and invaluable chunk of family history, but it was his aunt's family's history, not his, Al recognized with a sickening thud. He had held these letters in his possession for so long, but it was really his first cousin Etta—only daughter of Reva Anolik—who should have been the rightful heir.

Etta Ansel had never owned any documentation of her mother's experiences in the Holocaust. As the child of a survivor, she had been branded by osmosis, but the letters were the first tangible representation she'd seen of all her mother had gone through and transcended. When Al Anolik presented his first cousin with the sheaf of letters, he offered her a glimpse into her mother's life that she had never had before.

"This is our family history," Al told her when he handed them to her. "But it is more yours than mine. These letters tell the story of your mother's suffering, her fears, her hopes, her triumph of survival. They belong to you."

Etta wishes she could personally thank Skipper for the inestimable gift he gave to her by returning the letters, but no one has seen him around for a long time. Perhaps he's busy in a different alleyway somewhere in San Francisco, digging up precious jewels from other reeking Dumpsters, proving beyond a shadow of a doubt that all men seek redemption, and that anyone can be its messenger.

Postscript: Etta Ansel continues to treasure the letters from her mother as a gift from beyond. Mike Brod continues to counsel and help both immigrants and street people alike. Al Anolik continues to employ Johnny Bertolucci, who defies all the doctors' prognoses and remains alive several years after he was supposed to be dead. Skipper disappeared and was never seen or heard from again.

THE GOLD PENDANT

The drill was always the same. After days of traveling in urine-drenched, oppressively dark, and suffocatingly cramped cattle cars into which they had been shoved, squeezed, and crushed, the Jewish prisoners arrived at their final destination: Auschwitz. The Jews tumbled, or were pushed, off the trains, after which they were whipped, beaten with truncheons, and pulled into lines where they were ordered to strip naked and discard all their possessions. "You will get them back soon," the Nazis always promised, to avoid riots and ensure compliance. "We just need to get you deloused and disinfected, and then they'll be returned to you. Just go into the showers first, and get cleaned up." All lies.

It was 1944. Although Polish Jews—those who had not yet been killed—had been suffering the travails of the Holocaust for over five years, Hungarian Jews had just begun their journey into hell, Hungary being the last country invaded by Hitler. One morning, a new transport of wealthy Hungarian Jews rolled onto the tracks of the Auschwitz train station, and as they were being roughly herded off, two gentile women watched with intense interest. They were not camp prisoners, but day laborers who toiled in the vast warehouses where the prisoners' cast-off clothes were sorted and shipped back to Germany. The two women were sisters, Polish citizens recruited from the local countryside, whose hearts had not yet hardened to the Jewish prisoners' plight.

In fact, Anna Kosinski* had just recently told her younger sister Christina* that she didn't think she could stay in Auschwitz much longer: "I can't take it anymore," she had said. "The screams from the crematoria when the Jews realize it's gas pouring from the showers, not water—those screams haunt me every night. I don't think I can do this anymore." Still, avarice glittered in their eyes. As they watched this particular transport of elegantly dressed Jews, who had no idea that they were riding to their deaths, spill out of the trains, their attention was drawn to one woman dressed in a stunning silver fox coat who stood out in the crowd.

"Ooh, I love that coat," Christina said, practically salivating. "I want it. I'm going to take it for myself." Although pilfering was strictly prohibited, it went on nonetheless. Anna and Christina were among dozens who regularly raided the warehouses for clothes, jewelry, and food—items their Jewish owners would no longer be able to use. "I'm going to go get it right now," Christina said.

The two sisters rapidly approached the ground where the elegant woman had dropped her coat. Their job included collecting the clothing and then bringing it to the warehouses for sorting, so no one gave it a passing thought when Christina seized it. As she grasped the fur coat, she felt something wiggle inside its luxurious folds. She opened the coat's hooks carefully and beheld a tiny, tightly swaddled infant, only about a week or two old. The two women's jaws dropped.

"Oh, my good Lord in Heaven!" Christina screamed, almost dropping the baby. Christina motioned for her sister to join her in a secluded spot out of the Nazis' range of vision.

"What should we do?" Anna asked.

The hearts of the Nazis had always been stone, and they treated Jewish infants, toddlers, and children with the same ruthless punishment as they did adults. Their behavior toward infants was especially heinous. They often threw them up into the air and used them for target practice, just for kicks. They deliberately murdered them in front of their mothers to prolong their sadistic pleasures. And, for an extra measure of fun, they threw them—alive—into bonfires and furnaces.

But these two women were not Nazis, and their hearts melted at the sight of the pink-cheeked, blond-haired, blue-eyed little girl. Especially Christina. Whereas Anna had been blessed with children, the forty-four-year-old Christina and her husband were childless, and yearned for a baby. The two sisters' eyes locked.

"The baby will go straight into the gas chamber if I don't take her," Christina said. Anna was silent. "I feel that G-d has given me this child," Christina said. "The mother is already dead. We both know that this entire transport went straight into the crematorium. This child was destined to be mine."

"But how are you going to pull this off?" Anna asked.

"This is the one time I bless the fact that I am heavy," Christina thought quickly. "I will go lie down in one of the rooms in the warehouse, cut myself so that blood will pool around me, undress the child, and scream that I have just given birth. We'll say that I was pregnant all along, and went into labor suddenly. I had the baby so quickly, I couldn't get to the hospital in time. No one will question it! No one would ever suspect that a newborn baby could have survived a trip on the cattle cars, that we found a baby bundled up in a fur coat, or that we would think of taking a Jewish child."

As it turned out, she was right. Christina was driven home in a wagon with the baby cradled in her arms—in full view of the soldiers and Nazis at the watchtowers, waving joyously to them as she left the G-dforsaken grounds of Auschwitz forever—with the hidden coat.

Although Christina's husband instantly agreed to keep the infant and adopt her as his own, he had one question for his wife: "But how are we going to get enough money to support the child?"

Christina was a shrewd woman who had learned many tricks in Auschwitz. "You know," she said thoughtfully, "many Jews hide money in secret pockets and the linings of their coats. Let's open up this one and see what we find." Sure enough, the coat yielded tens of thousands in Hungarian currency, enough money to last a lifetime. It also delivered up a beautifully crafted gold pendant, from which a little locket dangled. Eagerly opening the locket in the hopes of finding a photograph of the baby, Christina was disappointed to find that it only contained some Hebrew words engraved inside. *Well, it's real gold, and maybe one day I'll want to give it to her, so I'll keep it,* Christina thought as she tossed the pendant into a drawer.

With their newfound cash reserves, after the war Christina and her husband moved to Budapest where they raised Lila* in the lap of luxury. The girl was never told she was Jewish, and adopted. They indulged her every whim, educated her at the best schools, and nurtured all of her creative impulses with lessons in music, dance, drama, and art. Lila grew up to be an accomplished and serious young woman who attended medical school and ultimately became a pediatric surgeon with a flourishing practice. Eventually, Lila married a fine young Christian man named Hans, became pregnant, and delivered a beautiful set of twins.

"Lila, let's throw a party to celebrate!" Hans exclaimed in the hospital room, adding, "When you feel up to it, of course."

"How about in a month from now?" Lila said, smiling weakly. "That should give me ample time to recuperate."

"Perfect!" her husband enthused. "We'll celebrate their four-week-old birthday, and I'll insist that my parents come in from Czechoslovakia to join us as well."

A month later, Hans left their home to pick up his parents, who were scheduled to arrive at the Budapest train station. With him were Lila's mother and father, who wanted to be present with him to welcome his parents. Lila and the babies stayed home. The train station was only a short trip away, and Lila expected Hans to return home within an hour. When two hours passed, she became impatient. *What's taking so long?* she wondered. By the fourth hour, Lila became frantic and called a neighbor to babysit the twins. She had just pulled on her coat to go down to the train station herself when a police officer appeared at her door.

"Are you Mrs. ———?" he asked quietly, avoiding her eyes.

"What's happened?" she screamed.

"I'm very sorry to have to give you this news, Madam. You know, it's been a very foggy and rainy day, and apparently on the way home from the train station, your husband's car went out of control. He hit an oncoming train, and there was a terrible accident. Everyone in the car was instantly killed—your husband, your parents, and your in-laws. I'm terribly sorry."

* * *

A few months after the tragedy, Anna—Christina's sister and Lila's aunt—came to visit the bereaved daughter and widow.

"Lila," she said, taking the younger woman's hands in her own, "I know that you are still very much devastated, very numb, from everything's that happened to you. And I feel very reluctant to do or say anything to add to your trauma, to cause you more pain. But long ago, your mother made me promise that if anything should ever happen to her, I should give you this. I feel uncomfortable and unhappy about adding to your anguish, but how can I not honor a promise I made to my beloved sister? I've waited several months, but I feel that

I have to fulfill my promise now. I am sorry for the suffering this is going to cause you, truly I am. Here . . ." With that, Anna handed Lila an envelope that she had secreted in her home for well over a decade.

Lila opened the envelope, inside which was a letter written in her mother's familiar spidery handwriting. "My dearest Lila," the letter began, "as I am instructing Anna to give you this letter only in the event of my death, I feel that it is fair and just that at this time you know the truth about your real background . . ." What followed was a detailed account of how Christina had come to find and adopt Lila.

"I . . . I'm Jewish?" Lila asked, trying to digest this piece of impossible news. "I-I'm not their daughter? How can this be? It can't be true!"

"Lila, my darling girl," Anna said kindly, "you will always be my sister's child. That is how she thought of you, and she loved you as her own. Surely, over all these years, you've read the accounts that appear in the newspapers from time to time about the Jewish children who were hidden during the war, the young adults who suddenly discover they're Jewish. You came to us under unusual circumstances, to be sure, but the phenomenon itself, we are discovering more and more everyday, is not so unusual. I felt that I had to honor my sister's wishes, and so I did. But nothing has to change. You were raised as a good Christian, and you *are* one. You can keep on living exactly as you did before."

"I don't know . . . I don't know what to say or do," Lila said. "I need time to absorb all this, to think it through. It's—it's such a shock. I'm in shock . . ."

"Of course," Anna said, compassionately patting Lila's arm. "You need time. After all you've been through, poor child, I had to burden you with more suffering. Tell me, is there some way I can help, something I can do to ease your pain?"

"Thanks, my sweet aunt, but this is something I have to do myself. Wait . . . there is one thing. Do you have *any* idea who I am? Do you know the names of my parents? Anything?"

"Oh, Lila, I wish I could help you. But it all happened so quickly . . ."

"Nothing? Not one single clue?" Lila cried.

"One minute, one minute . . ." Anna thought hard. "Something is coming back to me. . . . Yes, I remember now. Besides the cash, there was one more thing in the fur coat's lining. A pendant. I think your mother kept it hidden in her dresser. I know you haven't had the strength to clean it out yet. Let me go to her apartment and see what I can find."

Later that day, Anna presented Lila with the pendant. She opened the locket and hoped for a photo of her parents, but instead, found only a few foreign words—Anna told her it was Hebrew—engraved on the inside. Overcome with emotion, she buried her face in her hands, until dusk turned to evening, and evening turned to night.

* * *

Several weeks later, Lila visited with a rabbi in Budapest to find answers.

"So, what should I do?" she asked after telling him her story. "What religion am I? Am I the religion of my birth, or the way I was raised? I don't know anything about Judaism; I never met a Jew before until this moment. Now I find out my parents were Jewish, I'm Jewish. Should I continue to live as a Christian and ignore my Jewish roots?"

"I truly feel for you," the rabbi said. "I can't tell you what to do. It's a very hard decision for you to make. But listen . . . There is a very famous rabbi in Brooklyn. He is known as the Lubavitcher Rebbe, and people from all over the world turn to him for help. I will give you his address, and you can write to him. Tell him your story. He will tell you what to do."

A few weeks later, two strangers—a man and a woman—stood outside Lila's door. The man—clearly a rabbi—wore a long beard, a black suit, and a black hat; the woman's hair was covered by a scarf, and she was modestly dressed.

"The Lubavitcher Rebbe asked us to get in touch with you," they said. "He wanted us to personally deliver his answer to your letter. He recommends that you try to return to your Jewish roots. You should go to Israel, and we will do everything to help you move and begin anew. We will take care of everything for you: We will arrange the flight, find you an apartment, hire a babysitter for your twins, get you a position in your field. Israel desperately needs pediatric surgeons, and your expertise will tremendously benefit the country and its people. We will personally accompany you to Israel and not leave your side until you are completely settled."

"Can you do me a favor?" Lila asked, pulling off the pendant that she now wore constantly around her neck. "Can you tell me what is written inside my locket?"

The rabbi examined the pendant and smiled broadly at her. "Well, now at least we know your name. "It's Leah, *bas* (daughter of) Miriam."

"What about a last name?" Lila asked hopefully.

He shook his head.

"Sorry, no last name."

* * *

Lila, now Leah, moved to Jerusalem, became observant, fluent in Hebrew and Judaism, and eventually married Shmuel,* a *baal teshuvah* (returnee to Judaism) with whom she had two more children. Her twins believed that her new husband was their biological father. Leah went on to become one of the most prominent pediatric surgeons in Israel.

One day, the kids clamored for pizza—not just any pizza, but Jerusalem's best. This meant a trip to Jerusalem's bustling pedestrian mall on Ben-Yehuda Street, where the pizzeria was located. Parking spots are at a premium in Jerusalem's downtown district, and Shmuel circled endlessly until he finally gave up. "Leah, why don't I just go in myself and order out? You stay in the car with the kids so the police won't give us a ticket, and we'll just eat the pizza at home, okay? I'll be back soon."

The pizzeria was one of the most popular eateries in Jerusalem, and long lines of customers stretched out across the store. Inside the car, the children fidgeted restlessly; inside the pizzeria, customers grew impatient. Shmuel nervously tapped his foot and checked his watch as the line inched forward. After what seemed like an interminable wait, he finally reached the counter, made his order, and pulled out his wallet to pay. It was precisely then that the Arab suicide bomber wearing an explosive belt containing nails, nuts, and bolts, detonated his bomb.

There were dozens of victims that tragic day and Shmuel was among the dead.

"Dear G-d," Leah cried and cried until there were no tears left, "what do you want from me? My life is so full of tragedies and heartbreak. I finally found a wonderful husband, and he, too, is taken from me? I am so alone in the world. So alone . . ."

And then Leah was asked to do the hardest thing she had ever done in her life. She was asked to put her grief and shock and pain on hold, and head immediately to the emergency room of the hospital where she worked.

"Leah, dozens and dozens of mortally wounded children are pouring into the ER who need surgery *now*," she was told by a coworker who found her standing dazed in the rubble-strewn area cordoned off by the police. "I feel horrible to have to come get you now, at such a terrible time, but these children will die if we don't operate immediately. We're terribly shorthanded right now. There just aren't enough pediatric surgeons to go around. Please come."

The day was a blur of blood and blackened faces as endless stretchers were rushed into the operating room. Leah worked heroically to save them all, despite the fact that she had lost her own husband. Her own pain and grief and horror had to be set aside so that she could save others. She concentrated so hard on the mangled bodies before her that she didn't even notice a frantic nurse arguing with an elderly man who had defied hospital rules and barged into the operating room.

"Where is my granddaughter?" he screamed. "I am not leaving until I find her . . ."

"*Zayde*," a voice called weakly from a stretcher. "I am here."

The elderly man rushed over to a young child lying on a gurney lined up with the others, waiting for their turn. The most critical cases had been taken first, and although the little girl presented a terrifying specter drenched in blood, her condition had not been deemed as serious as many of the others.

"Please, *adoni* (sir), you must get out of the operating room now," the nurse begged.

"No!" he roared back, intractable. "Absolutely not! I'm not moving from her side!"

Having just finished another surgery, Leah went over to speak to the man. "Don't worry, *adoni*, I will take care of her. She'll be fine; despite all the blood, her injuries are not that bad."

"No!" he shouted again. "I'm not going to let you go near my granddaughter until you promise that I'll be allowed to be with her every step of the way." Leah sighed. She was not going to waste precious time arguing. "Let him scrub in," she told the incredulous nurse. "I'll undress the child myself."

She pulled off her surgical mask for a moment to grab a drink of water. She hadn't eaten all day. The elderly man looked at her, startled. He had seemed oblivious to her presence before, but now his eyes seemed to bore into her.

Leah gently undressed the young girl, and as she pulled off her outer garments, her hand paused in midair. Her heart skipped a beat as she surveyed a beautiful gold pendant around the little girl's neck. A pendant that was *an exact replica of her own.*

Leah was shaken, but set aside her feelings to tend to the girl's injuries, which didn't require surgery, after all. After the girl was treated, Leah left for a breath of fresh air. All the horrible events of the day converged on her at once. She felt as if she was about to faint. She hadn't noticed the elderly man following her out the door.

"Miriam?" he called after her, his voice quivering.

"What?" She stared at him, muddled, feeling the brightly lit hospital corridor grow dim, the walls closing in on her.

"Miriam?" he asked again, and then peered at her more closely. "Oh, I'm sorry, I've made a mistake; you're too young to be Miriam. She would be in her seventies by now. . . . You look exactly like someone I knew very well before the war. Exactly. The resemblance is uncanny. When you took off your surgical mask, you gave me a shock. How is this possible?" He began to walk away, shaking his head in disbelief.

"Wait a second," she ran after him. "My name is Leah *bas* (the daughter of) Miriam. Does that mean anything to you?" Then she yanked off the pendant around her neck, the pendant she perpetually wore, the pendant that was an exact replica of the one worn by the man's granddaughter. "And does *this* mean anything to you?"

"Where did you get this from?" he asked slowly.

"From my mother."

"Yes," he answered numbly, "you *do* look *exactly* like your mother. That pendant is an original design—I should know. *I* am the one who handcrafted it. I used to be a jewelry designer and I have made this same necklace for each and every one of my grandchildren. But the first one that I made was for my only child of my first wife, who perished in Auschwitz. All these years, I was sure that *you* had perished, too. Leah, I am your father."

At the funeral for her husband and during the *shivah,* Leah was surrounded by her newfound family—aunts, uncles, nephews, nieces, cousins . . . and, of course, her father. As she leaned forward to catch their gently murmured words of comfort, bowed her head solemnly when they chanted the requisite Hebrew prayer to the bereaved, and raised her eyes in gratitude as they crowded around her protectively, the morning sun streaming through the windows glinted off the gold pendant circling her neck. Leah touched it lightly every now and then, thinking of the magic it had wrought, in the most tragic of times.

Like the mythical baby phoenix born from its mother's own ashes, so too do the Jewish people mystically survive over the millennia, sparks of light arising from the deepest depths of darkness, in a constant cycle that never seems to end. Good mixed with bad . . . just like the world.

Postscript: Leah's incredible story lives on through an esteemed educator and lecturer who wishes to remain anonymous.

THE TRAIN OF LIGHTS

As told by Arnold Geier to Pesi Dinnerstein

Every year, Hanukkah arrives just when we seem to need it most. When the days are at their shortest and the nights have grown unbearably long, the menorah casts its glow upon a people hungry for light. In 1938, the entire world found itself sinking into a darkness unlike any it had known in modern history. If ever there were a need for light to guide our way, it was on this cold December evening in Germany, as the eighth and final day of Hanukkah was about to begin.

The Geier family was sitting in their second-class compartment on a train headed from Berlin to Holland as they watched the winter sun slip beyond the horizon. It had been a long and terrifying trail that led from *Kristallnacht* (The Night of Broken Glass) to this moment. They could still hardly believe they had managed to obtain an American visa and were now finally on what they prayed would be an uneventful journey to freedom.

Judah and Regina Geier and their two children, Arnold and Ruth, spent the duration of the train ride staring out the window, nibbling on sandwiches, reading, dozing, and trying to behave as if the world were still a normal place. But unlike most of the other passengers, the Geier family remained acutely aware of the dangers that awaited them as the train approached the German-Dutch border. There, Nazis, German police, and officers of the Gestapo would all be present for a final check of passports and travel papers.

For Judah Geier, however, there was an additional heaviness that weighed on his heart. As an Orthodox Jew and a cantor, his whole life had been devoted to following the ways of the Torah. Yet, here it was, almost nightfall, when the flames of the Hanukkah menorah should have been rising to spread their light, and he was forced to sit quietly in his seat with only the harsh glare of a naked bulb to illuminate the graying sky. Surrounded by strangers, he was afraid to strike a match or recite a blessing for fear of calling undue attention to himself and his family. Regina Geier, sensing her husband's inner struggle, tried to reassure him that G-d, who sees and knows all, would surely understand his situation and, no doubt, grant him many more Hanukkahs to celebrate properly.

Judah nodded gratefully, but did not seem comforted. In a place and time of such spiritual darkness, the light of the menorah seemed more important than ever—especially on this eighth night of Hanukkah, which represents the culmination of the holiday, when all the candles are lit simultaneously to proclaim the miracle of Jewish survival. Under these dangerous circumstances, how could he possibly light the menorah? But, then again, how could he possibly *not*?

Judah turned the issue over and over again in his head as the train continued onward. Suddenly, the train screeched to a halt at the German-Dutch crossing, where it sat in the station for the longest ten minutes of Judah's life as the border police and the Gestapo prepared to check everyone's documents. He felt his wife's body go still next to his, and even his children sat frozen in fear. One wrong answer, one nervous twitch, could mean the difference between escape and imprisonment, between a new life and certain death.

Then, it happened. A Hanukkah miracle arrived at the German border just in the nick of time. With no warning, the entire station and every corner of the train was thrust into total darkness. All the lights were extinguished at the very same instant, leaving the passengers and the approaching officers groping in the darkness.

Without a second's hesitation, Judah seized the moment and reached for his overcoat on the luggage rack above. He put his hand into one of the pockets and pulled out a small package. Before anyone realized what was happening, he struck a match, lit a candle, and quickly warmed the bottom of eight other candles. He then planted them firmly in a neat row upon the windowsill and, in a breathless whisper, recited the Hanukkah blessings. As his family looked on in amazement, he carefully lit each candle and placed the ninth one—the *shamash*—off to the side. In the bright warmth of the menorah, his face radiated joy and peace for the first time in months.

Seeing the unexpected light in the window, the Gestapo and the border police came running. The sound of their boots striking the pavement with intensified blows echoed throughout the stillness. Nevertheless, Judah continued to focus his thoughts on the Hanukkah lights while his heart pounded as loudly and rapidly as the quickening footsteps.

When the officers burst through the door, Judah was braced for the worst, perhaps even the end. However, instead of responding with rage to this brazen display of Jewish ritual, the officers only noticed the opportunity that it provided. By the light of the flickering candles, they would now be able to see clearly enough to begin checking passports and papers; and, so, with characteristic Nazi efficiency, they set to work. As soon as the process was completed and they were about to leave, the chief officer of the border police turned to Judah and thanked him personally for having had the foresight to carry "travel candles" on his trip.

Meanwhile, the Geier family sat in stunned silence for close to half an hour, unable to take their eyes off the windowsill. Just as the candles were beginning to grow dim, every light in the station suddenly flashed back on. Judah, still in awe at what he had just witnessed, put his arm around his twelve-year-old son. With tears in his eyes, he drew him close. "Remember this moment," he declared softly. "As in the days of the Maccabees, a great miracle happened here."

MIRACLE AT THE GALLOWS

Cantor Leo Fettman and Linda Ackerman

Leo Fettman was an unlikely candidate to become a hero. He was a pale, skinny, erudite yeshiva student of nineteen when the Nazis invaded his hometown of Nyiradony, Hungary, in the spring of 1944. Hungary's leader, Horthy, a longtime friend to the Jews, had made public assurances to them that they would always be safe, so the Fettmans were unprepared when, the day after *Pesach*, Nazis stormed into their home and ordered them to get ready to leave in ten minutes. Leo and his family—his parents, grandmother, and one brother—were transported first to the local synagogue and then, two days later, by wagon to the Nyirjespuszta ghetto. Suddenly, the Nazis' malevolent intentions were becoming increasingly clear.

I have to do something, Leo kept thinking. *I have to do something to help my family, my people. The leaders are gone, the rabbis are dead. My parents and their peers are middle-aged and lack the energy. I can't wait for someone else to do something; I have to do it myself.* Leo didn't know exactly what he could do to help, but he waited for an opportunity. And, one day, it came.

"We are looking for Hungarians to help us manage the Jewish prisoners," he heard a loudspeaker blare one day, right outside the ghetto walls where he stood. The sound quality of the loudspeaker was of such high caliber that it pierced the ghetto walls and reverberated in its streets. Most residents of the ghetto ignored the messages, but Leo took heed. This was the opening he had awaited. He began to formulate his plan.

That night, Leo's father cut off his son's yellow star, and Leo crawled underneath the ghetto fence. In the morning, he brazenly approached the commander of the ghetto, masquerading as a non-Jew. Fluent in Hungarian and possessing a Hungarian birth certificate given to him by a non-Jewish boyhood friend, Leo was able to pass the commander's cursory inspection. (The Nazis certainly didn't anticipate this type of audacity from a Jew.) Leo was recruited into the Nazi organization, the "Arrow Cross," where he pretended to assist the Nazis in their mission. But what he was really doing—as a "mole" inside the vipers' nest—was looking for opportunities to help his fellow Jews. Leo knew that the undercover role he maintained was fraught with danger, but even more difficult was the emotional vulnerability he felt, the loneliness of being the only Jew among a rabid, Jew-hating throng.

One morning, Leo happened to walk past a fellow soldier who was humming a tune as he worked. Leo stopped in his tracks, did a double take, whirled around, and retraced his steps to where the soldier stood. He listened intently to the music that pulsated in the air. *Could it be?* He listened again. The melody was unmistakable, achingly familiar. He gathered his courage and approached the young soldier, who, like him, was blond-haired and blue-eyed—a perfect "Aryan specimen."

"Excuse me, but isn't that melody you're humming the *Avinu Malkeinu?*" Leo asked, naming one of the most beloved prayers from the High Holidays liturgy.

The man looked around, saw that they were alone, and clasped Leo to him in a surge of joy. "A *landsman* (a fellow Jew)!" he exclaimed.

"What are you doing here?" Leo asked.

"Exactly the same thing you are," the man said wryly.

Eventually, Leo discovered that there were *eighteen* other Jewish boys, who, just like him, had smuggled themselves into the Nazi den "outside," in order to help their fellow Jews "inside" the ghetto walls. The nineteen boys joined forces and worked together to improve the lot of their brethren in any way they could. Despite the risks they faced, they resolutely continued leading their double life—until the day came when they learned that the entire ghetto was to be liquidated. An impromptu meeting of all nineteen boys was hastily convened.

"I can't do it," Leo said. "I can't stay here, relatively safe, while my family is deported who knows where."

"Me neither," said a second boy. "My parents are old; they need me. I can help them. I *must* help them."

"I agree," a third chimed in. "I couldn't forgive myself if I didn't go with them."

All nineteen boys felt the same way. One by one, they stole out of the soldiers' camp, crawled under the ghetto fence, dropped their Nazi uniforms in a pile, burned them, and returned to the ghetto apartments where their families lived. When the Nazis were summoned to the fire, they were livid, and rounded up all the ghetto residents in an attempt to find the culprits.

"Who is responsible for this fire?" the commander thundered at the two thousand residents assembled in the ghetto square.

"We are!" all two thousand voices roared in unison, putting their own lives in peril to protect their nineteen sons.

Save for Leo and his brother Sandor (who were both plucked out for slave labor in Auschwitz), the entire Fettman family was sent to the gas chambers. When he learned his family's fate, Leo was so devastated that he tried to commit suicide by climbing a tall tree and jumping off, but he surprisingly survived the fall with nary a scratch on his body. All that he accomplished was being sent—without his brother—to the punishment camp, as retaliation for his attempted suicide. In this camp, Leo worked under heinous conditions with brutal taskmasters. One day, when he didn't work fast enough to satisfy a Nazi, the soldier took a severed tree limb and hit Leo so hard with it that he broke Leo's leg. Leo was sent to the camp hospital where nothing was done to ease his pain other than wrapping up his leg. As he lay there in agony for several days, he was certain that he was marked for death.

The Nazis have no use for a man who can't work, he thought. *What's the point? I might as well kill myself right now. They're going to gas me anyway, and maybe I can find a method a little less painful. And better that I take my own life than they take mine. This way I'm in control, not them, and it would be some kind of statement of defiance . . . wouldn't it?*

But before Leo could find the means by which to execute his second attempt, he had to deal with someone else's actual suicide: his hospital roommate, who shared his sentiments. Knowing that Leo had already attempted suicide once before, the Nazis blamed him for inciting his roommate to kill himself, and decreed that Leo would be hung in punishment. Leo felt almost giddy with relief when he heard the death sentence pronounced over him. *Finally, it was over. Finally, the endless suffering would come to an end.*

The next morning, Leo heard his number, "37276," announced over the camp loudspeaker. Two SS men dragged him out of the infirmary toward a gallows that waited for him. Hundreds of prisoners, assembled for roll call, stood nearby. The Nazis wanted them to witness the hanging in order to teach them a lesson. Leo was led up a short flight of steps and ordered to stand on a small stool. A noose was tightened around his neck. He felt no fear. He was ready to die.

With nothing to lose now, he didn't hold back in his last conversation with the SS officer who was charged with hanging him, a man prisoners had nicknamed "Come Come" for all the times he had chided prisoners who were moving too slowly with his customary reprimand, "Come, come."

"Do you know why you are being hanged?" Come Come taunted him.

"Because I am a Jew, and it is a crime to be a Jew," Leo replied.

"Do you have a last wish?" Come Come asked.

Leo felt completely calm. "Not a wish, but a statement. This is my statement: G-d is in heaven and G-d is looking down now and seeing what is happening, and you won't get away with it. I have a question for *you*: Do you have a wife? And children? How about a dog? When you go home after murdering people here, how can you show love to your family?" It was strangely satisfying to Leo to see how angry Come Come was getting. When Leo said, "My family members are all human beings, compared to you," and then, "Am I not a human being?" Come Come screamed, "No, you are not a human being—you are a worm!"

With his statement to Come Come articulated proudly, Leo felt ready to meet his maker.

Come Come summoned a Jew by the name of Oscar to approach the gallows and kick the stool over, which would result in Leo's immediate death. Even though Oscar knew he could lose his life for refusing, he did so anyway. He would not kill a fellow Jew. Come Come then directed another Jew to do the job, but he, too, refused. By now, Come Come had reached a fevered pitch of fury. "I'll do it myself!" he screamed, incensed. He kicked the stool with all his strength, and a second or two later, the rope snapped and broke, leaving Leo lying on the ground, stunned, but very much alive. There had been many hangings in the camp, but as far as Leo knew, this had never happened before.

"I knew at once that G-d had intervened on my behalf," Leo remembers sixty-four years later. "And that with His blessing, I would survive *everything*. The suicidal feelings that had been inside me for so long completely vanished, and I was suddenly filled with tremendous resolve *to live*. Death as an escape was no longer an option. Against all odds, I had survived both a suicide attempt and a hanging. G-d had clearly ordained that I should live, and right then and there, I told myself that I must live a life dedicated to Him and the fulfillment of His commandments."

Postscript: A lifelong cantor and Hebrew school teacher in Omaha, Nebraska, *chazzan* Leo Fettman has served as an inspiring role model for the hundreds of Jewish students he has taught, and for the hundreds of non-Jewish students he has spoken to about the Holocaust. He did indeed fulfill the promise that he made to G-d on that fateful day at the gallows, a day he sees as his personal miracle—and not a . small one, either.

THE WAR ARTIST

At one time, Olga Rosenberger had been robust, brimming with energy and vitality, pink-cheeked and pretty. Now, she was withered, a desiccated mass of all bones and no flesh, more dead than alive. The cover on her bed engulfed her, dwarfed her skeletal frame. She weighed just 29 kilos (63 pounds), the hospital nurse—who was also a fellow survivor—had told her. She was eighteen years old. It was April 15, 1945, and Bergen-Belsen concentration camp had just been liberated.

From outside the window of the makeshift sick bay at the camp, Olga could hear the joyous whoops of the survivors as they welcomed the Allied troops with *hurrahs* and *bravos* in different languages; she could hear the crunch of the soldiers' feet on the gravel and their loud exclamations of horror and disbelief as they made their grisly discoveries; she could hear the blaring horns of the military vehicles and the noisy *putt-putt* of their motors as they steam-rolled into the camp. She wanted to join the celebrants, but she couldn't. She was too sick and frail. She lay limp on the bed, rivulets of tears streaming down her cheeks. Before the war, she had been part of a large family. Now, she was the only one left.

The hospital door opened, and a young man wearing a British uniform stood framed in the doorway. He looked at the skeletal figures on the stretchers in the sick bay and shuddered. He approached each survivor gently, reaching for their hands, caressing their cheeks, letting them know by his mere presence that they were finally free. He tried to murmur soft assurances to all of them, but he realized that his speech was unintelligible to them. Finally, he asked aloud: "Does anybody here speak English?"

Olga had been born and bred in Bratislava, Czechoslovakia, but she came from a family that had always put a premium on education and culture. "I do," she answered weakly.

"Can you tell me what happened here?" the man asked.

As Olga described life in Bergen-Belsen, she realized that it wasn't mere curiosity that had made him ask. He took scrupulous notes as she spoke, and asked her detailed questions. Every now and then, when she would pause to catch her breath, he would take out a camera and snap photographs of the patients.

"What are you doing?" Olga asked, her own curiosity piqued.

"I'm sorry," the man apologized. "I should have introduced myself. My name is Alan Moore, and I am what people call a 'war artist.' I have been commissioned by the government to document war events and what we find here now with sketches and photographs. I know you must be terribly tired and weak, and I very much appreciate your willingness to talk to me at such length. And I am also exceedingly grateful that you speak English! Believe me, I'll remember *you* for a long time to come!"

Although his was the first kind face she had encountered in a very long time, and they spoke extensively, Olga would forget Alan Moore soon enough. Many other soldiers would follow afterwards, sharing their army rations and asking many, many questions, until her voice became raspy from talking so much. Since it was a British and Canadian unit that had liberated this camp, the soldiers were all directed to Olga, the only English- and French-speaking patient in the camp sick bay. She obligingly showed them the blanket she had been given by a former Kapo of the camp—sewn from human hair gathered at Auschwitz—and the tattooed number on her forearm. She related the litany of horrors that inmates had faced on a daily basis, and everyone who visited her that day wore stunned expressions on their faces and shook their heads in disbelief. Soon, all the soldiers who had approached her bedside blurred into one.

Olga was repatriated to her hometown of Bratislava, Czechoslovakia, where she found no one and nothing. Every member of her immediate family had been killed. "It was not a homecoming in the normal sense," she remembers. "There was no one to welcome me home. And my 'home' itself had changed drastically: It was war-torn, strewn with rubble and despair, and the population was still anti-Semitic. The one bright note was my encounter with another Bratislavan Jew who had come back to search for *his* family, a man named John Horak, whom I hadn't known 'before.' We married in 1947, and in 1949 moved to Sydney, Australia.

"Australia *wasn't* our first choice," she says. "We applied for landing permits to both the United States and Canada, but were told that all quotas had been filled. After waiting in Switzerland for more than ten months, we finally decided to accept Australia's warm invitation to emigrate there. At that time, Australia desperately needed people, and it extended open arms to immigrants of all stripes, including war criminals.

"Like other survivors, we slowly rebuilt our lives. We established a manufacturing business and had two beautiful daughters. I also studied sculpture at East Sydney Technical College to fulfill my love for art that had been temporarily quashed by the advent of the war. As awareness of, and interest in, the Holocaust became more widespread in Australia, I joined the Association of Australian Jewish Holocaust Survivors and became an active volunteer guide and speaker at the Sydney Jewish Museum following its establishment. I also found myself often called upon to give lectures to public school students throughout Sydney and its suburbs. I never said no to these invitations, because I am a firm believer in transmitting the legacy of the Holocaust to the next generation. We are a dying generation—there are less of us every day—and we must tell our stories before it is too late."

Life was relatively good for Olga during these postwar years, with one irksome exception. "The German government refused to give me the financial reparations that other survivors were receiving. My application always seemed to be tied up in some bureaucratic red tape. I was told by various officials that I needed a non-Jewish witness to testify that I had been incarcerated in Bergen-Belsen. Since I could not produce any such witness, my application for reparations was denied. During the early years, when we were young and struggling, we needed the money to establish ourselves. Then, in middle age, it didn't matter as much. But as my husband and I aged and retired, and my husband became increasingly ill, it began to matter a great deal.

"In 2005, the Sydney Jewish Museum decided to stage an exhibition commemorating the sixtieth anniversary of the Liberation. Although various camps were liberated at different times, the Museum scheduled the opening event for April fifteenth—the date of *my* liberation from Bergen-Belsen."

Roslyn Sugarman—the new curator of the Sydney Jewish Museum who had recently joined its staff—started to amass various materials and artifacts for the exhibition. Someone told her that there were some graphic and gripping paintings of the Liberation that hung in the War Memorial Museum in Canberra, and that she could temporarily acquire them on loan for the duration of the exhibit. When

Roslyn traveled to Canberra to view the paintings, she was overcome by their power. They were utterly compelling. Roslyn asked who the artist was, and learned that he was a ninety-one-year-old man who lived in Melbourne. His name was Alan Moore.

"She called Alan to talk to him about his work," Olga recalls, "and in the middle of the conversation, apropos of absolutely nothing relevant or related, he suddenly blurted out to her: 'Would you happen to know the whereabouts of a Holocaust survivor named Olga Rosenberger?'

"Roslyn was stunned. The question had come out of left field, and had no connection to previous remarks. She hadn't talked to Moore about the survivor community in Australia, and since she was so new to the museum and Sydney, didn't know most of the survivors by their maiden names.

"Roslyn stammered that she didn't really know the Jewish community of Sydney all that well, but she would ask her staff if anyone knew a survivor by this name. For fifty-eight years, I had been known as Olga Horak, *not* Rosenberger, but Roslyn just happened to ask someone who remembered my maiden name.

"Somehow, word got out to the media, and *Sixty Minutes of Australia* decided to cover this unusual story so that Alan Moore and I could be reunited at the opening-night ceremony commemorating the Liberation.

"I, my family and friends, staff members of the Holocaust museum, invited guests—and a full television crew—waited tensely for my liberator to walk through the iron portals of the Holocaust Museum. I was barraged by an onslaught of mixed memories from that never-forgotten day: the hope that had pulsed in my veins; the dread in my heart that my family was gone; the tremendous void and sorrow that never quite left me. I wanted to put a face to the name Alan Moore, but I couldn't. And sixty years later, he would be unrecognizable.

"He walked toward me with alacrity. I was overcome to meet my liberator after all these years. He was ninety-one, and I was seventy-nine, but at the moment that we clasped arms and embraced, I was eighteen again and he was thirty. So many years ago . . . but the memories kept rushing up at me. I remembered how gently he had stared into my eyes, and waited patiently while I sobbed. I sobbed now, too, but from joy rather than sadness, from the poignancy of our first and now this second encounter, and from the fact that after sixty years I was vindicated: I had finally found my non-Jewish witness who could testify that yes, I had indeed been interned at Bergen-Belsen.

"All these years, I never knew that my liberator lived a mere city away. I never knew that Alan Moore's unsophisticated camera and raw sketches of that momentous day had been parlayed into powerful paintings that hung in mute testimony in a nearby museum in Canberra. And I never knew what an impression our meeting had made on the young man that day.

"For, along with the paintings on loan, Alan Moore lent an old diary to our Sydney Jewish Museum, a diary in which he had transcribed notes of his experiences during those heady yet horrific weeks of Liberation at Bergen-Belsen. And in that diary was *my* name, together with his detailed recollections of our encounter. Although the paintings were ultimately returned to the museum in Canberra, the diary became a fixture on loan to the Sydney Jewish Museum. As have I.

"Now more than ever, I feel driven to tell the story. Alan Moore told it with his photographs and paintings. I tell it with words."

During their reunion, Olga was so overcome by her emotions that she never thought to ask these questions of Mr. Moore: *What had prompted him—after sixty years —to suddenly ask a stranger if she knew Olga Rosenberger?* In the camp sick bay that day, Olga had told the young uniformed photographer that she came from Bratislava, Czechoslovakia, and that she would be returning home to search for her relatives. Most survivors from Czechoslovakia had emigrated to Israel, Canada, and the United States; only a handful had wended their way to Australia. *Was it some kind of premonition, intuition, that made him ask Roslyn Sugarman that question when she called? Why was she still on his mind after all these years?*

Sadly, Olga could not pick up the telephone or fly to Melbourne to ask. Only a few weeks after they met, Alan Moore became very ill. But just before he succumbed to his sickness, he had given Olga Horak the vindication she had sought for six decades. It was there, all along, in the diary that now calls the War Memorial Museum in Canberra its permanent home.

Postscript: Olga Horak continues to widely lecture on the Holocaust and serves as a docent for the Sydney Jewish Museum. She is the author of *From Auschwitz to Australia*, published by Simon & Schuster of Australia. This book has now been translated into German as *Von Auschwitz Nach Australien*, by German publisher Hartung-Gorre in Konstanz, Germany.

THE CONVERTED

As a fifty-year veteran of the pulpit, Rabbi Berel Wein knows that everybody has a story, every human being *is* a story, and that some stories are stranger than others. He thought he had heard them all. But Jerusalem—a city with a different slant of light, a magnet for mystics, saints, penitents, holy beggars, prophets—never fails to surprise. It was here that he first met an Orthodox Jewish man who confided that he was a convert to Judaism, and that his father had been a Nazi during the war.

"When I was in my early twenties," the man told Rabbi Wein as they walked home from synagogue one Shabbos afternoon, "I learned my father's secret. He had been an SS man during the war, and had participated in many massacres of Jews. I was so angry at him, so devastated, that I immediately fled my home, never to return. I turned my back on my family, completely severing my ties and renouncing them fully. I never saw my father again.

"Of all places, I decided to travel to Israel to gain some perspective on the people whom Hitler had hated so much and whom my father had killed. I fell in love with the country and decided to pursue graduate studies in microbiology at the Hebrew University in Jerusalem. As my stay lengthened, I became increasingly interested in the Jewish religion, and started studying its texts. Eventually, I converted to Judaism. I married another German convert—with a similar background to mine—and we had three children, all boys. They studied in Jerusalem yeshivas where they received an excellent Jewish education, and we raised them as Orthodox Jews. Although they were blond and blue-eyed, they looked and acted exactly like their peers in all other respects—cute little yeshiva boys with *yarmulkes* perched on their heads and *tzitzit* dangling from beneath their shirts. No one would ever have guessed their genetic heritage.

"Many years passed, and my resolve not to communicate—ever—with my family only hardened over time. But one day, I was startled to find in my mailbox a note from my father telling me that he was dying, and pleading to see his grandchildren just once before he died. I consulted with a venerable rabbi in Jerusalem, and asked him what to do. He instructed me to fulfill my father's dying wish, to allow him to see his grandchildren before he died.

"I was thunderstruck that a former Nazi—who had tortured and killed Jewish children himself—would even *want* to encounter grandchildren who looked like the yeshiva boys who resembled his past victims. Our meeting was difficult. My father, gaunt and ghostlike, looked shriveled as he leaned toward us, his shrunken eyes studying my children's faces most carefully. The atmosphere was strained and pensive. He coughed intermittently and his voice was raspy. He hugged my children tightly, planted tender kisses on their cheeks, and wept. The room smelled of decay and death. I knew it would not be long. And I knew that whatever he had to say to me that day could only be the truth. 'I want to tell you something,' he said. 'I think you will appreciate it.'

"My father went on to tell me this story: 'One day, during the war, in a small village near the Eastern Front, my comrades and I were rounding up all the Jewish residents and throwing them into trucks bound for the gas chambers. Before we left, we made one last tour of the village to make sure we had caught every single one.

"'It was during this last round of inspection that I saw them: three sets of round, frightened black eyes peering out at me from underneath one of the trucks. Their eyes locked with mine as I made my triumphant discovery. I was about to call out to my cohorts, to tell them of my find, when something stopped me. Those eyes implored me. For the first—and only—time in my Nazi career, my heart was touched. I couldn't do it. Those eyes bore into me. I walked away from the truck and shouted to the others, *We're done here. No one left. Let's go!*

"'I will never forget them,' my father told me. 'They were three little Jewish boys with sweet faces and innocent eyes. Just like yours.'

"'You know,' my father mused, a sudden light glinting in his cloudy eyes, 'I am sure that if there had been four of them hiding underneath the truck that day, I would have *four* grandchildren, not three.'"

Postscript: It is estimated that there are approximately three hundred such converts now living in Israel, among them Hitler's nephew's grandson.

THE NAMESAKE

For Lisa and David Skolnik, the world was complete. Little Sabena was a perfect baby, with adorable features and a sweet temperament. They dreamed of giving her everything, never tiring of proclaiming their love into her little ears. When they moved from their home in Pittsburgh to Kansas, they searched for a house that would suit the needs of their little family. As Conservative Jews, they also sought a synagogue that would reflect their values. When Lisa's lactation nurse, Cheryl Gold, suggested that they try a local Orthodox synagogue, they were a bit intimidated, and told her as much. She assured them that the rabbi was warm and engaging, the people friendly, and the atmosphere open and nonjudgmental. They decided to give it a try.

The next Shabbos, they attended services at the synagogue and were pleasantly surprised. The rabbi was indeed wonderful, and the people truly welcoming. The small Skolnik family started to feel like they might have found a congregation where they belonged. After the services were over, people gathered in little groups, making small talk and wishing each other the traditional "Good Shabbos." David and Lisa were greeted by the rabbi, who welcomed them to Kansas and asked them about their occupations and interests. Then he turned to Sabena and smiled. "What's the little princess's name?"

"It's Sabena," they said proudly.

"And may I ask what her Hebrew name is?"

David paused. "Um, she doesn't really have a Jewish name. You see, she was named for my great-grandmother, Sabena, and we don't know what her Jewish name was. We are still searching for more information about her life so we can find out her Jewish name and give it to our little Sabena as well."

"Where was your great-grandmother from?" asked the rabbi.

"A town in Poland."

The Rabbi looked around the room, his gaze resting on a short, plump man in his seventies. The Rabbi indicated the man and said, "That gentleman over there is Sam Nussbaum. He is a Polish war survivor. Do you mind if I introduce you to him?"

The Skolniks welcomed the opportunity to meet someone who represented their past, and the rabbi called Sam over. A jovial, cheery man, they would discover that Sam was always ready with a quip or a clever remark. After the rabbi made polite introductions, he said, "Their baby is named Sabena for a great-grandmother who was killed in the war. We're trying to figure out what the Jewish name would be."

Sam, an accomplished cantor, burst into a chorus of a popular Polish choir piece, singing "Sabena, Sabena, Sabena," to the delight of the small baby. "Where did your great-grandparents live?" Sam asked.

"In a small town called Przemys'l."

Sam Nussbaum looked at David in astonishment. "Przemys'l? That's my hometown!" Suddenly, Sam Nussbaum was no longer the cantor with the booming voice or the man who made children laugh. He was a child, back in Przemys'l, running home from the *cheder* to his Mama's apron. "Przemys'l," he repeated softly. "Was your great-grandmother Sabena Rhind?"

It was David's turn to be astonished. "Yes, that was her name."

A look of the deepest pain crossed Sam's face. "Sabena Rhind was my neighbor. I buried her."

And as Sabena Rhind's great-grandson and and his family listened, Sam told her sad tale. "Sabena and her husband were old and tired by the time the Nazis arrived in Przemys'l. We all knew our destiny; there were no more secrets, no more false hopes. They were rounding people up and herding them off to the cattle cars. Sabena and her husband had no more strength, no more fight left in them after months of privation and want. They asked their son, a physician, for some cyanide capsules. They bid each other farewell and begged the Almighty for forgiveness before swallowing the pills, their tickets to a world of peace. They were my neighbors, my friends. I buried them with these hands. We prayed for them at the gravesite . . .

"Of course I know her Hebrew name. Oh, how we said it then! It was *Shaindel*."

A DREAM ESCAPE

The two bullets that simultaneously felled their parents and rendered Esther and Yidel orphans had been fired by a trigger-happy Nazi who didn't think twice about executing the middle-aged couple in front of their children. In the streets of Chelm, Poland, once a vibrant Jewish village but now flooded with members of the SS, Jews were fair game—easy prey. You could pick them off one by one, or murder them en masse, for no other reason than that they were Jews. Law and order had ceased to exist. Reason and sanity had vanished; madness reigned instead.

There was no time for the siblings to scream in horror, or cry out in anguish. They had to prepare for the next round of bullets aimed at *them*. Esther shut her eyes tightly; Yidel stared defiantly into the barrel of the gun. They waited. The Nazi laughed, grabbed them both, and hurled them roughly onto a truck bound for a labor camp. It was 1941, four years before the end of the war. All Esther and Yidel had left was each other.

For two years, they clung tightly to one another, and miraculously, were never separated. They were shipped from one labor camp to the next, but by some extraordinary fluke, they were always transported to the same place at the same time. Four years his junior, Esther looked to Yidel for guidance and support. They bolstered each other's spirits, and nursed one another when they fell ill. In many ways, Yidel had become Esther's surrogate father. He was her world.

And then, one night, the unspeakable occurred. Esther and the women in her barracks heard a cacophony of loud noises coming from the men's camp: the excited barking of dogs, shrill screams, the sharp crack of bullets piercing the night. "Someone must have tried to escape," one woman whispered to the others as they strained to hear in the darkness. "Misguided fool," another muttered. "With electrified fences everywhere, tall watchtowers, Nazi guards, and German shepherds, how could anyone hope to escape?"

The next morning the women learned that it had not been *one* man but *several* who had tried to escape together. As the woman in the barracks had predicted, the attempt had been doomed from the start. All had been shot and killed. "I'm so sorry, Esther," someone said. "Apparently, your brother Yidel was among them." Esther's pitiful world crashed down around her. Yidel gone? *Dead?* It was inconceivable. It had to be some terrible mistake. But when she slipped away to the fence separating the men's barracks from the women's, the men inside confirmed her greatest fears. "At least he died a hero," one man tried to console her.

"Yes," Esther said sadly, "better a bullet in the back than death in the gas chambers."

This would become her constant mantra when she was moved again—this time to the infamous camp, Sobibor. All of the other camps in which she had been interned before had been labor camps, where Jewish slaves replaced German manpower siphoned off by the war. But Sobibor's sole *raison d'être* was death itself. Its only industry was extermination. Whereas the odds for survival were fairly good in the labor camps, here they were nil. "We'll be dead by the end of the day," everyone told each other as they lined up for selection one last time.

Esther knew it was incongruous, inexplicable, really, but suddenly, for some strange reason—in Sobibor, of all places—she felt a faint flutter of hope. *I'm going to escape from here!* she felt intuitively. *I'm going to survive!* Eight hundred Jews had arrived at Sobibor that morning, and by evening, only seven would remain.

Although Sobibor was a death camp, the Nazi staff who lived on its premises frequently required products and services for their own personal needs. Sometimes the call came for a dentist or a goldsmith or a carpenter. On this particular day, a Nazi officer had walked up and down the line asking if anyone knew how to knit, a skill at which Esther was particularly proficient. So she lived.

"But not for long," warned one of the seven survivors. "Everyone gets replaced. No one leaves Sobibor alive."

"Then we must try to escape," a second survivor replied. "We have nothing to lose."

Thus were the seeds sown for the greatest escape attempt and revolt in concentration camp history—the famous Sobibor uprising, the fabled act of resistance and defiance that still stands out in the annals of the Holocaust.

Almost immediately upon her arrival, Esther was recruited into the ranks of the insurgents. All of the Jewish prisoners were urged to participate, but many were too ill, weak, or dispirited to take the formidable leap toward freedom. So on the eve of the revolt, Esther sorrowfully bade farewell to her friends who had chosen to stay behind and tried to sleep. It was a troubled, restive sleep at first, but when Esther entered the dreaming state, it turned serene. Her mother appeared to her in the dream; she looked exactly as Esther remembered her. She gazed deeply into Esther's eyes with tenderness and love.

"Mama, what are you doing here?" Esther asked her. "Don't you know that we are revolting tomorrow?"

"Yes, I know, dearest one," her mother replied. "I came to tell you that you *will* escape, and I came to tell you *where to go* when you do." In the dream, Esther and her mother floated into the air—out of Sobibor and into the lush countryside where a weather-beaten barn stood, surrounded by bales of hay. They floated into the barn, and Esther's mother pointed to the hayloft. "This is where you must hide. You'll be safe here." And then, she vanished.

Esther's eyes flew open, and she blinked away the tears that had formed. The dream had seemed so real; her mother had felt so palpably close. Was it only an illusion? Esther roused her bunkmate to share her dream. *"Bubbe meise!* (fairy tale)" the girl scoffed. "Dead people don't talk. It was only a meaningless dream. It's just your nerves playing on you, because of tomorrow. Try to get some sleep."

"You don't understand," Esther said, standing her ground. "I recognized the barn in my dream. I know that barn. It belongs to my father's friend, a Christian farmer who lives outside Chelm. My father took us to visit his friend all the time. I played in that hayloft as a child."

"Don't be ridiculous," the girl said. "It's just a coincidence."

"I have had no reason to think about that barn all these years. Why would I suddenly remember it now?" Esther protested. "I'm telling you, if I do escape, that's where I'm going. My mother didn't travel all the way back to this world for nothing. I have to follow her instructions."

"You're crazy," the girl said as she turned her back to the wall and fell asleep.

On October 14, 1943, the most successful and famous concentration camp uprising took place at impregnable, formidable Sobibor. Using munitions smuggled into Sobibor by sympathetic partisans, three hundred Jews—including Esther—escaped into the forest. But while the others joined up with the resistance fighters, Esther struck out alone. "I'm sorry, but my mother came to me in a dream and told me where to go," she told the incredulous group. "I have to follow her instructions."

For five days and nights she walked, until she came to a clearing in the forest. Beyond the clearing stood the old farmhouse and the adjacent barn—exactly as her mother had shown it to her. She darted into the barn, climbed up into the hayloft, fashioned a makeshift bed out of hay for herself, and promptly fell asleep.

She awoke the next morning suffering from hunger and thirst. She knew she had to find food, even though straying outside represented a clear danger. Esther slipped out of the barn and wandered down the dusty road until she came to a house where a compassionate farmer gave her bread and milk. Returning to the hayloft, she ravenously tore at the bread and then reached for the jug of milk to quench her raging thirst. But the jug, which she had placed on top of the hay, had disappeared! *It must be somewhere in the hay*, Esther thought. *How could it have gotten swallowed up so fast?* Esther dug into the hay but couldn't find the milk. *Maybe it dropped to the floor below*, she guessed, as she climbed down into the main section of the barn. As she hunted for the missing jug, her frantic movements became increasingly louder and louder, until they wakened the sleeping figure curled up in a corner of the barn.

"Who's there?!" The figure sprang up in alarm.

I'm finished, Esther thought.

"Who's there?" The voice was unmistakable, one she knew and loved.

"*Yidel?!*" Esther screamed. "Yidel, is that you?"

"*Esther? Esther'le?*"

They ran into each other's arms, sobbing, delirious with joy.

"But how can this be?" Esther asked after they finally broke apart. "You're supposed to be dead."

"Everyone else was killed, but I escaped," Yidel said. "But you . . . Esther . . . someone told me that *you* were dead! I am overjoyed to see you! But how did you know to come *here*?"

"Mama told me to," Esther said, describing the dream and her mother's precise instructions. "She must have known that you were here, and sent me to you!"

"This is incredible." Yidel shook his head in disbelief.

"How long have you been here, Yidel?"

"Ten months. I knew Papa's friend wouldn't betray me. He's let me hide here all this time. We'll talk to him in the morning. I'm sure he'll let you stay here, too."

The farmer was visibly moved when Yidel approached him the next morning and recounted the story of his sister, her dream, and her escape from Sobibor. "Well, if G-d brought you together, who am I to tear you apart? Of course, your sister can stay."

Esther and Yidel safely hid in the barn together for the remaining nine months of the war, until they were finally liberated by the Russian army. Today, there are only thirty survivors of Sobibor left to tell the story, but more than six decades later, Esther is among them—all thanks to a mother's love that transcends both time and space, and is eternal.

"DER KRANKE YINGELE"
(THE SICK BOY)

"It must have been terrible for someone your age to go through such a nightmare," the Red Cross worker said compassionately as she gazed, stricken, at the emaciated figure in the infirmary cot, a few short days after Liberation.

"What do you mean?" the patient asked weakly, confused. "How old do you think I am?"

"Sixty-five, seventy?" the Red Cross worker suggested, striking a few years off her real estimate, for the sake of politeness.

"I am fourteen," the patient answered. "Fourteen years old. But I have lived a thousand years."

Had the Red Cross worker done her homework, she would have quickly learned that in the aftermath of the Holocaust, there *were* no seventy-year-olds who still lived. Neither were there sixty-year-olds or fifty-year-olds, for that matter. The middle-aged and elderly had been instantly exterminated by Hitler's death machines, and only the young had been plucked out to work for the war effort. If a handful of middle-aged Jews or small children still survived, it was only because of extraordinary circumstances, or because they had been hidden during the war.

The typical survivors of Hitler's war were teenagers and young adults who emerged from the ashes to learn that their entire support system had been completely wiped out: their parents slaughtered, their aunts and uncles and grandparents sucked into the vortex of the Holocaust and obliterated; extended family members, friends, a town's entire Jewish population—all gone. As the young survivors feebly tried to reenter life, they found that they only had each other, and in their compelling need to banish their aloneness, it was only normal that they would turn to their peers. In the early aftermath of the war, it was almost incongruous how quickly new attachments were being formed, how many love affairs were sparked, how many matches were made. It was called the life force.

* * *

Twenty-one-year-old David Rybowski, interned in the Lodz Ghetto in 1939, had received orders to join a work crew bound for the Berlin-Moscow highway, then in the early stages of construction. As a farewell gift, his friend gave him a ticket to a performance at the Lodz Ghetto Theater, one of the props used by the Nazis to convince the world that the Jews enjoyed a good life inside the ghetto walls. Despite the uncertain future that loomed ahead of him, David was able to lose himself in the evening's performance. The music, the acting, the scenery, the costumes—all created an enchantment that cast its spell on the audience and removed them, at least temporarily, from the nightmare world in which they lived.

David, too, was enthralled by the magic spun by the actors, but actual goose bumps erupted over his arms when a young woman who was unfamiliar to him walked onto the stage and began to sing a heartrending song called *"Der Kranke Yingele"* (The Sick Boy). The pathos of the song's lyrics, its haunting melody, bewitched him—as did the singer's beauty.

He nudged the man sitting next to him. "Who is that actress?" he asked. The man didn't know, but after the performance, David was determined to find out. Eventually, after many inquiries, David learned that her name was Jenny, and that she was sixteen years old. He wanted to find her and declare his love for her, but there wasn't time; he was deported before he could track her down.

In 1945, after six harsh years of Nazi terror, David was liberated by the Allied soldiers. His body barely recovered, he stole a bicycle and began to look for for surviving relatives. Hope beat faintly in his breast: *Maybe at least one of his parents still lived, or a sibling?* His frantic search was being reenacted all over Eastern Europe. The survivors' joy in being liberated was tempered by the dawning knowledge that whole families, indeed, entire villages, had been wiped out, and that there was no one to go home to, no one to welcome them back. No one wanted to believe, no one *could* believe, that they might be the only member of their family who was left. The emptiness, the loneliness of that stark realization was simply too much to bear.

After weeks of futile searching, David finally learned that one sister had survived, and that she was interned at the Bergen-Belsen camp, which had been turned into a makeshift DP (Displaced Persons) center. The diseased prisoner barracks had been burned down, and the Jews had been moved to the infinitely more livable quarters in which their Nazi tormentors had previously dwelled. David's sister was overjoyed to see him, and she quickly arranged to host an impromptu "Welcome Back" party for him. She scrambled to find food and drink, and invited the new acquaintances she had made at the DP camp to join them. All that was lacking was musical entertainment.

"Jenny, can you sing something?" David's sister asked one of her new friends.

Of all of the hundreds of Yiddish songs Jenny knew, she chose the same one she had sung in the Lodz Ghetto six years before: *"Der Kranke Yingele."* At first, David didn't recognize Jenny's face. After all, six brutal years had elapsed. But her voice was unforgettable. Shivers went up and down his spine, and he fell in love with her all over again.

David ran to Jenny's side in frenzied excitement and told her his story.

"What do you want?" she asked suspiciously.

"I want to be your husband!" he declared passionately.

"I don't *want* a husband," she said sadly. "I want a father, a mother. You can be my brother."

"I don't want to be your brother; I want to be your *husband*."

"No, you can be my brother," Jenny said, dismissing him.

Shortly after this conversation, Jenny became very sick and lost her beautiful voice. David nursed her, constantly at her bedside. He prepared her food, fed her chicken soup, and brought her back to health. Even after she had rallied, Jenny still looked at him with a jaundiced eye and stubbornly repeated: "You're still going to be my brother."

David wouldn't take no for an answer. When she threw him out the window, he came back in through the door. When she threw him out the door, he came back in through the window. Eventually, her feelings for him awakened. She fell in love with him, too, and they married. And today, if one were to visit the home they have made together for over six decades, it is very likely one would hear the strains of *"Der Kranke Yingele"* playing softly in the background.

Postscript: This story is based on a segment of the award-winning documentary film *Undying Love: Stories of Courage and Faith,* directed by Helene Klodawsky and Ina Fichman.

FUNERAL FOR BARUCH

Rabbi Binny Friedman

Chaim Shapiro went through the seven levels of hell, surviving four concentration camps, not to mention the ghetto and forced marches. He began the war with eight children and a wonderful family, and, in little over a year, he lost his wife and seven of his children, without ever having the chance to even sit *shivah* for them. He was finally liberated from Buchenwald with Baruch, his only surviving son, and they wallowed in the DP camps for nearly three years until finally, in 1948, they found places aboard an immigrant ship and arrived in Israel a week later.

Baruch Shapiro volunteered to fight in the War of Independence, Israel's desperate battle for survival against overwhelming odds. With no previous training, he was taken to a ravine, handed a rifle, taught how to shoot a few bullets, and sent off to war. Baruch distinguished himself in battle, joining Yitzhak Rabin's Harel Brigade. While fighting to break the Arab siege on Jerusalem, Baruch received a field commission as an officer and was awarded a medal for bravery under fire.

One day, while sitting in his tiny living room in Tel Aviv, Chaim Shapiro glanced out the window and saw one of those terrible delegations heading up the path to his apartment. They say that Chaim Shapiro opened the door before they knocked, and they say that he never even read the telegram, just crumpled it over and over in his hands. He knew his son was dead.

When a soldier in Israel is killed, the army takes care of everything, including the funeral arrangements. Chaim Shapiro had only one request: He wanted his son to be buried in Jerusalem, on Mount Herzl, the national military cemetery.

The next afternoon hundreds of mourners gathered at Mount Herzl. Most of them had never known Baruch Shapiro or his father Chaim, but they had heard of the terrible tragedy and wanted to pay their respects. Yigal Yadin himself, the IDF chief of staff (who would later discover Masada), stood by Chaim Shapiro's side. What Hitler had not finished in the crematoria had ended at the hands of an Arab bullet; this was the last Shapiro son, the end of a line. As the coffin was being lowered into the ground, Chaim Shapiro began to sing.

People thought he had lost it. Yadin put his arm around Chaim's shoulders and someone ran to get him some water, but he shrugged them all off and continued his song. People had no idea what to make of it, so finally, Chaim Shapiro looked at them and said, "You know, I have been through a hell the likes of which most people cannot imagine; I lost over seventy relatives in a little over a year, including seven children, my wife, and my parents. I have no place to mourn them, no grave; they are ashes in the skies over Europe, and I have no idea *why* they had to die.

"But this son—at least *this* son—I know why he died. He died so we could have a home for the Jewish people in the land of Israel, and he has a grave, here on Mount Herzl in Jerusalem. And that is not a reason to cry—it is a reason to sing."

When Chaim Shapiro finished speaking, he began to sing once more, and, grabbing people's hands, to dance. Three hundred mourners joined him, singing and dancing against the setting sun of the Jerusalem sky.

The next time you visit Israel, go to Mount Herzl, Israel's national military cemetery. When you walk through the wide stone gates, head up and then down to the right, where the graves from 1948 lie. It is there you will find the lonely grave of one Baruch Shapiro. Close your eyes and you will understand why the Jewish people will never be destroyed.

Am Yisrael Chai.

AN OSCAR FOR OSKAR

Eric Saul

It was a sweltering day—105 degrees Fahrenheit, hot even by Los Angeles standards. Thomas Keneally, a prominent Australian novelist, had just finished a book tour for one of his novels, and was wandering around Beverly Hills killing time before his flight back to Australia the next day. A luggage and leather store named The Handbag Studio caught his eye. The owner of the store, Leopold Page (who had changed his name from Poldek Pfefferberg), spotted Keneally and took pity on the withered-looking man, asking him to come inside and cool off.

Keneally carried a worn-out briefcase with a loose handle and asked if it could be repaired. Examining the briefcase, Page said it might be better if he simply bought a replacement. Keneally agreed and selected a new briefcase. He handed Page his American Express card. In 1980, it took nearly a half-hour to get authorization for the card. While he was waiting, Page asked Keneally what he did for a living. Keneally replied, "I am a writer."

Page inquired, "A good one?"

"Some think so. I manage to make a living from it."

"If you are a writer, then I have a wonderful story for you; it is a story of humanity, man to man," Page said. He then proceeded to regale Keneally with the story of German businessman Oskar Schindler and how he saved 1,200 Polish Jews from almost certain death. Schindler, a member of the Nazi Party, had come to Cracow, Poland, in 1939 to make his fortune as a war profiteer, and, with the help of local Jews, set up a factory in the city. It eventually became their safe haven.

Leopold took Keneally to the back of his store to show him his personal archives on Schindler. There were two full file cabinets, stuffed with papers. Leopold told Keneally that both he and his wife Mischa had been saved by Schindler, a larger-than-life hero whom both had worshipped. "Not that he was a saint," Leopold added. "Schindler was an all-drinking, all-black-marketeering, promiscuous man. Okay? But he got Mischa out of Auschwitz, so to me, he is G-d."

Keneally was intrigued by this Schindler story. Page quickly ran across the street and made a little bit of a scene in the bank when he implored the tellers to make copies of the documents for Keneally to read in his hotel. Keneally recalled, "I began reading the papers Page had given me. They were instantly engrossing."

Still, Keneally insisted that he was not the right person to write the book. He was an Irish Catholic from Australia and was only three years old when World War II started. He knew nothing of Jews and the Holocaust. Page said that was precisely why he *should* write the book. After much prompting, Keneally agreed to write a biographical novel about Oskar Schindler.

Leopold Page considered Schindler not only his savior, but also his best friend. Early in their friendship, Page promised Schindler that someday, everyone would know his name. He told Schindler, "You protected us, you saved us, you fed us—and we survived the Holocaust, the tragedy, the hardship, the sickness, the beatings, the killings—because of you! We must tell your story." He also said, "Schindler gave me my life, and I tried to give him immortality."

He and fellow Schindler survivor Moshe Bejski regularly took up a collection from their fellow survivors and sent Schindler a pension every year for the rest of his life. Leopold Page continued his friend-ship with Schindler until Schindler's death in 1973. Page and Moshe Bejski, along with other Schindler Jews, arranged for Schindler to be buried in Jerusalem. Page had promised Schindler that he would arrange for him to be buried in Israel so that Schindler could be near "his children."

Page and Bejski were also responsible for having Schindler honored as a Righteous Gentile by Israel's Holocaust Museum, Yad Vashem. The citation about his rescue efforts included the following facts:

* Schindler transferred 700 Jewish men and 300 Jewish women from the Plaszow camp before its final liquidation, bringing them into his factory and saving their lives;
* he saved 300 Jewish women who had already been transported to Auschwitz;
* he got about 100 Jewish inmates from the Golleschau camp out of frozen train wagons and saved them, with the help of his wife;
* he constantly worried about the health of his Jewish workers and repeatedly supplied them with additional food and medicines;
* he provided his Jewish workers with humane living conditions and medical treatment to ease their suffering;
* he allowed the Jewish dead to have Jewish funerals; and
* he constantly endangered his life to do these things.

"By doing them," the citation concluded, "Mr. Schindler has obtained the deepest gratitude of the hundreds of Jews that he saved and is worthy of recognition by the entire Jewish people."

Keneally finished the book in 1982. It was published as *Schindler's Ark* in England and as *Schindler's List* in the United States. At first, sales in the United States were very poor; only a few thousand copies were sold. Page was disappointed. He purchased thousands of the unsold books at remaindered prices and began handing them out for free. Eventually, *Schindler's List* would become an international best-seller, selling millions of copies.

In an interview with Polish author and filmmaker Franciszek Palowski, director Steven Spielberg explained how he had learned about the story of Schindler. "I had never heard of Oskar Schindler. I had heard of Wallenberg [a Swedish diplomat who rescued Jews, and who after the war disappeared into the Russian gulags], but I had never heard of Oskar Schindler. I remember that one day Sidney Sheinberg, who is, and was at the time, the head of Universal Pictures in Hollywood, sent me a book review from *The New York Times* reviewing the Thomas Keneally novel, *Schindler's List*. I read the book review, was fascinated with the story—just based on three pages of review—and based on that, I read the book. Then, based on that, Universal bought the rights in 1982 for me to film the novel. That's how I came across the Oskar Schindler story."

After Spielberg obtained the rights, he realized it would be a difficult film to make, unlike any he had made previously. He informed Page that he was not ready to make the movie; he needed time to mature. "In the 1980s, I started to build a family, to have children. I needed time to mature within myself and develop my own consciousness about the Holocaust. I had to wait until a time when I really felt that I was ready to express myself on the subject of Oskar Schindler and make a very serious movie about his life and deeds."

While Spielberg waited for the right time to make the movie, Leopold fretted. Leopold met with Spielberg and predicted that he would certainly get an Oscar for making a movie on Oskar Schindler. "An Oscar for Oskar!" he punned.

Until then, Steven Spielberg had not received an Oscar for his work as a film director, even though several of his films were among the top box office films of all time. Spielberg's producers told Leopold not to repeat his pun, as Spielberg was superstitious and sensitive about not having received an Academy Award.

Page frequently visited Steven Spielberg's mother, who owned a kosher restaurant called the Milky Way in Los Angeles. Page would politely pester Leah Spielberg Adler to tell her son to make the movie already. Leopold also called Spielberg's office every week for eleven years. He told Spielberg, "I want this film made in my lifetime . . . enough with [the movies with] little furry animals."

In 1992, Spielberg informed Page that the time had come: They would begin filming in Cracow, Poland, in early 1993, using many of the original locations, including the site of the original Schindler factory. Leopold Page returned to Cracow to witness the filmed re-creation of his life of fifty years before. It was especially moving for him to see the re-created factory—one of the few safe havens in a world gone mad. Spielberg filmed *Schindler's List* in black and white, and the budget was very small compared to other epics he'd made. Spielberg was haunted by the notion that no one would want to see a three-and-a-half-hour Holocaust movie, and doubted that the film would break even.

Schindler's List opened in December 1993. The film received almost universal rave reviews from critics, and grossed $321 million. No one was surprised when it received eleven Academy Award nominations and was honored with seven: Best Picture, Best Director [Steven Spielberg], Art Direction, Editing, Original Score, Cinematography, and Screenplay.

Leopold Page and his wife, Mischa, were in the Dorothy Chandler Pavilion, in Los Angeles, on the night that *Schindler's List* was honored by the Academy. Steven Spielberg went to the podium and thanked, before anyone else, "a survivor named Poldek Pfefferberg . . . I owe him such a debt. He carried the story of Oskar Schindler to all of us."

During the ceremony, Page remembered, "I was jittery because I had promised Spielberg ten years earlier that if he made *Schindler's List*, he would get an Oscar for Oskar. When they announced that Spielberg had won as Best Director, I jumped so high, and when he talked about my wife and me, we were crying. When *Schindler's List* also won the Best Picture award, everybody cried."

The American Film Institute voted *Schindler's List* among the top ten best films of all time.

Steven Spielberg's experiences while making *Schindler's List* became a catalyst for another one of his major inspirations. While making the film in Poland, Spielberg was continually meeting survivors. At an interview, he recalled, "Well, it's unusual to be making a film on the streets where the events actually happened and to have a woman come over to me as a woman did a couple of weeks ago. She said, 'I was an eleven-year-old Jewish girl working in Oskar Schindler's DEF, Deutsche Emailwaren Fabrik.' . . . I've had people come up to me on the streets to say, 'I was at Emalia'; 'I was in Plaszow camp'; or 'I went to Oskar Schindler's factory in Brinnlitz.' It's just incredible to meet the people from that former time who are still here—the people whose stories we are telling in this film."

Even after the film, Holocaust survivors approached Spielberg with their many personal stories of the war. Spielberg made $65 million on the film, but felt that the profit from *Schindler's List* really didn't belong to him. He donated the money to create both the Righteous Persons Foundation and the Survivors of the Shoah Visual History Foundation, which would ultimately interview more than 52,000

Holocaust survivors worldwide. Video testimonies were recorded in thirty-two languages, in fifty-six countries. This constituted the largest oral history collection in the world. Spielberg donated much of the $126 million for the project.

This project gave voice to thousands of Holocaust survivors whose testimony would otherwise have been lost forever. Many survivors who were reluctant to talk about their wartime experiences were proud to share them with Steven Spielberg's foundation. The foundation distributed tapes to the survivors, who then gave them to their families, many of whom were hearing their loved ones' stories for the first time. Spielberg later remarked that this was the most important work of his life.

Poldek Pfefferberg (Leopold Page) died on March 9, 2001. He kept his promise to Oskar Schindler, to make him immortal, and to Steven Spielberg, to help him get an Oscar for Oskar, and finally, he fulfilled his promise to the world, to "remember to remember."